THE BIG 50
DETROIT RED WINGS

The Men and Moments That Made
the Detroit Red Wings

Helene St. James

TRIUMPH
BOOKS

No part of this publication may be reproduced, stored in a retrieval system, or transmitted in any form by any means, electronic, mechanical, photocopying, or otherwise, without the prior written permission of the publisher, Triumph Books LLC, 814 North Franklin Street, Chicago, Illinois 60610.

Library of Congress Cataloging-in-Publication Data available upon request

This book is available in quantity at special discounts for your group or organization. For further information, contact:

Triumph Books LLC
814 North Franklin Street
Chicago, Illinois 60610
(312) 337-0747
www.triumphbooks.com

Printed in U.S.A.
ISBN: 978-1-62937-777-3

Design by Andy Hansen
Page production by Patricia Frey
All photos courtesy of *Detroit Free Press*

To my parents, Helle and Poul

[Contents]

[Foreword]

I didn't see much of the Detroit Red Wings when I was young. I didn't even know much about them. I grew up watching Edmonton, Calgary, Vancouver, and Winnipeg. This was back in the day when there was just one game on TV a week, on *Hockey Night in Canada*. Then one year the Wings played the Oilers in the playoffs, and I actually liked the Wings. Being a goalie, I liked Greg Stefan and Glen Hanlon, their goalies. I grew up watching Grant Fuhr and Andy Moog. From then on I followed the Wings as much as I could. I would look in the newspaper and see where they were in the standings. I would watch TV and watch for highlights of their games.

For me to be drafted by them was huge. They were an Original Six team. When I got there, I saw the passion people had for hockey in Detroit. There is a pressure to it. Expectations are higher when you play for a team like Detroit. They live and breathe hockey, and that's why you love it so much as a player. I loved playing there because it was just pure hockey. That's what Joe Louis Arena was.

I agreed to write this foreword because I wanted to tell people what it is like to be a Detroit Red Wing—what it meant to me, what it meant to players. It's one of the most storied franchises in sports.

To be a Red Wing was more than an honor. You felt a responsibility to show up and play—not only for the fans but for the guys who were there before you. You felt a responsibility to Ted Lindsay and Gordie Howe and Terry Sawchuk—to all the guys that put on the winged wheel in years past. It was something that carried a lot of weight.

Those guys who were there before, you think of their perseverance. And I saw the perseverance of Steve Yzerman. I roomed with him one year in the playoffs, in 1998. He expected a lot out of his teammates, as a captain should. He expected you to do certain things, and he did all those things himself.

When you are a Red Wing, you feel a responsibility to give it your all. You feel a responsibility to your teammates and to the fans, because the fans were there to watch hockey and that was it. Watch hockey and drink beer. It was a great spot.

I had a lot of fun playing for the Wings. We had a lot of guys who were great, really funny guys. Marc Bergevin was great. Kirk Maltby was naturally funny—still is. Tomas Holmstrom—he'd go home to Sweden in the summer and he'd come back and his English would be atrocious. It would get better as the season went along and then we'd have to start over again the next year. Jamie Pushor was a lot of fun too. Kevin Hodson would imitate other goalies in the league. He was hilarious.

I miss the competition of the playoffs. When you get older the seasons get long, but the playoffs never did. Those times are what I miss the most, being with the guys and playing the same team for two weeks. I miss the aftermath of winning too—whether it's being in the dressing room celebrating or being on the bus with the guys.

—Chris Osgood
Detroit, November 2019
NHL goalie, 1993–2011
Detroit Red Wing, 1993–2001, 2005–11

[Acknowledgments]

In the summer of 2002 it was my great good fortune to tour the Czech countryside in Red Wings defenseman Jiri Slegr's Mercedes. He drove and his wife sat next to him. Next to me in the backseat, strapped in by a seat belt, was the Stanley Cup. That is one of many marvelous memories I have from more than two decades covering the Detroit Red Wings for the *Detroit Free Press*.

I covered the Stanley Cup championships in 1997, '98, '02, and '08. The Wings were an amazing team in the mid-1990s to late aughts, the rosters populated by superstars and role players who were a delight to interview. I think hockey is the most entertaining sport to watch, and on top of that, hockey players are almost universally pleasant to deal with. I started covering the Wings around the time of the Russian Five, and Slava Fetisov—a legend in the game—couldn't have been kinder and more helpful. I've never met another player who knew the right thing to say quite like Steve Yzerman. There's a funny anecdote in his chapter about that gap-toothed smile of his from the '97 Cup. To this day I remember watching him leave Joe Louis Arena that June night, carrying the Stanley Cup and placing it in his car.

Covering the Red Wings means covering hockey legends. Gordie Howe once snuck up on me at Joe Louis Arena and gave me a gentle nudge with one of those famous elbows of his. "No girls allowed in the locker room," he said with a wink and a laugh. It was such a pleasure to be around him.

I relished writing this book and greatly appreciate those who aided in the effort. Gene Myers, my friend, former editor, and fellow snowshoe enthusiast, provided invaluable advice and encouragement. Michelle Bruton, my editor at Triumph Books, was supportive at every stage.

I am grateful to the people who spent time talking to me for this book—Yzerman, Scotty Bowman, Mark Howe, Kirk Maltby, Kris Draper, Chris Osgood, Nicklas Lidstrom, Bruce Martyn, Ken Holland, and Jimmy Devellano. They were all very gracious and shared great memories of their time with the team.

I was thrilled when Osgood said yes to providing the foreword, because I know how much playing for the Wings meant to him. He was one of the wittiest players I covered. I usually walked away from interviewing him laughing.

Going through the *Detroit Free Press* archives reminded me of how much fun I had covering the Wings with former colleagues Keith Gave, Jason La Canfora, Nick Cotsonika, and George Sipple. Their reporting contributed to this book, as did that of Mitch Albom, Drew Sharp, Bill McGraw, and John Lowe.

Most of all I am grateful to my family, especially my parents, Helle and Poul. I have been fortunate to have great adventures in my life, and that started with their love and support.

—Helene St. James
Detroit, December 2019

THE BIG 50
DETROIT RED WINGS

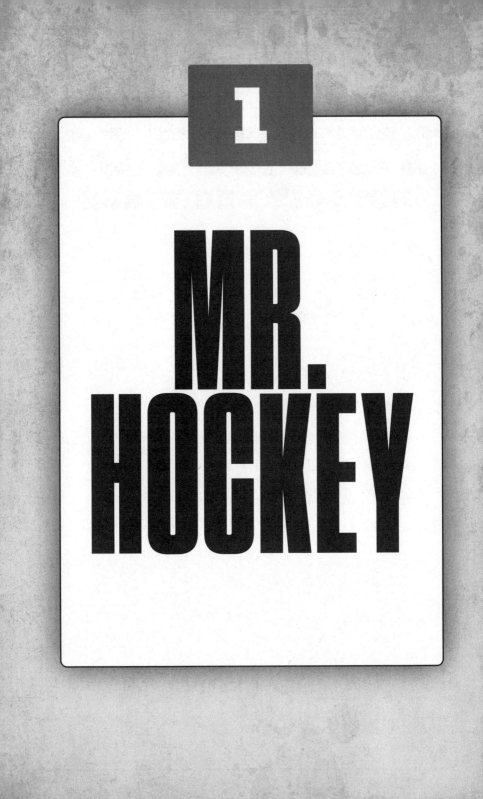

1

MR. HOCKEY

Gordie Howe was 51 years old yet he fit right in among the players, some of whom weren't even half his age. It was February 5, 1980, and Scotty Bowman was coaching the Wales Conference team in the All-Star Game at Joe Louis Arena.

"I remember it like it was yesterday," Bowman said in 2019. "I was coaching that year in Buffalo and Howe was with Hartford. I put him in that All-Star Game, and seeing how he just blended in as a fifty-something-year-old—he ends up getting an ovation that's louder and longer than anything I had heard. I saw him later on when I coached the Wings. He always went out of his way to thank me for putting him on the team. What a nice way to come back to a brand-new arena. He was the franchise's best player for 25 years. That's my favorite story about Gordie."

It speaks to how encompassing Howe's reach was that seemingly everyone in hockey has a story to tell about him. A good one. Many of them are about what a great player he was, this giant of hockey whose legacy with the Red Wings spanned a quarter of a century as a player and endures as a beloved legend. Howe was a 23-time NHL All-Star, won the Art Ross Trophy as the league's leading scorer six times, led the league in goal scoring five times, won six Hart Trophies as the league's most valuable player, and helped his teams capture four Stanley Cups. His wife, Colleen, knew what she was doing when she trademarked Mr. Hockey as his nickname (and hers as Mrs. Hockey).

Many more stories are about Gordie Howe the man, who would stay to sign autographs until every fan had one, who used his fame to raise money for charity, who had time for everyone, who was always the most modest guy in the room.

"I was 18 years old when I first met him in the hallways at Joe Louis Arena," Steve Yzerman said. "He introduced himself to me, and I was kind of in awe. He was very nice and very humble and very down-to-earth. You're talking, at the time, to the best player ever to play. It was a neat thing for me."

Gordie Howe with a trophy from the Sports Guild in Detroit in January 1954.

One summer the two were at a charity game in Halifax, Nova Scotia, when Yzerman realized he had forgotten his shin pads. Howe lent him his. "I don't even think he played," Yzerman said. "So I wore Gordie's shin pads, and he just left, and I carried them around all summer long."

Then there was the time in June 2007 when Nicklas Lidstrom, his wife, and their four young sons ended up on a private plane with Howe because their scheduled flight to Toronto for the NHL Awards Show had been cancelled. "He took time to talk to my kids and explain how he worked out in the summertime to get in shape for the hockey season, which they thought was very cool," Lidstrom said. "He was kind and funny."

Encouraged by Colleen, Howe embraced public appearances. Gordie's son Mark Howe was out running errands when a stranger recognized him. The man told Mark he just had waited in line three hours to meet Gordie for the 22nd time. "The guy told me, 'Every time I meet him, it's like the greatest thrill of my life,'" Mark recalled. "That's the impact my dad had on people. He was always accessible. He never turned anyone away. We grew used to having to wait for him. We'd go to a store with him, and we'd sit and wait while he signed autographs. 'That's just what you do,' he would say. 'That's how you repay the people.' Dad would always say, 'Hey, these are the people that pay my salary. I'm going to give them everything they deserve.' That's who he was."

Howe's amazing career was anchored by 25 years in Detroit. He was handsome, strong, and skilled, a hard worker who played an incredibly demanding game until he was 52. Wayne Gretzky, growing up across the border in Ontario, wanted to wear No. 9 when he played junior hockey in honor of Howe. When that wasn't available in the NHL, he chose 99.

Born in the rural community of Floral, Saskatchewan, on March 31, 1928, Howe grew up during the Depression in Saskatoon, one of nine children born to Ab and Katherine Howe. Katherine was chopping wood when she went into labor, and Gordie would later tell the story that his mom was so self-reliant and resilient that she tied the umbilical cord herself after giving birth at home.

Howe learned to skate on frozen potato patches. During especially tough times, the family would eat oatmeal three times a day. (Oatmeal was a staple of Howe's life; even after he suffered a stroke on top of having dementia in his eighties, son Murray said his dad's daily breakfast consisted of four eggs, toast with butter, a banana, four sausage links, and a bowl of oatmeal.) Howe was a strapping boy, reaching six feet as a teenager. Life at home was hard, and Howe was convinced hockey was his salvation. He would sit at the kitchen table practicing his autograph for hours. There would be rumors years later that he could sign his name a thousand times an hour.

Howe left school after eighth grade. He was 15 when he was invited to a Wings camp in Windsor, Ontario. He signed a contract for $2,300 and a team jacket and went to play for the Galt Red Wings, an affiliate junior club based in Galt, Ontario. A year later the Wings promoted Howe to the Omaha Knights of the United States Hockey League, where Howe finished the 1945–46 season with 48 points in 51 games. He was 18 years old. It would be the last time Howe played for a minor league team until he took a spin for one game with the Detroit Vipers of the International Hockey League in 1997—at age 69.

On October 16, 1946, Howe made his Red Wings debut against the Toronto Maple Leafs. He scored a goal, the first of a franchise-record 786. At 18 he was the youngest player in the NHL. The Wings' annual press guide described him as "a typical teenage youngster. He enjoys swing music and malted milks. He is shy and afraid of the opposite sex."

Jack Adams, the general manager, "knew what he had in Dad," Mark Howe said. "He looked out for him, looked after him." What Adams had, what the Wings had, was an ambidextrous right wing who was good at everything. Howe was a smooth skater with an accurate shot, a savvy playmaker with soft hands and hard elbows. Opponents came to fear and respect him; he was the most complete player in the league, and if a defender tried to get the puck off of him, Howe would elbow him in the head.

Howe had attitude and brawn, and although the fights diminished as his stardom expanded, his ability to score and his punch bequeathed the Gordie Howe hat trick: a goal, an assist, and a fight. (Howe only had two of them himself. The first was on October 11, 1953, against the Maple Leafs when he set up Red Kelly's goal, scored to make it 2–0, and fought Fernie Flaman. The second came on March 21, 1954, also against the Leafs, when Howe scored the first goal, set up two by Ted Lindsay, and fought Ted Kennedy.)

Howe turbocharged the juggernaut Adams had assembled and the Wings emerged as a dynasty. They finished first in the regular season in

MARK HOWE

Amusingly enough, the Howes rarely talked hockey at home. So Mark Howe relished when his dad would take him to the rink and let him watch practice. He knew he'd be in for a long treat, because days with his dad never ended early. They ended only after Gordie Howe had signed an autograph for every fan who mobbed him.

His dad already had won the Stanley Cup four times when Mark was born in May 1955, and Gordie's career with the Red Wings lasted into Mark's teenage years. But at home they "always talked about fishing and being able to do other stuff like that together," Mark said. "Family was everything to my dad. When my son Travis was born in '78, I was living in Connecticut. This was before cell phones. My dad called on a pay phone and said, 'I'm in the neighborhood. Can I stop by for five minutes?' Well, it turned out he was two hours away and had to drive an hour out of his way to come visit for 10 minutes and then go home. That was the kind of father he was."

Mark Howe forged a highly successful hockey career of his own, playing junior hockey in the Detroit area. When he was 16 years old he was part of the U.S. team that won a silver medal at the 1972 Winter Olympics in Sapporo, Japan. In 1973 Mark signed with the World Hockey Association's Houston Aeros, joining his dad and older brother, Marty. Together the three Howes helped the Aeros win the WHA championship in 1974 and 1975. In 1974 Mark represented Canada at the Summit Series (Mark is a dual citizen of the U.S. and Canada). He played on a line with Gordie, who was 46 by them. Mark, Marty, and Gordie played together in the NHL with the Hartford Whalers in 1979–80.

In 1982–83 Mark began his career with the Philadelphia Flyers. He joined the Red Wings in 1992, aged 37, and finished his NHL career where his dad had started his own. Mark played 122 games for the Wings before retiring in 1995. In all, he logged 929 games in the NHL, plus 426 in the WHA. The Flyers retired his No. 2 jersey in 2012.

Mark Howe segued into a job as video coach with the Wings before finding a niche as a scout and serving as the Wings' director of pro scouting. In November 2011, he was inducted into the Hockey Hall of Fame—with his dad by his side. "I wish my mom could have been there to see it too," Mark Howe said. "But to have my dad there, after all the years we played together, all the stuff we did together, it was very special."

seven straight years, from 1949 to 1955. After losing in the Stanley Cup Finals in 1948 and 1949, the Wings won the Cup in 1950, '52, '54, and '55.

Howe starred for the Wings from 1946 to 1971. He finished in the top five in NHL scoring for 20 straight seasons and garnered headlines alongside Sid Abel and Lindsay as the Production Line, named after Detroit's prolific car industry. In 1949–50, Lindsay, Abel, and Howe finished first, second, and third, respectively, in scoring. Howe endured a life-threatening scare in the first game of the 1950 playoffs when he attempted to check Toronto's Kennedy and instead crashed headfirst into the boards. Howe lost consciousness and suffered a fractured skull, broken cheekbone, and lacerated eye. Team officials, fearing the worst, called his family in Saskatoon, urging them to come to Detroit. Howe missed the rest of the playoffs, and fans cheered when he came onto the ice to touch the Cup, his head wrapped in bandages. It is estimated Howe received some 400 stitches to his face during his career.

The next season Howe led the league with 43 goals and 86 points to capture his first Art Ross Trophy. He won the Art Ross again the next season, and added his first Hart Trophy when he posted a league-leading 47 goals and 86 points. Howe kept outdoing himself: in 1952–53, he led the NHL in goals (49), assists (46), and points (95), becoming the first NHL player to reach 90 points in a season.

Howe won the Art Ross Trophy each year from 1951 to 1954 and again in 1957 and 1963 and was the league's leading goal-scorer in each of those years except 1954, when Maurice Richard's 37 goals were four more than Howe had. Richard retired in September 1960 as the league's career leader, with 544 goals. Howe broke the record on November 10, 1963, and finished that season as the NHL's career leader with 566 goals, 719 assists, 1,285 points, and 1,189 games played.

Howe was determinedly accessible to fans as his fame grew, but in his early years with the Wings he was still very much a shy farm boy in a big city. He slept on a cot at Olympia Stadium. He entertained himself by people-watching along Woodward Avenue and hung out at a nearby bowling alley named Lucky Strike Lanes. It was there in 1951 that Howe met Colleen Jaffa, whom he would marry in 1953. She was a tremendous influence on Howe, a trailblazer who took control of the business side of his career. In 1968–69, the first season the schedule had expanded to 76 games because the league had doubled to 12 teams, Howe recorded a career-high 103 points (he topped 100 points in the last game of the season, recording two goals and two assists on March 30, 1969, the day before his 41st birthday). When Howe complained that his $45,000 salary was only the third-highest on the team, owner Bruce Norris more than doubled Howe's salary to $100,000—and blamed Colleen.

In their book *Net Worth*, authors David Cruise and Alison Griffiths portrayed Howe as one of the most underpaid stars in professional sports because of his reluctance to demand more money. Howe loved causing trouble on the ice, but it was not part of his DNA off the ice. "Dad always respected his bosses," Mark Howe said.

After retirement in 1971, Howe took a front-office job with the Wings, with the title of vice president, but it was a figurehead position. He was 43—an old age in sports—but sitting still didn't sit well with a man as vigorous as Howe. The Wings celebrated the end of Howe's playing days— or so they thought—by flying in vice president Spiro Agnew to attend the ceremony to retire Howe's No. 9 in March 1972. Howe was inducted into the Hockey Hall of Fame five months later.

When the Houston Aeros of the upstart World Hockey Association called in 1973, however, Howe was game. He still wanted to play hockey, and the Aeros offered him the opportunity to do so alongside sons Marty and Mark, two of Gordie and Colleen's four children. Although 45, Howe recorded 100 points in 70 games (31 goals, 69 assists), was voted the WHA's most valuable player, and led the Aeros to the league championship. They repeated in 1975 when Howe notched 99 points. He added 102 more in 1976.

All three Howes relocated to Hartford in 1977 to play for the New England Whalers. For his six WHA seasons, Howe finished with 508 points (174 goals, 334 assists) in 419 games. In 1979, the WHA folded and four teams—including the Whalers—joined the NHL, and Howe played one last season in the NHL. It was a fitting farewell for Mr. Hockey: 41 points in 80 games, and an invitation to the 1980 All-Star Game in what was then a brand-new Joe Louis Arena. Howe was treated to a long ovation from 21,002 fans chanting "Gor-*die*, Gor-*die*."

Howe retired in 1980 having scored 801 goals and recorded 1,049 assists in 1,767 NHL games. His 1,850 points rank fourth all-time, after Wayne Gretzky, Jaromir Jagr, and Mark Messier. Howe ranks second in all-time goals, behind only Gretzky. His numbers with the Wings are the

MRS. HOCKEY

Colleen Howe was the tough and tenacious counterpart to her husband, a woman who recognized what she had in Gordie and wanted to share. Born Colleen Joffa in 1933 in Sandusky, Michigan, she was living in Detroit when she met Gordie Howe in April 1951 at the Lucky Strike Lanes, near Olympia Stadium. She was 20 years old when they married in 1953 and together they had four children: sons Marty, Mark, and Murray and daughter Cathy. That was her nucleus.

"She believed in her family," Mark Howe said. "Part of that was what she did for my father—making sure that he got the recognition but also making sure he gave back. She was an incredible, great mom and always a great wife."

"She didn't have a great childhood," Mark Howe continued. "She was basically raised by her great-aunt Elsie and her upbringing was difficult compared to what we have. So I think she used that to foster her family, to have a really good family life, and she would fight like the devil for that."

Colleen Howe would fight for many, especially fellow hockey wives. Today's NHL arenas have rooms designated specifically for families, where wives, girlfriends, parents, and children can eat, socialize, and hang out before and after games. Players today receive an allotment of tickets for home games; that wasn't the case for hockey wives in the 1950s. "They were all treated like second-class citizens," Mark Howe said. "She tried to make it more of a family thing, to not be on the outside. Mom pushed hard to make the wives, to make the children, part of their husbands' and fathers' lives in hockey as the years progressed. She wanted them to be recognized. When she believed in something, she went at it 100 percent. When she had an idea, it was very hard to deter her. And generally all her ideas were about making the quality of life better in hockey."

It was Colleen Howe who trademarked Gordie as "Mr. Hockey" and herself as "Mrs. Hockey." She served as a sports agent for her husband as well as sons Mark and Marty, both of whom would go on to play professional hockey. She orchestrated Gordie's return at age 45 after a two-year retirement to play with Mark and Marty on the Houston Aeros of the World Hockey Association.

She also founded the first Junior A team in the United States, the Detroit Junior Wings; developed the first private indoor rink in Michigan, Gordie Howe Hockeyland in St. Clair Shores; created the Howe

Foundation, a charity to bring hockey to the less fortunate; and became the first woman inducted into the U.S. Hockey Hall of Fame.

She fought to ensure Gordie was recognized for his greatness—and she was equally staunch that he was approachable. "She wanted people to know what a great person Gordie was," Mark said. "Back in the day before TV, players weren't very well known. My mom always made my dad available to the fans, to the people everywhere. He was a generous guy and always made sure he signed every single article after every game, which I loved because I got to sit at the rink for an extra hour. It was great for the people. They got to meet him. At the same time, it helped build my dad's image. My mom knew what she had in my dad and she wanted other people to know."

stuff of legend. He leads the franchise with 786 goals, 1,809 points, and 1,687 games played, and he ranks second with 1,023 assists, behind only Yzerman.

Howe spent 15 seasons in the Hartford Whalers organization, 10 of them as a special assistant to the managing general partner. When Mike Ilitch purchased the Wings from the Norris family in 1982, there was talk of the Howes moving back to Michigan even though Howe still had five years left on his Whalers contract. Howe was delighted at the prospect. "I've always wanted to come back to the Detroit area," he said in June 1982. It was the second time in five years a Howe homecoming was mulled—in 1977, Colleen Howe negotiated with team officials only to have talks break down when owner Bruce Norris suddenly hired Lindsay to be general manager. When fans spotted Howe at Detroit's airport, they chanted his name.

It didn't happen, though Howe would eventually become a regular sight at Joe Louis Arena, milling about the locker room talking hockey with players, trainers, and reporters. In older age as in younger, Howe had time for everyone. "You wanted to hear Gordie's hockey stories," said Kirk Maltby, who played for the Wings from 1996 to 2010. "You wanted to be within an ear's length so you could hear him, but at the same time you didn't want to be right next to him because he'd get his fists and his elbows up. He'd get so animated. Thankfully there was never a hockey stick nearby."

Mike Modano, who grew up in metro Detroit and finished his Hockey Hall of Fame career with the Wings, wore No. 9 for much of his career in honor of Howe. He was a "great storyteller," Modano said. "Certain guys can just go on and on, and Gordie was one of those guys. He just had a gift."

In 2002, Colleen was diagnosed with Pick's disease, a neurological disorder that resembles Alzheimer's. Gordie took care of her, tenderly looking after his wife as her memory faded into a fog. She died March 6, 2009, aged 76, at the family's home in Bloomfield Hills, Michigan. The Wings had a moment of silence for her before their next game.

Howe's own health deteriorated in his eighties. He suffered a stroke in October 2014, compounding health problems stemming from his own battle with dementia. During the winter months he lived with his daughter, Cathy Purnell, and her husband, Bob, in Lubbock, Texas, because the milder weather allowed Howe to be outdoors. He still wasn't one to sit still. He liked to rake the garden, finding comfort in the repetitive motion and in knowing he was helping out one of his children. He still loved fishing, just as he did as a young boy when he used wooden, handmade lures to catch northern pike in Saskatoon.

Mark Howe, a Hockey Hall of Fame inductee like his father, was by then a scout for the Red Wings. Based outside Philadelphia, Mark sometimes took Gordie with him to games. Hockey was integral to Gordie's life, a balm against the ravages of dementia. The sights, the sounds, the smells were ingrained in his brain. The Wings arranged for Howe to drop the ceremonial puck during the second alumni game as part of the celebration surrounding the 2014 Winter Classic. Yzerman and Mark Howe attempted to assist Gordie, but he would have none of it. Mark received a nasty look for his intentions, which made him smile. "Dad knew the difference between me and Stevie and only got mad at me," he said, "And 30 seconds later, it was forgotten."

Spurred by son Murray, a doctor specializing in radiology, the family took Howe to a stem-cell clinic in Mexico and deemed treatments beneficial to Howe's quality of life. He attended his last Wings game on March 28, 2016, at the Joe, where fans sang "Happy Birthday to You" three days before his 88th birthday.

Howe passed away June 10, 2016. His death drew national and international headlines. President Barack Obama released a statement lauding that Howe's "productivity, perseverance, and humility personified his adopted hometown of Detroit. The greatest players define their game for a generation. Over more than a half a century on the ice, Mr. Hockey defined it for a lifetime."

A public visitation took place on June 14 at Joe Louis Arena. Thousands of fans and admirers paid their respects as Howe lay in repose, his closed casket adorned with red and white flowers. Fittingly for a man who never turned anyone away, fans could walk right up to the casket and touch it.

Gretzky was among those in attendance. He was 10 years old when he first met Howe, and his generosity made a lifelong impression. "I was really lucky," Gretzky said. "Not everybody gets to meet their hero. And sometimes when you meet them, it wasn't as good as you thought it would be. I got so lucky that the guy I chose happened to be so special. He was very humble."

Howe is one of the greatest hockey players ever, but his legacy is grander for the man he was. The shy farm boy from Saskatoon was a joy to watch play, a delight to meet, a memory to cherish. "Wherever I go, anywhere in the world," Yzerman said, "if people talk about the Red Wings, they talk about Gordie Howe."

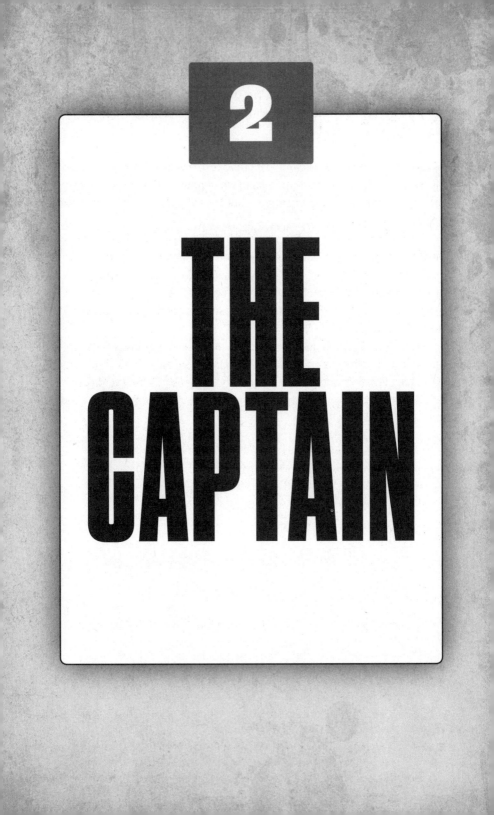

2

THE CAPTAIN

He finally left Joe Louis Arena sometime after 3:00 AM. He had been up for nearly 24 hours, his arms hurt, but the prize he carried out of the arena that June night was worth the aches. Steve Yzerman placed the Stanley Cup in the backseat of his silver Porsche, slid into the driver's seat, and took off. He had realized a dream, but he still had to convince himself it was real.

"I had just won a Cup and I had been there for 14 years," Yzerman reflected in 2019. "Sometimes you wonder if it can be as good as you dream about."

Yzerman had longed for this moment since he was a child growing up in Ontario. He joined the Red Wings in 1983, and as early playoff exits mounted he wondered whether a season ever would end with such joy. He was the face of a franchise that had hoped to draft someone else, and, under the most revered coach in the NHL, he had changed the way he played. He had endured trade rumors and trash talk and terrible disappointments.

Yzerman may not have been who the Wings originally wanted, but his arrival transformed the franchise and galvanized the city. He built a career on quiet excellence, evolving from a draft-day consolation pick into "The Captain." He was a reserved teenager when he first pulled on a winged wheel sweater and a gap-toothed veteran when he first hoisted the Stanley Cup. His homecoming on April 19, 2019, was heralded as another resurrection for the franchise.

"He was ultracompetitive," Hall of Fame coach Scotty Bowman said in a 2019 interview. "That's the first thing that comes to mind. I don't know many players like him. He scored big goals, he blocked shots, he played with injuries. You put a package like that together, it wears off on the rest of the players. There's nobody that knows a player better than the other players on the team."

But back in 1983, the Wings famously coveted Pat LaFontaine with the fourth overall pick in the draft. He was a homegrown star player out of Waterford, Michigan, seemingly a slam dunk as a box-office draw and a guy to build a team around. New owner Mike Ilitch was so intent on making that happen that he made a draft-day decision to offer the New York Islanders $1 million to flip spots. The Wings would have picked third had the Islanders taken the money.

Minnesota drafted Brian Lawton first overall. Hartford drafted Sylvain Turgeon second. At the Wings draft table in Montreal, Ilitch and general manager Jimmy Devellano anxiously waited for the New York Islanders to make their choice. The hope was the Isles would pass on LaFontaine because he was only 5'10" and 180 pounds. When Islanders general manager Bill Torrey called out LaFontaine's name, the Wings were crushed. Ilitch hung his head and stared at the floor.

Out in the crowd, another hopeful teenager wearing a bright red tie lit up when he heard his name called next. "Detroit is a super club with a lot of class," Yzerman said later that day. "They still haven't forgotten the days when they were the greatest."

Yzerman was scouted as an excellent puck handler and a fine skater. He had spent the previous two seasons in the Ontario Hockey League with the Peterborough Petes, but on draft day that June 8, 1983, Yzerman was all about the Wings. "They're rebuilding," he said. "I think I have a chance."

Devellano wasn't so sure. Yzerman looked small (he was listed on draft day as 5'10", 177 pounds). Surely the best thing would be to send Yzerman back for another year of junior hockey. "But two shifts into camp," Devellano recalled when Yzerman retired in 2006, "we knew he was our best player." Yzerman made the Wings, and moved in with Lane Lambert, a fellow 1983 draft pick, on Detroit's riverfront. Devellano would drop by to make sure the young men were eating properly. Sometimes he would take them out to dinner.

LaFontaine was forgotten (for now). The Wings were smitten. Yzerman was quiet but effective. He tallied a goal and an assist in his NHL debut October 5, 1983, a 6–6 tie at Winnipeg, and he finished the season with 39 goals and 87 points. Yzerman was the youngest player in NHL history selected to the All-Star Game when he played for the Campbell Conference on January 31, 1984, at 18 years, eight months, and 22 days.

He was a finalist for the 1984 Calder Trophy. The night of the NHL awards, before Buffalo Sabres goaltender Tom Barrasso was announced the winner, Ilitch handed Yzerman an envelope on which he had written, "You're my rookie of the year." Inside was a check for $25,000.

ABOUT THAT SMILE

Steve Yzerman was one of the most photographed men in the NHL in June 1997, when the Red Wings finally ended a 42-year drought and won the Stanley Cup, dispatching the Blues, Ducks, Avalanche, and Flyers en route. Yzerman had lost one of his front teeth two years earlier, and it had been replaced with a crown by team dentist Chet Regula. When a toothache became gradually more unbearable during the spring of 1997, Yzerman ended up in the dentist's chair the day after Game 1 against the Ducks. "I was feeling lousy all the time and the doctor said I had a bone infection and should have it removed," Yzerman said at the time.

The tooth was taken out May 17. Before a new one could be put in, the Wings were Stanley Cup champions. The image of Yzerman hoisting the Stanley Cup while grinning a gap-toothed smile became an iconic image. "Here I am looking like a hillbilly," Yzerman said of the photo. "Not that there's anything wrong with that."

Yzerman was appointed Wings captain on October 7, 1986. He was 21 years old, the youngest captain in franchise history. Coach Jacques Demers presented Yzerman a Wings sweater bearing the "C" at a news conference after a practice in Oak Park, Michigan. "The captain has to be a guy who can play, a guy who on and off the ice shows some class; a guy who wears the Detroit Red Wings sweater with some pride, and a guy who the other players look up to and respect," Demers said. "He doesn't have to necessarily be a rah-rah guy, but someone who will stand up when times get tough and say, 'Let's go, guys. This is it.'"

Former teammate Gerard Gallant recalled Yzerman's reaction as muted. "He was pretty excited, but he didn't show it much," Gallant said. "That's just the way Steve is. He doesn't show a lot of emotion."

That was at the start of Yzerman's fourth season. When he scored 50 goals in his fifth season, Ilitch gave Yzerman a $50,000 bonus. Alas, the game in which he scored his 50th goal, on March 1, 1988, was the same game in which he crashed into a goal post and tore ligaments in his right knee. Ilitch chartered a private jet to fly Yzerman for a consultation with a specialist at the University of Wisconsin Hospital in Madison. He avoided reconstructive surgery. But the knee would give Yzerman problems throughout the rest of his career.

Still, more personal success followed. In 1988–89, Yzerman tallied 155 points, third in the NHL behind Mario Lemieux and Wayne Gretzky. Yzerman won the Lester B. Pearson Award (MVP selected by the players) and was a finalist for the Hart Memorial Trophy (MVP selected by writers covering the NHL). The following season, Yzerman reached 62 goals and 127 points. He topped 100 points again in 1990–91 and 1991–92.

Playoff success was elusive, though. There were back-to-back Campbell Conference finals appearances in 1987 and 1988, but the '89 playoffs ended after six games and the Wings failed to make the cut in 1990. They lost in the first round in '91 and were swept in the second round in '92.

A 1993 first-round playoff loss to the Toronto Maple Leafs after a team-record 103-point regular season prompted ownership to bring in a new taskmaster. Bowman already had coached six Stanley Cup winners. By that time Yzerman's teammates included Sergei Fedorov, Nicklas Lidstrom, and Vladimir Konstantinov, all culled from the Wings' amazing 1989 draft.

"He had a decade of having to score goals and not win," Bowman reflected in 2019. "I mean, 60 goals, 120 points and you don't win a round in the playoffs. The playoffs are what make the season in hockey. I could sense the disappointment when I got there in '93. I mean, how much disappointment can you have? And what else can you do to change it? He wasn't drafting the players. He wasn't making trades. It's a pretty tough situation if you're not making progress."

Early in the 1993–94 season, Yzerman suffered an injury to his spine. He needed two cervical discs fused together and spent six weeks in a halo-shaped device that immobilized his spine. He rejoined the lineup in December and helped the Wings win 46 games and finish first in the Western Conference with 100 points. Yzerman injured his left knee in the regular season finale but appeared in the final three games of the first-round series against the upstart San Jose Sharks. In Game 7, Chris Osgood mishandled the puck on the series-clinching goal and once again the Wings were one and done.

Spurred by the defeat, Bowman demanded more of his players. He knew the team had to become harder to play against, had to buy into team defense. If every player on the ice checked, Bowman was certain the Wings would fare better when it really mattered.

"Scotty wasn't just asking me to change my game," Yzerman said in 2019. "He asked our entire team—well, he didn't ask us, he told us—that we had to be a good defensive hockey team and he wanted us all to buy into it. I remember for myself, we had one particular conversation where he talked about his teams with the Canadiens and Jacques Lemaire's role. Basically, Scotty said that he knew our team in Detroit could score a lot of goals, but we needed to become a really good defensive hockey team. He was counting on everybody, including me, to do that. We all wanted to win, and that was what we were going to do. We all committed to it."

At his retirement ceremony in 2007, Yzerman credited Bowman for making him mentally tougher. "Playing under him, my confidence grew," Yzerman said. "My stats declined, but my confidence grew. I will be forever grateful for Scotty's coaching abilities, his ability to bring us together and what he did. He changed me as a hockey player in a lot of ways and made me a much better leader and a much better captain."

Yzerman's willingness to adapt his style was further evidence of the competitiveness that so impressed Bowman. Yzerman had rounded into his thirties, he had suffered through injuries that would have felled a lesser player, but had become a force to deal with at both ends of the ice. "He became a very good defensive player," Bowman said. "He knew what he had to do to improve the team. He was very focused on playing two-way hockey. It hurt him production-wise, but he'd produced before. I think he knew what he was doing."

The 1994–95 season was reduced to 48 games because of a labor dispute between the NHL and the Players' Association. The Wings finished with a league-best 33-11-4 record and went into the '95 playoffs as Stanley Cup favorites.

Yzerman, though, injured his right knee in Game 4 of the second-round sweep of the Sharks and underwent arthroscopic surgery May 29 to repair cartilage damage. As part of his rehabilitation, Yzerman spent an hour a day in a hyperbaric oxygen chamber. He grew so sick of it he wanted to throw it in a lake.

A trying summer—the Wings, despite losing only two games in their first three series, were swept in the Finals by the New Jersey Devils—segued into a testy fall. For the second time in his career, rumors swirled that Yzerman was on the trading block. (In 1992, general manager Bryan Murray had explored trading Yzerman for LaFontaine, the Detroit-area native the Wings originally hoped to draft in 1983. Although his career was cut short by concussions, LaFontaine was inducted into the Hockey Hall of Fame in 2003.)

In October 1995, just as the season was about to start, Yzerman's name was linked to the Ottawa Senators and New York Islanders. Yzerman publicly ripped the Wings organization for not telling him first, while sounding wistful about the possibility of leaving. "I can't say I'm upset about the possibility of being traded," he told reporters. "I just expected to be treated like an adult. I would have thought that at some time somebody would have come to me and said, 'Here's what we're thinking. Here's why we're doing this.' I guess they're not adult enough to do that. I thought I knew people in the organization well enough. I've always tried to be upfront and honest and I thought I deserved that in return—the good or the bad. I love this city and I love this hockey team. But life goes on. Hockey goes on. Careers go on. We'll just wait and see what happens."

What happened was the home opener, when fans shared their feelings about the trade rumors. Even before public address announcer Budd Lynch finished introducing Yzerman, fans were on their feet, roaring and cheering and clapping and chanting, "Ste-*vie*, Ste-*vie*." Yzerman raised his stick to salute the crowd.

Describing the moment later, Yzerman said it was "a thrill." A thrill for Yzerman, a chill for Bowman: the coach was booed, soundly and thoroughly. Afterward, talk of trading Yzerman died down.

Shortly after he had been drafted, Yzerman and Devellano joked about how Yzerman would play until he was 35 and win five Stanley Cups. It was a longer wait than either man predicted, but in 1997 Yzerman finally hoisted the Cup and Devellano finally made good on the promise to win the Cup that he had made when Mike and Marian Ilitch hired him in 1982.

Yzerman was 32 years old. He already had topped 1,000 games and had reached 500 goals, but playoff disappointments had racked up as fast as his personal accomplishments. There were summers when Yzerman didn't want to go outside, didn't want to be recognized. As disheartening as the early playoff exits of the late 1980s were, part of that was the roster. By the early 1990s, the Wings had three superstars on the team in Yzerman, Fedorov, and Lidstrom—and still the playoffs disappointed.

"The last five years there have been a couple of times you don't want to go out, you don't want to be recognized," Yzerman said the night of

Steve Yzerman hoists the Stanley Cup, June 7, 1997. (Mary Schroeder)

the '97 championship. "You put a hat on or put sunglasses on. It was embarrassing. I was in Las Vegas and a couple of guys from Windsor came by. They said, 'Hey, Steve Yzerman. I'm going to stay away from this table. There's no luck here.'"

In 2009, the year he was inducted into the Hockey Hall of Fame, Yzerman revealed the toll that losing in the playoffs all those years had taken on him. "You're trying to get over the hump and questioning yourself and questioning your confidence, questioning if you're good enough, if the team is good enough," he said. "It was a real challenge to remain confident."

The double-overtime goal Yzerman scored against the St. Louis Blues in Game 7 of the 1996 playoffs was a career highlight, but one of his personal favorites was the goal he scored in Colorado in the '97 playoffs in Game 2. "It was late in the game and it was kind of a fluky goal. I just banked it in off Patrick Roy's leg and it went in," Yzerman said. "We ended up winning the game and winning that series."

An exhilarating Stanley Cup Finals against the Philadelphia Flyers followed. Yzerman scored to secure a 4–2 victory in Game 1. He scored his sixth goal of the playoffs in Game 2 and his seventh in Game 3, both Wings victories. In Game 4, he picked up an assist on the Cup-clinching goal by Darren McCarty. Finally, on June 7, 1997, Yzerman lived his childhood fantasy by hoisting the Stanley Cup. He flashed a gap-toothed smile as he lapped the ice at Joe Louis Arena.

"As I went about halfway around, I thought, 'This thing is getting heavy,'" Yzerman said that night. "My arm about fell off. I was looking for my parents and my wife and a friend in the corner. I wanted to make sure I saw them as I was carrying it around the rink. I just tried to take it all in."

It took Yzerman 14 years to win his first Stanley Cup, and 15 to win two. When the Wings repeated as champions on June 16, 1998, it was a second opportunity to really appreciate what it meant to come so far in the playoffs. "In '97, as exciting and fun as it was, it was really nerve-racking," Yzerman said. "We were up 3–0 in the Finals and before that Game 4, you could hear a pin drop in the locker room. We were in total control, but we were so nervous. In '98, we were able to enjoy it more. We were confident."

Yzerman's career continued to flourish. On November 26, 1999, he became the 11th player in NHL history to score 600 goals. On June 15, 2000, he was awarded the Frank J. Selke Trophy as NHL's best defensive forward. On February 24, 2002, Yzerman won an Olympic gold medal with Team Canada. On June 13, 2002, he hoisted the Stanley Cup for the third time in his career. His right knee was in such pain that Yzerman only played one regular season game after the Salt Lake Olympics, but he gutted it out through the 23 playoff games it took the Wings to secure another championship.

"His strong suit is he's ultracompetitive," Bowman said. "He is not going to accept half measures. Players saw what happened to him with his knee and found out that he was going to play again and saw how he played. If he did that, how could they not do it?"

Yzerman set up two goals in the Game 5 finale against the Carolina Hurricanes, a 3-1 triumph, but his biggest impact came when he addressed his teammates after they lost the first two games of the playoffs—at the Joe, to boot. "The one thing that we're going to keep talking about is what he had to do in 2002," longtime teammate Kris Draper said. "We're down 2-0, and he just nonchalantly and casually addresses the team. Next thing you know, we go out and win four straight. That's how legends are made. There are times he got knocked down and he had to lean on his stick to get up. He couldn't just stand up. But he had so much desire to win, and that's what makes him so great."

Yzerman looked for his family in the stands when he won his first Cup. When he won his third, he brought his oldest daughter, Isabella, then 8, onto the ice at Joe Louis Arena.

Once into the off-season, Yzerman had to do something about his right knee. It had ached on and off since the injury in 1988. In August 2002, Yzerman underwent an osteotomy, a realignment procedure so radical that there was no guarantee he would be able to play again. This time it took 66 games to recover, but on February 24, 2003, Yzerman returned to the ice at Joe Louis Arena to a thunderous ovation. Once again, Yzerman had accomplished something almost superhuman.

Yzerman played 75 games the next season, in 2003–04. He waited through the labor dispute that wiped out the following season and returned for his final season in 2005–06. The Wings won 58 games and coasted to the Presidents' Trophy with 124 points. Yzerman suffered a torn oblique muscle that sidelined him for Games 4 and 5 of the first-round series against the Oilers, but he returned to play in Game 6 and set up a

ALMOST TRADED?

Steve Yzerman wearing another NHL team's uniform? It boggles the mind. The Wings did talk to teams about trading The Captain. The first time was in 1992. Jimmy Devellano had been pushed upstairs to a senior vice president role, and owner Mike Ilitch brought in Bryan Murray as general manager and coach. Ten years had passed since Ilitch purchased the Wings, and there was still no Stanley Cup championship. Pat LaFontaine—the Waterford native the Wings really wanted to draft in 1983—had forced the Islanders to trade him in October 1991. He put up 46 goals in 1991–92, his first season with the Buffalo Sabres.

"There was talk between Buffalo and Detroit about LaFontaine for Yzerman even up," Devellano said in 2019. "There were talks. We didn't make it happen. But it was considered." Ultimately, Ilitch nixed the trade.

The second time the Wings explored trading Yzerman was 1995. Scotty Bowman was in charge. Ken Holland was the assistant general manager. The Ottawa Senators were newly minted and having a terrible time; they weren't competitive and they weren't a draw. Their arena at that time, the Ottawa Civic Centre, only seated 9,500 —and still there were often more empty seats than filled ones.

"They were an awful team and they weren't selling tickets," Devellano said. "Randy Sexton, their manager, made an inquiry to Scotty Bowman telling him basically, we need to improve the team, we've got a lot of tickets to sell in the new building. The one guy that would really allow that to happen is Steve Yzerman."

Yzerman grew up in Nepean, on the edge of Ottawa, Ontario. Just as the Wings coveted LaFontaine because he was from the Detroit area, the Senators saw Yzerman as someone who could fill the seats in the new arena they were building, the Canadian Tire Centre. "Sexton asked Scotty if he would ever entertain such a deal," Devellano recalled. Bowman did entertain the idea. He would have had to receive permission from Ilitch to trigger such a trade, but it never came to that. What Bowman did was let it be known Yzerman was available. After all, Bowman pointed out, even Wayne Gretzky was traded. The New York Islanders and Washington Capitals also expressed interest.

When Yzerman found out his name had come up in trade talks, he fumed to reporters about how much it bothered him. It is unlikely Ilitch would have okayed a deal, but Bowman let it play out until it petered out. "Ken Holland and Scotty were in on the discussions," Devellano said. "They would report back to me. There were tons of names involved. At the end of the day, that trade didn't get done because they couldn't even afford to pay Yzerman. It was a wasted effort."

goal. That was May 1, 2006, eight days before his 41st birthday. That was Yzerman's last game, a 4–3 loss in Edmonton. He retired that July, the longest-serving captain in league history.

"I should have done it earlier, actually," Yzerman said in 2009. "I think if I did it all over again, I'd have retired after '02, just because with the condition of my knee, I should have just hung it up after '02. My last year, it was a real struggle just to stay healthy. I was relieved to retire. I knew I couldn't keep up anymore. I was falling apart."

The Wings retired Yzerman's No. 19 in a 90-minute ceremony on January 2, 2007. He was inducted into the Hockey Hall of Fame on November 9, 2009, alongside 2002 teammates Brett Hull and Luc Robitaille. In fact, Hull was part of one of Yzerman's favorite memories. Reflecting on his career in 2009, Yzerman had this to say when asked about his favorite lines: "Playing with Paul MacLean and Gerard Gallant was a lot of fun. We had success on the ice, but they were both really witty guys. Darren McCarty and Bob Errey and I were a line, and we had zero chemistry—like, we couldn't make a pass, we just fumbled around out there, but we used to have a lot of fun laughing on the bench about our ineptitudes. It was a lot of fun. In '02 playing with Brett and then Sergei in the playoffs was really memorable."

After retiring, Yzerman joined the Wings' front office and set about learning the managerial side of an NHL club. Gradually, his life changed. Instead of skating, he worked out on elliptical machines. He stopped carrying around crossword puzzles, a habit he developed early in his career. "Joey Kocur got me started on them and then there was a whole group of guys that would do them," Yzerman recalled in 2019. "Joey was the only guy smart enough that could do the *New York Times* crossword puzzle. We were all *USA Today* guys. I would just grab one in the morning. As you get older you don't sleep in as much and you get up early and you get to the rink early and you put on your hot pack or your ice pack and grab a cup of coffee and kill time doing a crossword puzzle. I liked doing them before games and before practices because it took my mind off the game. For whatever reason, when I retired I stopped doing them. Most of time I watch hockey. And if I'm not watching hockey I'm watching European soccer, and if not I listen to audiobooks a lot."

As executive director for Team Canada, Yzerman, who became a U.S. citizen on his 36th birthday, led his homeland to gold medals at the

2010 Vancouver Olympics and 2014 Sochi Olympics. He left the Wings organization in May 2010, when he was offered the general manager position by the Tampa Bay Lighting. When he announced he was stepping back in the fall 2018, the last year of his contract, the Wings knew they had a chance to bring him back. On April 19, 2019, the man who wore No. 19 returned to where he belonged.

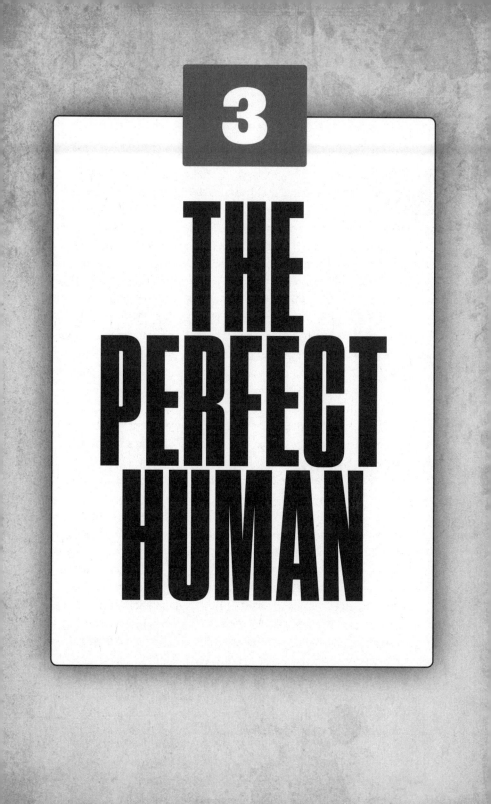

3

THE PERFECT HUMAN

Nicklas Lidstrom was on his way to Toronto for the NHL Awards Show, nominated, as usual, for the Norris Trophy. He, his wife, and their oldest sons boarded a flight at Detroit Metro Airport only to deplane with the rest of the passengers because of a mechanical issue. An hour passed, then another. Then four. The flight eventually was cancelled, but it took two more hours to arrange for the baggage to be unloaded. The Lidstroms ended up leaving Detroit around 5:00 PM on team owner Mike Ilitch's private jet, accompanied by Gordie Howe and Larry Murphy, who also were on the scheduled 10:26 AM flight. That night, Howe presented the Hart Trophy to Sidney Crosby. Murphy presented Lidstrom his fifth Norris Trophy, recognizing his superiority among NHL defensemen.

Throughout the boring, unpredictable delay, Lidstrom's sons behaved like model children, not a single fit thrown even as time dragged on. Like their famous father, their behavior was perfect. That June day in 2007 is a snapshot of what made Lidstrom so special: it wasn't just that he was never out of position on the ice; he was never out of sorts anywhere. "I don't know if there has been a less flashier superstar player in hockey than Nick Lidstrom," Kirk Maltby said in 2019. "Nick just did everything great but he made it look so ho-hum."

Soon after he joined the Wings in 1991 (he almost rejected their overture because he wanted to play for Sweden in the 1992 Olympics, and was hesitant to turn pro), teammates started calling Lidstrom "Super Swede." Before long, he was known by the moniker "The Perfect Human." There was never a pile of equipment in front of his locker, because Lidstrom hung up all his gear in his stall. He was remarkably even-tempered. He was assessed just 514 penalty minutes in 1,564 games.

He never lost his temper off the ice either. Bob Rouse, who played with Lidstrom for four seasons, once borrowed Lidstrom's car—a leased Mercedes that Rouse estimated cost in the $90,000 range—and returned it with a dented bumper. "He was test-driving it to see if he liked it," Rouse said in 1997. "So I said, 'Hey, can I borrow it to take some friends out to eat?' We go to this restaurant, and when the valet parking guy brings it back—the bumper is just kind of hanging there. I call him and say, 'Nick, you wouldn't believe what happened,' and I told him what the car looked like." Many a person would have erupted. Lidstrom did not so much as curse.

While some players would chastise reporters on occasion, Lidstrom never did. When he was asked about failing to convert on a 5-on-3 power play during the 2009 playoffs, many a player would have scoffed because the two-man advantage lasted only two seconds. Not Lidstrom. He made note of the short duration, but still politely answered the question.

That was also the year Lidstrom missed his first playoff game, after taking a stick to the groin area. He underwent surgery on a testicle while his teammates played Game 4 of the Western Conference finals in Chicago. "We didn't know until we came to the rink before the game," Maltby said. "We're like 'What? Nick is not playing?' I think it helped us not knowing all day. We won the game but we were shocked he wasn't playing. We weren't used to not having Nick in the lineup. He was so dependable. I honestly think if you needed him to, he could have played an entire 60-minute game."

Everything Lidstrom did, he made look effortless. "From the minute he played his first NHL game, he looked totally comfortable," Steve Yzerman said in 2015, the year Lidstrom was inducted into the Hockey Hall of Fame. "I never saw him get rattled, he never had a bad day at the office, never reacted or acted inappropriately on or off the ice. He was the most low-maintenance player I have ever seen."

Lidstrom was the stealth Swede: unimposing, imperturbable, incredibly efficient. His poise was a running joke. A Detroit-based Swedish reporter who had known Lidstrom since his days playing for Vasteras IK would tell stories of how teammates would ask Lidstrom's dad how to get him mad before a game. His wife, Annika, had no answer either. "He's always so calm," she would say.

Lidstrom played against top lines, played in all situations, sometimes seemingly playing every other shift. His ability to read plays was superb. "If Wayne Gretzky anticipated plays offensively," Yzerman said in 1997, "Nick does that defensively."

Slava Fetisov, who began his legendary career as a defenseman for the famed Red Army, would point out that Lidstrom "controls the game. He's not flashy like Brian Leetch or Paul Coffey, but I think he is the most

Nicklas Lidstrom hoists the Stanley Cup, June 13, 2002. (Julian H. Gonzalez)

valuable defenseman in the league. His skill level is incredible. He is so good at both ends of the rink. He is very underrated. Maybe because he's so quiet, but he has so much presence."

Lidstrom won his first Norris Trophy in 2001, at age 31, and his last of seven in 2011, aged 41. He retired in 2012 having produced 1,142 points in 1,564 NHL games. In 20 seasons he missed just 44 games, and a dozen of those were in his last season, 2011–12. The Wings never missed the playoffs with Lidstrom. He played in 263 playoff games, a league record for most playoff games with a single franchise.

"Nick was so consistent and durable, I don't know if it will ever be duplicated," Scotty Bowman said. "He always played against the best players in the league, and his stats were terrific. He was just a consummate, consummate pro, and he will go down in history for his durability and performance. Considering he played against the best in the league, as a defenseman his offensive stats were terrific. He didn't go up the ice very often, and he never got caught up the ice. I have never seen another defenseman who could play in the O-zone and not get caught. Whenever he had the puck and made a play to a teammate, we generally kept the puck. Nick's possession game was fantastic."

Not only did Lidstrom play against the opponent's best line, he did so with an array of partners who ranged from Hall-worthy to *who?* There were Paul Coffey and Chris Chelios, Vladimir Konstantinov and Larry Murphy. Lidstrom made a defenseman out of converted forward Mathieu Dandenault, revived the career of Fredrik Olausson, and was the reason Ian White finished the 2011–12 season tied for the team lead with a plus-23 rating. "Nick made a lot [of] partners good," Bowman said. "They all had terrific seasons when they were with him. Without him, some were still pretty good, but not like they were with him. He was effortless. No maintenance at all. He did not need much coaching; he just played at a high level every game."

In 2006, Lidstrom scored the goal that earned his Sweden a gold medal at the Winter Olympics in Torino, Italy. He returned to the NHL and finished the season leading all defensemen with 80 points in 80 games. In 2008, he became the first European to captain a team to the Stanley Cup. Opponents never said a bad word about him, because what was there to criticize?

"He was just so unbelievably positionally good, you could never shake him," said Mike Modano, whose Hockey Hall of Fame career was forged with the Dallas Stars franchise but ended with the Wings in 2010–11. "At some point or other, you had to go through him, and you never could. There was no better defenseman I saw at that. He was never, ever out of position. He never put himself in a vulnerable position."

Teammates measured themselves against Lidstrom. 'We would do two-on-one drills and if it was me and Kris Draper, we didn't care if we scored," Maltby said. "We just thought if we could get a saucer pass from me to him without Nick batting it out of the air, to us that was a successful drill."

As a teenager, Lidstrom studied to become an electrical engineer and drove a truck for the Swedish army. He chose to do the former and had to do the latter, but hockey was his passion. While playing in Vasteras, young Lidstrom drew the interest of a scout named Christer Rockström, who in turn told Neil Smith, the assistant general manager who had recruited Rockström to work for the Wings in the mid-1980s. Lidstrom's numbers weren't anything special—two assists in 20 games in Sweden's top hockey league—but his hockey sense was obvious. The Wings made him their third-round pick, at 53rd overall, in the 1989 draft. "He wasn't very big or strong, but he was very talented," senior vice president Jimmy Devellano later recalled. "Christer really pushed him, and the rest is history."

Right before joining the Wings, Lidstrom played for Sweden in the Canada Cup. Sweden's 4–0 loss to Canada in the semifinals was less important than the confidence he gained from the series: if he could play against Canada's best, he could play in the NHL. His coaches—from Bowman to Mike Babcock—would say the same thing about Lidstrom: he didn't need them."He was pretty well what he is from the get-go," Bowman said. "He was more a self-teacher than anything."

Lidstrom finished 1991–92 as the runner-up for the Calder Trophy, awarded to the NHL's top rookie, losing to Pavel Bure. In 1993, Bowman replaced Bryan Murray as coach, moved Lidstrom from right defense to left, but otherwise left his young star alone. "He was very steady, both offensively and defensively, a very good player," Bowman said. "You never heard from him from one day to the next. He never missed any games, any practices. He didn't want much time off."

Lidstrom was 6'1", 190 pounds in his playing days. He used his brain to impact games—containing opponents, cutting them off, stripping them of the puck. When he had the puck, there was a good chance it would lead to a scoring opportunity. He was a great passer—he ranks third all-time in team assists with 878—and a deft shooter. Lidstrom loved to joke he would have more goals (he finished with 264 in his career) had Tomas Holmstrom not "stolen" a bunch of them by tipping the puck while in front of the crease. Then there were the times Lidstrom would shoot just wide, knowing how bouncy the end boards were at Joe Louis Arena, confident Holmstrom would be able to scoop up the rebound.

When he hung up his skates in 2012, Lidstrom's accomplishments included the record for most games played with a single franchise (1,564) and most regular season victories (900), among others. He holds virtually every record for defensemen in franchise history, including career goals (264), assists (878), points (1,142), playoff goals (54), playoff assists (129), and playoff points (183).

"I don't think there's ever been a better Red Wings defenseman," Bowman said. "I don't think anybody has ever had an impact playing defense like he has. I had great defensemen in Montreal with Larry Robinson and Serge Savard, and he's right there with those guys. If you were to make a mold of a defenseman to play in the NHL, it would be Lidstrom. There's not much else to say about him. He was so steady."

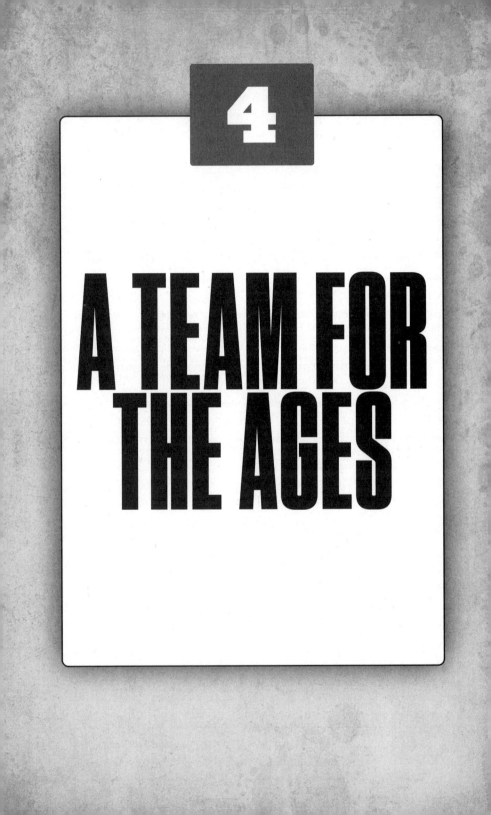

4

A TEAM FOR THE AGES

The locker room was crammed with people, with teammates and their families and friends hugging and chugging and celebrating the Red Wings' third Stanley Cup in six years. Brett Hull suddenly found himself next to Pavel Datsyuk. The young Russian looked at Hull, his brown eyes glistening, and spoke one of the few words he was comfortable with in English. "'Friend,'" Hull remembered. "That says it all. I feel the same way."

The 2001–02 Red Wings were one of the grandest teams ever assembled. When Nicklas Lidstrom and Sergei Fedorov were inducted into the Hockey Hall of Fame in 2015, they brought the number of inductees from that star-studded team to 10: nine players and coach Scotty Bowman.

The friendship, the camaraderie, that blossomed between Hull and Datsyuk began in December 2001, when Bowman paired them on a line with Boyd Devereaux, a fast, two-way forward. Hull, at 37 more than a decade older than Datsyuk and Devereux, dubbed the trio "Two Kids and a Goat."

It was not what Hull envisioned when he signed as a free agent the previous summer. He pictured himself on a line with Steve Yzerman or Fedorov or maybe Igor Larionov. "Instead," Hull said, "it ended up being with one of the greatest kids on earth. I am so happy we were a big part of this."

"This"—the team of teams—ignited with Dominik Hasek. The Buffalo Sabres needed to shed salary and Hasek wanted to chase the Stanley Cup, preferably with the Wings. General manager Ken Holland was ecstatic when Sabres GM Darcy Regier called with the news. Holland traded a first-round pick and forward Vyacheslav Kozlov for a goaltender with six Vezina Trophies and two Hart Memorial Trophies. It was one of the best trades of Holland's career.

The Wings already had superstars on the roster in Yzerman, Lidstrom, Fedorov, Larionov, Chris Chelios, and Brendan Shanahan, but the Hasek trade triggered a spending spree. Within days, Holland signed Luc Robitaille, who months earlier had been on the Kings team that eliminated the Wings from the 2001 playoffs. In August, Holland signed Hull, who openly campaigned to come onboard. Yzerman, Chelios, Lidstrom, Shanahan and Hull all deferred salary, but the Wings still stood to lose $12 million barring a long playoff run.

Hull's arrival gave the Wings something no other team had ever had: three 500-goal scorers, in Yzerman, Robitaille and Hull. Shanahan joined the list in March 2002.

Hull made fun of his age by referring to himself a goat, but the team could have used a herder. All the most important players on the team were grizzled: Larionov was in his forties and Chelios turned 40 midseason. Hasek was Hull's age, 37. Yzerman was 36, Robitaille 35. Fedorov, Lidstrom, and Shanahan were all in their thirties.

They might have been pensioners by pro sports standards, but they were perfect on the ice. The Wings started the season 12–2. Shanahan crammed 17 points into those 14 games. Fedorov contributed 16, Hull and Yzerman 13 points each. At Christmas, the Wings led the league with 26 victories. When the NHL paused in February for the 2002 Winter Olympics, they were in first place with 41 victories after 60 games. Shanahan had 57 points, and Yzerman, Fedorov, and Hull each topped 40. Shanahan, Robitaille, Hull, and Fedorov all had at least 20 goals.

Seven players returned from Salt Lake City with Olympic medals: Team Canada's Yzerman and Shanahan with gold, Team USA's Chelios and Hull with silver, and Russia's Fedorov, Larionov, and Datsyuk with bronze.

The Wings went winless in their last seven games of the season but it didn't matter. They had been so dominant up until the Olympics that they still finished with 116 points, 15 more than second-place Boston. They ranked second in goals per game (3.06), third in goals-against average (2.28), and second on the power play (20.3 percent).

Shanahan led the team with 75 points. Hull was third with 63 and Robitaille had 50 points. Shanahan, Fedorov, Hull, and Robitaille each had at least 30 goals. Yzerman had 48 points, but he played only one game after the Olympics because of nagging pain in his right knee. Hasek delivered an NHL-best 41 victories and a 2.17 goals-against average. He started 64 of the 65 games he played.

The Wings had not traded for Hasek and signed Hull and Robitaille because they wanted to have a good regular season. They did, of course, but the money was an investment in the playoffs. Yet it all began so very horribly. The Wings drew the Vancouver Canucks in the first round. They lost Game 1 4–3 in overtime. Then they lost Game 2, also at home 5–2. Hasek let in eight goals on 45 shots. His goals-against average ballooned to 3.60; his save percentage was .822.

Would the shocking upset of 2001 repeat itself? Fans were livid and let the team know it. The Wings were booed off the ice in Detroit—jeered when they arrived in Vancouver. "I remember riding the bus from the airport in Vancouver to the hotel—we were at the Pan Pacific—and I was

The 2002 Stanley Cup banner is raised in Joe Louis Arena, October 17, 2002.
(Julian H. Gonzalez)

genuinely like, *We put ourselves in a real bind*," Kirk Maltby reflected in 2019. "We got close to the hotel and the cars that had been following us disappeared. We were relieved. Well, they raced to park and meet us and as sure as we came off the bus, all these fans were around us and were giving it to us."

Trust in Yzerman. At practice in Vancouver the day after Game 2, he spoke to his teammates. He told them they had done many good things in the first two games, and not to be crushed because they trailed two games to none. He told them to relax, but also to treat Game 3 as a must-win scenario. There were no fireworks, no pom-poms, just the calm words of The Captain.

"He's the kind of guy, when he steps up the whole room just listens," Kris Draper said. "He picks his spots. That's why he's such a great leader. A guy can say things, but he goes out and backs everything up. When he speaks, it's great to hear him, because of the way he goes out and plays hard."

Yzerman, despite playing on a knee that needed major surgery, had a goal and an assist in Game 3, but the goal that turned the series was scored by Lidstrom. There were 24.6 seconds left in the second period, the game tied at 1–1. Lidstrom carried the puck up ice and fired it on net from the red line.

Improbably, impeccably, it went in. The Wings took the series in six games.

Their second-round series against the St. Louis Blues was a blur. That's how quickly it was over. The Wings won the first two games, got caught sleepwalking in a 6–1 loss in Game 3, woke up, and finished off the series 4–1.

Next up was archrival Colorado—the defending Stanley Cup champion. It was the fifth time in seven years the teams met in the playoffs. There had been blowouts and blow-ups, and this series did not disappoint.

The Wings won Game 1 at home 5–3. Darren McCarty recorded the only hat trick of his career—a natural one, no less—scoring the last two goals in 3 minutes and 11 seconds. Hats and octopi littered the ice at Joe Louis Arena.

The next four games were nail-biters. The Avalanche won Game 2 in overtime, then the Wings countered with an overtime victory in Game 3. When Peter Forsberg beat Hasek in overtime of Game 5 at Joe Louis Arena, it gave the Avs a 3–2 lead in the series heading back to Denver.

"This is a challenge to all of us, individually and as a team, to see what we can do here," Shanahan said at the time. What Shanahan did was score a goal. Yzerman had fired a short-range shot on net. Colorado's Patrick Roy thought he had the puck in his glove, rising in triumph and raising his

THE PROFESSOR

Teammates called him "The Professor" because with his glasses and suits and penchant for chess, Igor Larionov just oozed smarts. Larionov was less than six weeks from his 35th birthday when the Red Wings traded for him in October 1995. Scotty Bowman wanted him enough to send 50-goal scorer Ray Sheppard to San Jose in the trade, because Bowman remembered the impact Larionov had when the Sharks upset the Wings in the first round of the '94 playoffs.

"He was such a great player," Bowman said in 2019. "We lost to San Jose and he was the main reason we lost. If he wasn't around San Jose at that time, we would not have had any trouble beating them. He was a quiet guy, but boy, he knew how to play. And guys looked up to him."

During the 2002 playoffs, Larionov's son was a regular presence in the locker room. Igor Larionov Jr., known to teammates as Little Iggy or Iggy Two, was three years old and reached to his dad's knees. The two would work on drills after practices ended. "I know Igor Senior really enjoys the game, both playing it and watching it," Steve Yzerman said at the time "And his son, he is just hockey-crazy."

Larionov himself started skating when he was around six years old, on an outdoor rink in his home in Voskresensk, Russia. By the time he was 21, he had made it on to the elite Central Red Army team, where he would stay for eight seasons. Larionov won Olympic gold medals with the Soviet Union in '84 and '88, and he won gold at four World Championships. Together with Slava Fetisov, Larionov pushed Soviet authorities to allow hockey players to emigrate to North America.

After stops in Vancouver and San Jose, Larionov arrived in Detroit. He helped them win Stanley Cups in 1997 and '98, and authored one of the most memorable moments of the 2002 championship in the Stanley Cup Finals against the Carolina Hurricanes. In triple overtime of Game 3, Larionov took a pass from Tomas Holmstrom, stickhandled past a defender, and flicked a backhand shot into the Carolina net. Larionov was 41, the oldest player in the NHL.

"I think this is the biggest goal of my career," Larionov said at the time. And when Larionov ventured into the wine business after retirement, he marketed one of his wines under the label Triple Overtime.

left hand. Only the puck wasn't in the glove, it was in the crease, and then Shanahan poked it and it was in the net. What Hasek did was stop all 24 Avalanche shots to deliver a shutout. The Wings won 2–0 and headed back to the Joe for Game 7.

The mere mention of a Game 7 tends to chill spines. They have a reputation as thrillers. The one played May 31, 2002, at Joe Louis Arena thrilled because fans could relax 13 minutes into the game. Roy—whose "Statue of Liberty" flub had been the talk of the hockey world—gave up four goals in the first period. Tomas Holmstrom scored two; Fedorov and Robitaille beat Roy too. Roy didn't even last half the game—he was pulled after 26½ minutes, having allowed six goals on 10 shots. The Wings cruised to a 7–0 victory. Late in the third period, fans sang along as the Joe's loudspeakers blared Neil Diamond's "Sweet Caroline." The Wings had secured a date with the Carolina Hurricanes in the Stanley Cup Finals.

Carolina forward Ron Francis scored in the first minute of overtime in Game 1 at the Joe, but that ultimately worked in the Wings' favor. The most memorable game of the series—before the clinching one—was Game 3. It went on and on. The game began on a Saturday night in Raleigh but didn't end until Sunday morning, around 1:15, when Larionov, the oldest player in the NHL, went to his backhand and put the puck in Carolina's net 14:47 into the third overtime. It was the 41-year-old center's second goal of the game and secured a 2–1 lead in the series for the Wings.

Hasek shut out the Hurricanes on the road in Game 4, setting up the potential to clinch at home. This team of teams, this team of the aged for the ages, had rallied from a terrible start and had rallied against its archrival. On a Thursday night in mid-June, the Wings completed their journey. Holmstrom scored the first goal and Shanahan their last two and the Wings won Game 5 3–1. The Joe pulsed with joy, with cheers—and also with shock, as Scotty Bowman chose that moment to tell everyone he was done, that he had coached his last game.

The Wings would deal with that later. This night was about relishing the championship they had been favored to win since the previous summer, since a phone call set in motion a trade that triggered the greatest collection of hockey talent ever assembled on an NHL team. "The only thing that mattered was winning," Yzerman said after hoisting the Stanley Cup, "and the only thing that mattered was the team."

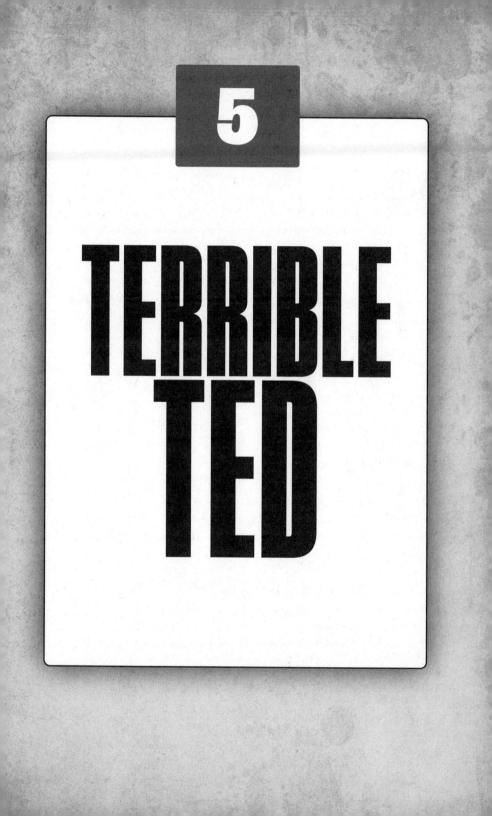

5

TERRIBLE TED

very picture of Ted Lindsay seems to tell a cherished story. Take the one among the mementos Henrik Zetterberg has on display commemorating his 1,000th game with the Detroit Red Wings. His son, Love, a few months from his second birthday, is tucked into his dad's left arm. Zetterberg's right arm is wrapped around Lindsay, who is reaching out to grab Love's little hand.

It was a special night that April 9, 2017: Zetterberg's milestone, and the last game at Joe Louis Arena. But what capped it for Zetterberg was having Lindsay there, a man who meant as much to the Red Wings organization as he did to NHL players everywhere.

Zetterberg looks forward to telling Love all about Lindsay. It's a story that can't be told in one night, and that's hardly fitting for bedtime. Lindsay was nicknamed "Terrible Ted," because as unimposing physically as he was in a suit, he was fearsome in uniform. He received some 600 stitches, mostly to his face, during a legendary career highlighted by four Stanley Cups. It was Lindsay who started the tradition of lifting the Cup and skating it around the ice.

When the Wings played in Montreal in the late 1940s, Lindsay—who stood 5'8" and weighed 165 pounds—caught the attention of a teenaged Scotty Bowman. "He was so good, a complete player who was good offensively and defensively," Bowman said. "He was an ultracompetitive player but also very skillful. He wasn't very big but he was completely fearless."

Robert Blake Theodore Lindsay was born July 29, 1925, in Renfrew, Ontario, a town about an hour west of Ottawa. His father had played professionally as a goaltender. An invitation to try out for the Wings in 1944 earned Lindsay a job, and he made his NHL debut at 19. That started one of the many feuds that would define Lindsay's career, as his decision to play for the Wings after having played amateur hockey in Toronto angered Maple Leafs owner Conn Smythe (who'd later side against Lindsay as he tried to build support for a players' association).

In 1947, Jack Adams stepped back from coaching the Wings to focus on being general manager. New coach Tommy Ivan put Lindsay and Gordie Howe with center Sid Abel, and the "Production Line" was born. Abel, the Wings captain, was 10 years older than Howe and seven years older than Lindsay, but the three developed tremendous chemistry. Lindsay and Howe were so fast they obscured Abel's lack of speed, and the line's success soared as they perfected the art of having one of the wingers shoot the puck into the offensive zone and the other winger chase the puck down, then either take a shot or pass to Abel. At that time, goaltenders rarely left their crease to play the puck. The three read one another with ease, their off-ice camaraderie on display as they tormented opponents from 1947 to 1952. Lindsay led the team with 52 points (in 60 games) in 1947–48, and Howe and Abel each had 44.

"Gordie Howe was the toughest player in the league, and they were on the same line, but Ted didn't need Gordie to protect him," Bowman said. "He looked after himself. He was a wonderful skater and a great finisher."

In 1949–50, Lindsay (78 points), Abel (69), and Howe (68) were the top three scorers in the NHL, something no line since has accomplished. The season culminated with the Wings winning the Stanley Cup. Three more Cups would come over the next five years. Lindsay and Howe appeared on the cover of a 1957 issue of *Sports Illustrated*, their smiles as cocky as their play. After Abel was hired as Chicago's coach in 1952, Lindsay served as captain until 1956.

In 1,068 regular season games, Lindsay scored 379 goals and had 472 assists for 851 points. He had another 47 goals and 49 assists for 96 points in 133 playoff games. He also logged 1,808 penalty minutes (plus 192 in the playoffs). He used his elbows, his knees, whatever it took, to harass opponents. He was a trailblazer for the "love to hate him unless he's on your team" type of player. As Lindsay would put it over the years, "I hated everybody I played against and they hated me. That's the way hockey should be played."

Another favorite phrase encapsulated his approach to every shift. Lindsay would tell players and their coaches: "If they go into the corner with another guy, and if they don't come out with the puck, they are a horseshit hockey player."

One of Lindsay's hardest-fought battles came when he took aim at the business side of hockey. As his career progressed, Lindsay grew concerned over the imbalance of power between players and team owners. At the time, teams owned players' rights for the duration of their careers. Lindsay's efforts to organize players to demand basic rights such as a minimum salary and a transparently funded pension plan so enraged Wings owner Bruce Norris in 1957 that he ordered Adams to trade Lindsay to the Chicago Black Hawks (the spelling changed to Blackhawks in 1986).

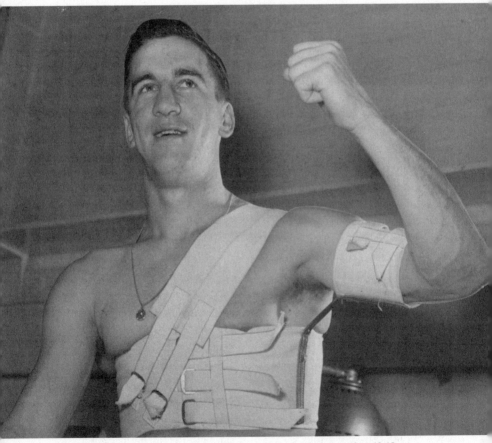

Ted Lindsay showing off his banged-up shoulder in December 1948.

"Jack Adams was a dictator. That's how it was in those days," longtime Wings executive Jimmy Devellano said. "He found out Ted tried to organize the players for an association, and he was banished to the lowly Black Hawks."

Together with Montreal Canadiens defenseman Doug Harvey, Lindsay set in motion what in 1967 would be formed as the Players' Association. "He really was the first guy to organize the players," Devellano said. "He's really the reason we have the NHLPA. The players playing today making their millions of dollars, god bless them all, they owe a debt of thanks to Ted Lindsay because he stood up to managers and owners and wanted more say in how the game was directed."

In a stroke of karma, Adams was fired in 1962 and Lindsay was lured out of retirement in 1964 to play one more season for the Wings by Abel, who by then was coach and general manager. Lindsay was 39 years old and put up 28 points in 69 games as the Wings finished the 1964–65 season with a league-best 40–23–7 record. In the final playoff series of his career, a seven-game, first-round loss to the Black Hawks, Lindsay ranked third on the Wings with three goals and first with 34 penalty minutes.

Lindsay retired for good in 1965. A year later he was inducted into the Hockey Hall of Fame, but he refused to attend the ceremony because women were not allowed at that time, and Lindsay wanted to bring his wife. The NHL changed the rule the next year.

Lindsay resurfaced with the Wings as general manager in 1977, hired by Bruce Norris, the same guy who'd ordered him banished 20 years earlier. Lindsay was named Executive of the Year after the Wings made the playoffs for the first time in eight years. He added coaching duties late in the 1979–80 season, but lost GM duties after that season to Jimmy Skinner. Under Lindsay's management, the Wings' payroll had grown to more than $5 million, the highest in NHL history at the time. Lindsay was gone the next season after the Wings won just three of their first 20 games.

In 1982 Bruce Norris sold the Wings to Mike Ilitch, who brought in Devellano as general manager. One of Devellano's first acts was to reach out to Lindsay and take him and his wife to dinner. Devellano wanted Lindsay back in the fold, recognizing his importance to the team's rich history. Lindsay soon became a regular at the Joe. He'd hang out and talk hockey with Devellano, with Bowman (who was appointed coach in 1993), with the players. Lindsay seemed to know everything about everyone in hockey, always kept up to date with current events. In 2015 he'd recently turned 90 when he came upon Dylan Larkin, the Wings' first-round draft pick from 2014, sitting in the locker room. Larkin was 19 and hadn't played a single game yet for the Wings. "He knew who I was, knew I was from Michigan," Larkin recalled. "For him to take the time to show interest, to know about me—looking back, I realize how special that was. There's a picture of me and him sitting at my locker. I didn't think it was a big deal at the time, but looking back, I realize what a cool thing it was." Larkin would go on to join the Ted Lindsay Foundation as a board member and spokesperson in 2018, and serve as a pallbearer at Lindsay's funeral.

Lindsay was inspired to start his foundation in 2001 as a result of working out with John Czarnecki, his physical therapist and trainer who had a nine-year-old son with autism. Through an annual golf outing, wine tasting, and other events, the foundation has raised more than $3 million to support autism research.

Lindsay would often say he played the way he did because it was the only way for a 5'8" guy to thrive. But his legacy comes as much from the person he was off the ice—from taking on greedy executives to fight for a better living for players to the humanitarian side revealed in the establishment of his foundation. In 2010, the NHLPA renamed the Lester B. Pearson Award—given annually to the NHL's most outstanding player as voted on by players—the Ted Lindsay Award.

Lindsay's legacy encompasses the NHL, but around Detroit, his greatness was personal. He had time, it seemed, for everyone. Lindsay's appreciation for forging a good living playing hockey was evident in how he gave back, in how he inspired Wings players who could have been his grandchildren with how fit he was mentally and physically even as he aged into his eighties. Players loved to hear him tell stories, cherished hearing Lindsay share his memories.

"I once asked him to sign a photo that I had of him skating with his stick as a rifle," Nicklas Lidstrom said. "I told him that I had it at my house but I would bring it down to the Joe so that he could sign it next time he came around. He said that he would come out to my house that afternoon and get it signed instead. I insisted that he wouldn't have to make the trip but he just said, 'It would be my pleasure.'"

As he signed the photo, Lindsay told Lidstrom the story behind the pose: Lindsay had received death threats in Toronto during the 1956 playoff series and after the Wings won a game at Maple Leaf Gardens, on an overtime goal from Lindsay, he came up with the idea of turning his stick over and aiming it at fans. The famous black-and-white photo of Lindsay holding his stick like a rifle hangs in the Wings locker room at Little Caesars Arena, just like it did at the Joe. A stall in one of the corners bears Lindsay's name tag. His No. 7 hangs in the rafters, retired since 1991. Lindsay passed away March 4, 2019, at age 93, but his feistiness lingers on.

6

THE PLAYOFF STREAK

The year was 1991. The Cold War ended as the Union of Soviet Socialist Republics dissolved into 15 sovereign republics. George H.W. Bush was president of the United States. *Thelma and Louise* ignited controversy at the box office while garnering critical and commercial success. Theatergoers flocked to see *Terminator 2: Judgment Day*, *Beauty and the Beast*, and *The Silence of the Lambs*. A first-class stamp cost $0.25, a gallon of regular gasoline cost $1.14, and a gallon of milk cost $2.80.

In April of that year, the Wings (34–38–8) advanced to the playoffs after finishing sixth in the Campbell Conference, setting up a first-round series with the St. Louis Blues. Steve Yzerman had a hat trick as the Wings claimed Game 1 6–3. The Blues took Game 2, but the Wings won the next two games at Joe Louis Arena to take a 3–1 lead in the series. They couldn't carry momentum, though, and wound up eliminated.

A rookie by the name of Sergei Fedorov had six points in the seven-game series, after producing 79 points in 77 regular season games. The Wings had drafted him two years earlier, in the fourth round of their fabulous 1989 draft. The following season, 1991–92, the Wings welcomed another of their 1989 selections in rookie defenseman Nicklas Lidstrom. The Wings were on the rise, a once-championship franchise emerging from decades of misery. But no one who was on the roster that made the playoffs in 1991 could have foreseen that it was the start of a piece of history that would last 25 seasons and yield four Stanley Cups. The streak lasted beyond the retirements of Yzerman and Lidstrom, the departure of Fedorov, the arrival of the salary cap era.

Only three teams have been able to accomplish the same or better in NHL history. The Boston Bruins hold the all-time record of consecutive playoff seasons at 29 (1968–96), with the Chicago Blackhawks next at 28 seasons (1970–97). The St. Louis Blues had a 25-season streak from 1980–2004. To put in perspective how rare it was to make the playoffs year after year when the Wings did it, consider this: when their playoff streak ended in 2017 at 25, the Pittsburgh Penguins had the longest active streak at 11 straight seasons.

The second year of the streak went a little better than the first. The Wings bested the Minnesota North Stars in seven games in the first round, but were swept by the Chicago Blackhawks in Round 2. The Wings stumbled in 1993, eliminated in the first round after again coming up short in a seven-game series, this time to the Toronto Maple Leafs.

Then Scotty Bowman was hired. He'd won five Stanley Cups coaching the Montreal Canadiens in the 1970s and one with the Pittsburgh Penguins in 1992. The decision looked as if it might pay off immediately. The 1993–94 Wings finished first in the Western Conference and were favored to win their first-round series against the eighth-seeded San Jose Sharks, making the first playoff appearance in their history.

It was 2–2 entering Game 5 in San Jose. The Sharks took a 4–2 lead in the third period and, despite two goals from Lidstrom, held on to win. In retaliation, the Wings crushed the Sharks in Detroit, winning Game 6 7–1.

In Game 7 at the Joe, the Sharks led 2–1 after the first period, but Vyacheslav Kozlov scored to make it 2–2 going into the third. The third period features in the history of both franchises: a celebratory one for the Sharks, a sorrowful one for the Wings. Two-thirds of the way through the period, 21-year-old goaltender Chris Osgood left his net to play the puck along the boards. He ended up clearing the puck to the stick of Sharks forward Jamie Baker, who flung the puck into the open net. The goal would seal the Sharks' victory. Osgood wept afterward as he spoke to reporters. Much later in his career, he'd talk about how important it is for a goaltender to forget bad goals, to flush them from memory. It was a lesson he learned that spring.

The Wings swept the Sharks in the second round of the 1995 playoffs, losing only once in the first round, to Dallas, and once in the third round, to Chicago, en route to meeting the New Jersey Devils in the Stanley Cup Finals. There the Wings' momentum crashed, as they were dismissed from their first Finals since 1966 in four games. Fedorov paced the Wings with three goals in the Finals; no teammate had more than one. Mike Vernon had a 4.07 goals-against average after giving up 14 goals on 96 shots. After losing Game 4 5–2, in New Jersey, Wings defenseman Paul Coffey said the stunning end to their season "is going to hurt for a while.... We've got to learn something from it."

Unfortunately, there was more pain in store. The 1995–96 Wings had a spectacular regular season, their 62 victories eclipsing the record 60 won by the 1976–77 Montreal Canadiens. The Wings spun together two nine-game winning streaks in the run and went the entire season without being shut out. That was the season they went into Montreal on December 2 and dealt the Canadiens an 11–1 loss, leading Patrick Roy to declare he'd played his last game for the team. The Wings topped the NHL regular season standings with 131 points, 27 more than the second-place Colorado Avalanche.

With Osgood in net, the Wings won the first two games of the first-round playoff series against Winnipeg by a combined score of 8–1. It was 3–1 after Game 4 and the Wings won Game 6 4–1 in Winnipeg to advance to meet the St. Louis Blues in Round 2. The Wings won the first two games of the series, but the Blues, who'd managed only 80 points during the regular season, ultimately forced a Game 7.

On May 16, 1996, Yzerman scored the most legendary goal of his career, collecting the puck after Wayne Gretzky lost it and firing a 55-foot slap shot that eluded Jon Casey, giving the Wings a 1–0 victory 1:15 into the second overtime. Fans erupted in deafening celebration. "Once we heard the noise, we all knew," defenseman Vladimir Konstantinov said.

Yzerman noted, "It wasn't the kind of goal I normally score. But we really enjoyed being in this game. We really believe in our team."

Three days later the Wings hosted Game 1 of the Western Conference finals, facing the now Roy-led Colorado Avalanche. The Wings lost in overtime, and then were shut out in Game 2. They trailed 3–2, going into Game 6 at Colorado.

Events during that May 29 game provoked a rivalry that lasted years. At 14:07 in the first period, Claude Lemieux took advantage of Kris Draper being down along the half-boards between the benches and hit him from behind, slamming Draper's head into the dasher. Draper suffered a broken jaw, shattered cheek and orbital bones, and a concussion. He required 30 stitches in his mouth alone. Officials assessed Lemieux a five-minute major penalty and a game misconduct. The Avs won the series, but Lemieux was suspended the first two games of the Stanley Cup Finals. It wouldn't matter, as the Avalanche swept the Florida Panthers.

Retribution came 10 months later. The emotional release earned during the March 26, 1997, game—when they beat the Avalanche and

THE OCTOPUS TRADITION

Opponents complain and tossers have received tickets for disorderly conduct, but if the Red Wings are in the playoffs, an octopus will land on the ice during home games, its slithery, eight-tentacled carcass a salute to a tradition that began in the 1950s.

Back then, a team needed to win eight games to capture the Stanley Cup. On April 15, 1952, Pete Cusimano, who with his brother Jerry sold fish at Detroit's Eastern Market, hurled an octopus onto the ice at Olympia Stadium. The Wings had swept the semifinals against Toronto and had a 3–0 lead on Montreal in the Stanley Cup Finals. That night the Wings became the first team to win the Cup without losing a game, capping their sweep of the Canadiens with a 3–0 victory. And a legend was born.

The Wings were so dreadful in the 1970s and early to middle-1980s that there wasn't a market for mollusks to be used as hockey tokens. During the 1985–86 season, in which the Wings finished a franchise-worst 17–57–6 season, a fan threw a bone on the ice during the season's final game to send the message the Wings were playing like dogs.

When the Wings made their first playoff appearance in six years in 1984, fans were wary of resuming the practice after reports surfaced a fan had been fined $100 for throwing an octopus onto the ice during the final week of the regular season. Finally, during overtime of Game 3 of the first-round series against St. Louis, a brave soul hurled one onto the ice during a stoppage in play. It slid to a stop to the right of Blues goaltender Mike Liut. The crowd roared in approval.

The practice regained traction in the 1990s, when the Wings once again were playoff regulars. Al the Octopus, a purple mascot, made his debut in the '95 playoffs, named in honor of Al Sobotka, the team's longtime Zamboni driver and building operations manager. Sobotka became a sensation when he began a tradition of picking up an octopus from the ice and twirling it overhead.

In 2002, before Game 7 of the Western Conference finals, the Wings invited Pete Cusimano to attend. When an octopus hit the ice after Karen Newman finished the anthem, Cusimano picked up the octopus and held it over his head. Fans roared and clapped.

Opponents pushed back. During the 2007 playoffs, Ducks general manager Brian Burke complained about Sobotka's octopus antics. During the first round of the 2008 playoffs the NHL informed the

Wings it would impose a $10,000 fine if Sobotka continued his traditional twirl. Only linesmen were supposed to clean up the critters. In an email to the *Detroit Free Press*, NHL spokesman Frank Brown explained the ban: "Because matter flies off the octopus and gets on the ice when he does it."

Bowing to protestations, the league eased restrictions and allowed Sobotka to pick up an octopus, bring it to the Zamboni entrance, and twirl away.

Darren McCarty led a fight-card's worth of brawls in beating up Lemieux—bolstered the Wings into the playoffs. They dispatched the Blues in six games. It took six overtimes (one in the opener, three in the second game, two in the fourth) but the Wings swept the Ducks in Round 2 to advance to the Western Conference finals.

The Avalanche advanced three days later to set up a second playoff series between the teams. The Wings took a 3-1 series lead with an emphatic 6-0 victory at home in Game 4 but were unable to withstand the Avalanche attack in Game 5, losing 6-0 in Colorado. Martin Lapointe and Fedorov made it 2-0 in Game 6 before Scott Young pulled the Avs to within a goal. Brendan Shanahan ensured this time it would be the Wings who celebrated, scoring an empty-net goal with 30 seconds left to play in regulation. One day earlier, the Philadelphia Flyers had won the Eastern Conference in a five-game series against the Rangers.

Proving they had learned from the 1995 fiasco, the Wings swept the Flyers, and on June 7, 1997, brought the Stanley Cup back to Detroit for the first time in 42 years. "I was glad when the game was over, but then I didn't want the game to end," Yzerman said. "I've been watching hockey since I was five years old. I always dreamed of the day I would get the Stanley Cup. Sometimes I wondered if I would ever get there. As the game went on, it almost was as if I wanted to sit back and watch it." That night, Yzerman described skating around with the Cup as "the greatest moment in my career, the most gratifying and the most rewarding."

Sadly, the celebrations came to a tragic halt one week later, when a limousine carrying Konstantinov, Slava Fetisov, and team masseur Sergei Mnatsakanov crashed on Woodward Avenue in Birmingham en route home from a team party to celebrate the Cup. The driver, Richard Gnida, who had a revoked license and a long list of violations, would later admit he had fallen asleep. The careers of Konstantinov and Mnatsakanov ended abruptly on June 13, 1997. The next year, when the Wings were on the verge of repeating as champions, they brought Konstantinov to the MCI Center in Washington. Celebrating their sweep of the Capitals, teammates pushed Konstantinov around the ice in his wheelchair, the Cup in his lap.

Second-round losses to the Avalanche followed in 1999 and 2000. In 2001 the Wings made the playoffs for the 11th straight year only to be upset by seventh-seeded Los Angeles in the first round.

The summer brought changes that turned the Wings into a superpower. General manager Ken Holland added goaltender Dominik Hasek via trade, and signed forwards Brett Hull and Luc Robitaille to create a roster that already included Yzerman, Fedorov, Lidstrom, Shanahan, and Chris Chelios. Then rookie Pavel Datsyuk joined the team in the fall.

The 2001–02 Wings won a league-high 51 games and finished first with 116 points, securing home-ice advantage throughout the playoffs. Then first round of the playoffs began ominously when the Vancouver Canucks took the first two games at Joe Louis Arena. It was 1–1 late in the second period of Game 3 when Lidstrom scored a most improbable goal: he carried the puck up the ice and ripped a slap shot from the red line that eluded Dan Cloutier. The Wings won the game, and the next three, to claim the series.

The Blues were taken care of in five games in Round 2, setting up another showdown with the Avalanche. The Avs took a 3–2 lead in the series, but Hasek stopped 24 shots to deliver a shutout in Game 6. "It doesn't mean anything if we don't win the next one," Hasek said afterward.

They would, on an epic scale. The Wings' 7–0 victory was the most one-sided Game 7 in NHL history. They scored on their first shot. Tomas Holmstrom scored twice in the first period. It was 4–0 in less than 13 minutes. "To be honest, we thought this would be an overtime game," Yzerman said.

One of the highlights of the Stanley Cup Finals happened in Game 3, when 41-year-old Igor Larionov took a pass from Holmstrom, stickhandled around a Carolina Hurricanes defender, and scored on a backhander at 14:47 in triple overtime. The Wings celebrated another Cup championship on June 13, 2002, winning the series in five games.

Bowman donned skates and took a lap with the Cup, then announced his retirement. During the off-season, Hasek—who'd delivered six shutouts in the playoffs—announced his retirement. The Wings promoted Dave Lewis to head coach and signed goaltender Curtis Joseph.

It was goaltender Jean-Sebastien Giguere who starred the following spring, as the defending champions and Cup favorites were swept in a first-round stunner by the Anaheim Ducks. Giguere made 63 saves in Game 1, which lasted until Paul Kariya scored at 3:18 of the third overtime. Giguere stopped 165 of 171 shots in the series, finishing with a .965 save percentage and 1.24 goals-against average.

When the 2004 playoffs ended in a second-round loss to the Calgary Flames, despite the league's best record, Holland let Lewis' contract expire after the 2004–05 season was lost to a lockout. The man Holland tapped to be the team's next coach was the guy who'd been behind Anaheim's bench during that 2003 upset: Mike Babcock.

Babcock's first season, despite the league's best record, ended with a first-round loss to the Edmonton Oilers, in what would be Yzerman's farewell season. The Wings, captained by Lidstrom and with Datsyuk and Henrik Zetterberg on the rise, advanced past Calgary and San Jose before falling in the Western Conference finals to the Ducks, who'd go on to win the Stanley Cup.

Zetterberg scored a league-best 27 playoff points in 2008 as the Wings bested Nashville, Colorado, and Dallas to meet the Pittsburgh Penguins in the Finals. Hasek was back for his third stint with the Wings, but he was replaced by Osgood after struggling against the Predators. Osgood backstopped the Wings to nine straight victories and Zetterberg was awarded the Conn Smythe Trophy as the playoff MVP after a six-game series against the Penguins.

The Wings made their 24th appearance in the Stanley Cup Finals in 2009, in a rematch of the 2008 contest. They won the first two games against Pittsburgh, and went up 3–2, with a 5–0 victory in Game 5.

In what ranks as a painfully squandered opportunity, they were not able to close it out, losing Game 6 and Game 7 by a score of 2–1. The last Stanley Cup Finals game to be played at Joe Louis Arena saw the Cup in the arms of Sidney Crosby.

The 2010 and 2011 playoffs ended in second-round exits. Had it not been for the luck of drafting Datsyuk in the sixth round in 1998 and Zetterberg in the seventh round in 1999, the playoff streak might have ended after Lidstrom retired in 2012, following a first-round loss to Nashville. But the Wings had two superstars in their prime and kept angling for playoff runs. In 2013 they upset Anaheim in a seven-game first-round series, and pushed the eventual Cup champion Chicago to overtime in a second-round Game 7.

Back surgery limited Zetterberg to two games in the 2014 playoffs, and his teammates didn't last much longer, as the Wings fell in five games to the Bruins. In 2015 the Wings finished third in the Atlantic Division and lost in the first round to the Tampa Bay Lightning. After the Game 7 loss, Babcock questioned the scarcity of the organization's depth, which had been depleted to stoke playoff runs. He left that off-season to coach with the Toronto Maple Leafs. The Wings promoted Jeff Blashill, who'd been an assistant for one year under Babcock before leaving to coach the AHL's Grand Rapids Griffins.

On April 9, 2016, the Wings played their last game of the regular season, meeting the Rangers at Madison Square Garden. The Wings could clinch a playoff berth by winning. The Rangers would avoid a first-round series against the Penguins by losing. New York started backup goalie Antti Raanta instead of Henrik Lundqvist. A few minutes after the buzzer sounded on a 3–2 loss for the Wings, they found out they had advanced to the playoffs because Ottawa routed Boston 6–1, clinching third place in the Atlantic Division for Detroit. The Wings lost in five games to the Lightning. (The Rangers, meanwhile, lost in five games to Pittsburgh.) Datsyuk departed that summer for Russia with a year to go on his contract, citing homesickness.

The streak ended on March 28, 2017, when the Wings lost 4–1 at Carolina, eliminating them from playoff contention. In total, it had lasted 25 consecutive seasons and yielded four Stanley Cups, six Finals appearances, and six Presidents' Trophies. "I think everyone in Detroit should be proud of it," Yzerman said. "It is incredibly difficult to make the playoffs in this league. Going back to the early '90s, this team was a legitimate contender for the Stanley Cup for a lot of years."

7

THE PRODUCTION LINE

In his first year behind the Red Wings' bench, Tommy Ivan assembled what would become one of the greatest lines in the NHL. Ivan replaced Jack Adams as coach in 1947, and decided to pair Gordie Howe and Ted Lindsay with veteran Sid Abel. The three—Abel at center, Howe on the right wing, and Lindsay on the left—had such great success that they spawned the nickname the "Production Line," in honor of Detroit's car industry.

Abel was 29, Lindsay was 22, and Howe was 19. During trips, they were inseparable, the young wingers eager to learn. "We used to sit there and listen to him for hours," Howe recalled of the veteran at Abel's funeral in 2000. "He'd rehash the whole game like a coach. He helped me because he used to stir us up."

That wasn't hard to do. In Howe and Lindsay, Abel had two of the toughest wingers of the day. Howe was 6'0", 200-odd pounds, and had a knack for using his elbows as weapons. Lindsay was 5'8", 160-odd pounds, and 100 percent tough. He didn't want anybody touching any of his teammates. Between Lindsay and Howe, they would take care of anybody. "Compared to Ted, Gordie was easygoing," Abel said in a 1991 interview. "We had to get him going, in fact. But Ted was always very fiery. He wouldn't back down from anybody."

Howe and Lindsay wreaked havoc in the corners, mixing it up with opponents and emerging from scrums with the puck. Abel would go to the front of the net and wait for the pass. In 1947–48, Lindsay led the Wings with 52 points in 60 games. Howe and Abel each had 44 points.

"We had talent, and by talent I mean the ability to anticipate plays," Lindsay reflected in a 1991 interview, shortly before the Wings retired his No. 7. "We were two seconds ahead of everybody else. We knew what was going to happen. The average guy waits to see what happens, and often it's too late."

Ivan tried other centers with Howe and Lindsay, but there was nobody who was a better fit than Abel. "It happened nearly every year," Abel said. "And I wouldn't get Gordie and Ted back until camp was over. At times it upset me, but I figured if they could find somebody who could do a better job, they ought to give him a whack at it. But invariably, they'd come back to me. I think we were together four or five years."

The Production Line produced for the Wings from 1947–48 to 1951–52. In 1948–49, the first of seven straight seasons when the Wings won the regular-season title, Abel and Lindsay tied for third in NHL scoring. In 1949–50, the line simply dominated the NHL. Lindsay finished the season with a league-best 78 points in 69 games, Abel had 69 points in 69 games, and Howe had 68 points in 70 games. Respectively they finished first, second, and third in NHL scoring, a feat also accomplished by Boston's Kraut Line in 1939–40.

The next season, in 1950–51, the Production Line ranked first, fourth, and seventh. Howe won the scoring title with 86 points, 20 more than Montreal's Maurice Richard. In 1951–52, their final season together, they were first, second, and seventh, with Howe scoring 47 goals and finishing 17 points (86 to 69) ahead of Lindsay. Abel, in eight fewer games, tallied 53 points. That spring the Wings celebrated their second Stanley Cup in three years. Lindsay and Howe were among four players tied with a league-leading seven playoff points. Lindsay had a league-high five goals.

Lindsay recalled Ivan as a stickler about positional play, but the Production Line was so dominant, Ivan didn't care. "He'd give hell to the other guys," Lindsay said, "but we'd be wandering all over the place."

Other players, including Alex Delvecchio, played with Lindsay and Howe after Abel left for Chicago in 1952, but there was nothing like the original Production Line.

8

1989

No NHL team has ever had a draft like the Red Wings did in 1989. On June 17 at the Met Center in Bloomington, Minnesota, the Wings made 14 selections spread across 12 rounds. Teams were only starting to dip into the European market for players, and most were scared of dipping into the Russian market for fear the Soviets would never release their players. The Wings played it safe with their first two choices and picked Canadians. By the time they took their turn in Round 3 and selected Nicklas Lidstrom, 19 defensemen already had been drafted. Lidstrom would become the greatest defenseman in franchise history. But in 1989 he wasn't the guy the Wings were most excited about drafting. That was a young Russian named Sergei Fedorov, whom the Wings took a chance on in Round 4, at 74th overall.

General manager Jimmy Devellano thought Fedorov was the steal of the draft—red tape and the Red Army be damned. He warranted a toss of the dice. Better to have the rights to Fedorov—even if getting him out of Russia was daunting—than to not have his rights.

Devellano was dead-on. Five years after the Wings drafted Fedorov, he was the MVP of the NHL. In the lead-up to the 1994 NHL awards, Devellano told the *Free Press* that he had "been involved with 11 entry drafts in Detroit, and out of those we've gotten two franchise players: Steve Yzerman and Sergei Fedorov. They often say if you get one every 10 years you're doing pretty darn good."

As it turned out, the Wings culled two franchise players in the same draft (and might have had a third in Vladimir Konstantinov but for the 1997 limousine accident that ended his career).

Lidstrom would anchor the Wings for 20 seasons and was a key part of four Stanley Cup championships. Fedorov was one of the best two-way forwards in the game and a key part of three Stanley Cup championships. All told, picks the Wings made in 1989 combined to play 5,995 games. Their first selection, at 11th overall, was center Mike Sillinger. He logged 1,049 games in the NHL, though only 129 for the Wings before being traded. Their next selection, at 32nd overall, was Bob Boughner, a

PAVEL BURE

The 1989 draft was an embarrassment of riches for the Red Wings—and they *almost* added Pavel Bure to the list. NHL teams were given the impression Bure had to be drafted within the first three rounds because at 18 he had not played the requisite number of games in his native Russia to be eligible in later rounds.

Teams were only just beginning to explore the Russian market, and were fearful the Soviet system would not allow its players to leave. "You felt you were wasting your pick, that he was never going to get out of Russia," said Ken Holland, who was a scout for the Wings at the time. "We took Sergei Fedorov in the fourth round, thinking we got one of the world's best players, and maybe we could get him over in two years."

The Wings' draft table was led by general manager Jimmy Devellano and assistant general manager and chief scout Neil Smith. Christer Rockstrom was among the scouts. "As the draft is going on, Christer Rockstrom is convincing Neil Smith and Jim Devellano that we should take Pavel Bure," Holland said. "Christer is convincing Neil that he could prove Pavel Bure played for Russia in Siberia, that he was eligible after the first three rounds."

Rockstrom—the man who made the case for Nicklas Lidstrom in Round 3—was convincing enough that Smith approached Gil Stein, the NHL vice president and counsel at the league's draft table. "Gil says Bure is an ineligible player, that if you pick him, you are going to lose the player," Holland said. "Neil comes back to the draft table and is scared off. Christer is persistent—he keeps pushing Neil, to the point we're now going into the sixth round. It's the sixth round. If we lose the pick, we're going to lose the pick. So we were all set to pick Pavel Bure. Three spots before we pick at 116th, Vancouver picked Pavel Bure."

Bure was considered a spectacularly talented player, and the Canucks' boldness in drafting someone other teams believed to be ineligible did not go without notice. "When Vancouver made the selection, the chief scout of the Washington Capitals, Jack Button—he had been in the business forever—he jumped up and he went flying towards the podium," Holland recalled. "He was ranting and raving that he is an ineligible player. Everybody thought he was ineligible."

NHL president John Ziegler initially declared the pick illegal after an investigation following formal complaints from multiple NHL teams. It took a year—until the eve of the 1990 draft, when Bure would have been available again—for the NHL to rule in favor of the Canucks, who had appealed by filing proof of Bure's additional games.

The Wings selected Dallas Drake at 116th. He spent most of his 1,009 career NHL games with other teams, but returned to help the Wings win the 2008 Stanley Cup. But had the Wings decided to gamble in the fifth round as they did with Fedorov in the fourth, then instead of Shawn McCosh, who appeared in nine NHL games with two other teams, they could have had Pavel Bure in their lineup by 1991. Bure was inducted into the Hockey Hall of Fame in 2012.

defenseman from across the river in Windsor, Ontario. He topped 600 career games, none with the Wings.

As the third round wore on, Devellano turned to Neil Smith, the chief scout, and Christer Rockstrom, the chief European scout. Devellano wanted to know more about the Swedish defenseman they were pushing. "I hadn't seen this player, so I did what all GMs do," Devellano said. "They ask questions. 'Who is he? Why can he make the NHL? Blah blah blah.'"

Rockstrom told Devellano he had seen Lidstrom play more than a dozen times and never saw him make a mistake. "Nick was described to me as a young boy who was a fluid skater, had fabulous hockey sense, and really knew how to play the game," Devellano said. "That all turned out to be true. The only question was, they felt—and they were correct—was that he needed to get bigger and stronger. So we let him be in Sweden a couple of years, and then he came over in '91, and boy oh boy, he really helped propel us to be a pretty good team for two decades."

It is interesting to look at some of the defensemen who were selected in the draft before Lidstrom. It proves how hard it is to fully judge a young player. The first one drafted, Adam Bennett, at sixth overall by the Chicago Blackhawks, played 69 NHL games in his career. The third one chosen, Jason Herter, played one. Lidstrom played 1,564. He is regarded as one of the best defensemen ever, with the hardware to prove it: seven James Norris Memorial Trophies as the NHL's top defenseman, four Stanley Cups, a Conn Smythe Trophy as the MVP of the 2002 playoffs, and 12 post-season All-Star team selections. Teammates called Lidstrom "The Perfect Human" because he made everything he did look effortless. He would play 30 minutes a night, if needed. He was always on the ice against the opponent's best line, and he made that look easy. The Wings never missed the playoffs during Lidstrom's career.

Had he been the Wings' lone steal, it would have been a great draft. Fedorov and Vladimir Konstantinov elevate it to legendary. Immediately after the draft, Devellano beamed as he told reporters, "We got the best player in the world." He was talking about Fedorov. Getting Fedorov into their fold took subterfuge and planning. The Wings staged a defection while Fedorov was in Portland, Oregon, with his Soviet national team for a warm-up match before the 1990 Goodwill Games. They bribed and they lied and it was so, so worth it.

In 13 seasons with the Wings, Fedorov tallied 400 goals and 554 assists in 908 games. His 954 points were second only to Steve Yzerman's 978. From 1990 to 2003, Fedorov led the Wings with 163 playoff points in 162 games (he was the only player on the team with a points-per-game average above 1.00). Fedorov had his best individual year in his fourth season, 1993–94, when he scored 56 goals and collected 64 assists, and his 120 points ranked second in the NHL behind only Wayne Gretzky's 130. At the end of the season Fedorov was awarded the Hart Memorial Trophy (league MVP), Frank J. Selke Trophy (best defensive forward), and Lester B. Pearson Award (most outstanding player as selected by players, later renamed after Wings great Ted Lindsay).

Fedorov played right wing on the Russian Five unit with center Igor Larionov and left wing Vyacheslav Kozlov, and Konstantinov and Slava Fetisov on the back end. Fedorov was an amazingly strong skater, which led to Scotty Bowman entrusting Fedorov to serve as a defenseman at times. Fedorov left as a free agent after the 2002–03 season to play for Anaheim, a decision that cost him goodwill with the Wings organization and fans. It wasn't until he was inducted into the Hockey Hall of Fame in 2015—alongside Lidstrom—that good relations were restored.

The guy the Wings picked in the fifth round, Shawn McCosh, played nine games in the NHL, none for them. Their next choice, Dallas Drake, from Northern Michigan University, played 1,009 games, beginning and finishing his career in Detroit, where he became an emotional linchpin in the 2008 run to the Stanley Cup.

The next five players selected, spanning rounds seven to 10, never made it to the NHL. Neither did the two picks the Wings made in the 12th round. But in the 11th round, Devellano gambled again and chose another

Russian, a 22-year-old defenseman named Vladimir Konstantinov. He was the former captain of the Soviet Junior National Team, famous for leading his squad in a brawl with Team Canada at the 1987 World Junior Championships.

The Wings fabricated a medical emergency in engineering Konstantinov's exit strategy from the Red Army. He joined them in 1991 and quickly became a fan favorite. He was the grit to Fedorov's glamor, using his 5'11", 190-pound frame to deliver bone-crunching hits on the open ice. Konstantinov was dirty and disruptive, aggravating opponents with his hard-nosed play. He took home the NHL Plus/Minus Award in 1995–96 with a plus-60 rating. He was runner-up to Brian Leetch for the Norris Trophy in 1997. Konstantinov played 446 games, plus 82 in the playoffs, for the Wings before his career was cut short by a limousine accident on June 13, 1997. He was 30 years old and in the prime of his career. Had that tragedy not occurred, it is easy to imagine he would have played into his late thirties and forged a Hall of Fame–worthy career.

The Wings didn't know just how incredible their draft choices would turn out that June day in 1989, but they were due a dose of karma. That was the year Bob Probert was arrested and sent to prison for cocaine possession, Petr Klima was arrested for his third drunken driving offense, and the Wings won the Norris Division only to be eliminated in the first round of the playoffs. There were more challenging years immediately ahead, but the 1989 draft ultimately transformed the team.

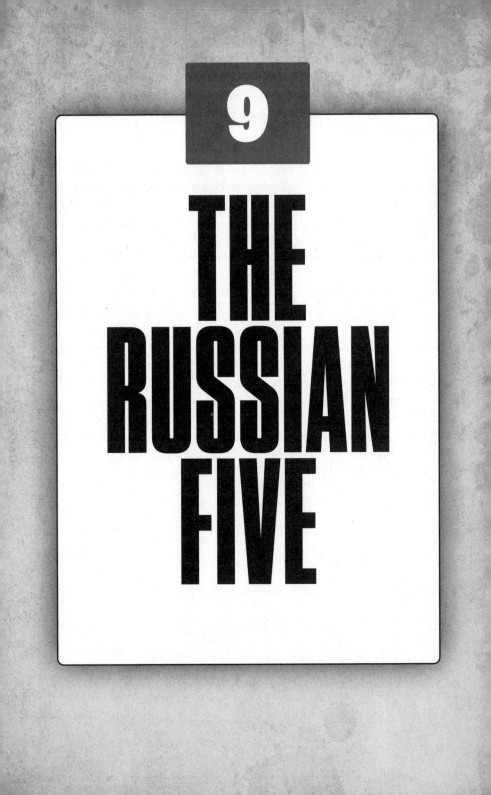

9

THE RUSSIAN FIVE

Had it been anyone else pushing to trade a 50-goal scorer for a smallish player in his mid-thirties, the move might not have happened. But such was the persuasion of Scotty Bowman, the best coach in the NHL, that he got what he wanted. The Red Wings had three Russian players when Bowman was named coach in the summer of 1993. He wanted more. The moves raised eyebrows within the organization for the price Bowman paid to orchestrate his Soviet reunion.

In April 1995, the Wings gave the New Jersey Devils a third-round draft pick to acquire Slava Fetisov, who was just a few weeks away from turning 37. He joined fellow Russians Sergei Fedorov, Vladimir Konstantinov, and Vyacheslav Kozlov, all of whom had been drafted by the Wings. Fetisov was a legend from his 14 years with Central Red Army, a savvy veteran whom Bowman saw as a beneficial addition.

"He has a lot of character," Bowman said at the time of the trade. "I've had experience with veteran defensemen before of this type. He was such a great player in his absolute prime." Fetisov had been part of a five-man unit with the Red Army, alongside defenseman Alexei Kasatonov and forwards Igor Larionov, Vladimir Krutov, and Sergei Makarov. In 1989, Fetisov was one of the first Russian players to come to the NHL. He put up 42 points his first season, but by 1995 the Devils no longer found him useful and limited him to four appearances. Bowman, who was also the Wings' director of player personnel, wasn't fazed by giving up a third-round pick.

If his cohorts in the front office, general manager Jimmy Devellano and assistant general manager Ken Holland, thought that was a pretty high price to pay for an aged defenseman who'd been been benched in Jersey, it was nothing compared with what happened when Bowman decided he wanted Larionov too. Larionov had impressed during the 1994 playoffs when he helped the San Jose Sharks upset the Wings in Round 1, but when Bowman pursued Larionov in October 1995, the player was closing in on his 35th birthday. The Wings forked over Ray Sheppard, a 50-goal scorer, to close the deal. "This is a real class player," Bowman said in explaining the trade. "We get a complete player."

Bowman pulled off acquiring two of the biggest legends in Soviet-era hockey, men who'd paved the path to the NHL for Russian hockey stars by standing up to Red Army coach Viktor Tikhonov, who controlled the team with an iron fist. Fetisov had captained the Red Army hockey team and been a major in the army; Larionov had been a lieutenant.

"He was the first guy who started to go against the Soviet sport system; nobody else had enough here to go against those guys," Fetisov said in an interview with the *Detroit Free Press* in October 1995. "That was before perestroika. We were under triple pressure—the army, the Communist system, and the sports system. It was pretty tough.

"The situation there, it was anti-human, and we paid a pretty high price," he continued. "Igor didn't play for almost a year. He didn't go abroad with his team. Then he writes a big letter against Tikhonov in a sports magazine. It wasn't easy, those times. Because we were in the Soviet army, they could send anybody anywhere, and they did. They could bury athletes."

Larionov was known as "The Professor" for his cerebral play and personality. He brought a chessboard onto the team plane. He introduced players to bandy. He also helped start the practice of players standing in a circle and kicking around a soccer ball before games.

On October 27, 1995, in a game at Calgary, Bowman played the comrades as a unit: Fetisov and Konstantinov on defense, Larionov at center, Fedorov on the right wing and Kozlov on the left wing (the forwards were so fluid, they could easily cover for one another). They clicked instantly. Kozlov scored in the first period, set up by Fedorov and Konstantinov. In the third period, Fedorov fed Larionov to clinch a 3–0 lead that would hold up as the final score.

It was the first time in the NHL that five Russians had been on the ice at one time for one team. They were a creative force, always thinking ahead two or three moves. "We really hadn't seen that kind of hockey since the Russian national team used to come over and play," Steve Yzerman said. "We used to practice against them, and there were drills we'd do five-on-five, and it was like, 'Geez, we have to go against that line?' Once they got the puck, you couldn't get it from them, so you chased them around for 45 seconds. They were totally unique to the NHL."

What made the Russian Five tough for opponents to handle was their mind-set that if one of them had the puck, there was no reason to give it away. North American players were raised to play dump-and-chase if the situation called for it; dumping the puck was anathema to the Russians. If a play required lateral passes to retain control, then that's what they did. "They're just so crafty you don't know what they're going to come up with," said Avalanche defenseman Adam Foote. "They'll do plays that other players don't seem to do, unbelievable plays."

Fedorov led the Wings with 39 goals and 107 points in 1995–96. Kozlov was fourth with 73 points and Larionov fifth with 71 points. Fetisov reached an NHL career high with 35 assists (and matched the 42 points he'd scored in his first year, 1989–90). Konstantinov scored a career-high 14 goals and matched his career-best 34 points. The Wings won a record 62 games to finish atop the NHL with 131 points.

In 1996 the Wings were smarting from being swept in the 1995 Stanley Cup Finals, and their awesome regular season came with heavy

The Russian Five (Slava Fetisov, Sergei Fedorov, Vladimir Konstantinov, Igor Larionov, and Slava Kozlov). (J. Kyle Keener)

expectations. When they exited the playoffs after a six-game series against Colorado in the Western Conference finals, some critics pointed fingers at the Russians. But Fedorov was tied with Yzerman for a team-leading 20 playoff points, and four of the five Russians were among the team's top seven scorers. As a unit, however, they struggled to dazzle like they had during the regular season, their high-speed style thwarted by increased clutching and grabbing. Bowman chose to break up the Russian Five during the playoffs.

Two games in particular stood out during the 1996–97 season: Fedorov's five-goal performance on December 26 and the brawl with the Avalanche on March 26. The former was a reminder of how dominant Fedorov could be. The latter unified the Wings, and served as a rallying point as they entered the playoffs the next month. Of all the unlikely people to serve as ignition points that night, it was Larionov and Colorado forward Peter Forsberg. "I'd never had any fights in my life," Larionov said afterward. He also capped his night with an assist on Darren McCarty's overtime goal.

PAPA BEAR

Slava Fetisov was 37 years old when the Red Wings acquired him in April 1995. He had a storied past in his native Russia, helping the Soviets to gold medals at the World Championships in 1978, 1981, 1982, 1983, 1986, 1989, and 1990. He won Olympic gold medals in 1984 and 1988, and a silver in 1980. In the late 1980s, Fetisov led the movement that successfully campaigned to give Soviet hockey players the freedom to leave for the NHL.

The respect he was given in the locker room was immediate. When the Wings added Igor Larionov in the autumn of that year, it enabled a Russian Five unit of Fetisov, Larionov, Sergei Fedorov, Vyacheslav Kozlov, and Vladimir Konstantinov. Fetisov ended up staying three years and helped the Wings win Stanley Cups in '97 and '98. Teammates called him "Papa Bear" in a nod to his nationality and his grizzled appearance.

"Slava was a like a coach on the ice with the young guys," Scotty Bowman recalled in 2019. "He was a tough loser. His temperament was outgoing, but he was ultra-competitive. He knew what it took to win.

"He wasn't the fastest skater, but he'd get there in time. He knew the game. He was such a great player when he was young. He had had a lot of hardships. Adversity never bothered him. He always had confidence."

All five Russians finished the season in the top 10 on the team in scoring. Konstantinov was a particular fan favorite because of his bone-crunching hits. Before the playoffs began, the Russian Wings treated their teammates to a Russian feast. Vodka flowed as toasts flourished. It was another experience that bonded the Wings as family.

The knock on European players, and Russians in particular, was that they hadn't grown up dreaming about winning the Stanley Cup like North American boys did. Such xenophobic nonsense was exposed in the 1997 playoffs. Fedorov paced the Wings with 20 points in the 20 games it took the Wings to beat St. Louis, Anaheim, Colorado, and Philadelphia to win the Stanley Cup for the first time in 42 years. Kozlov was third with 13 points. Larionov had 12. Fetisov had four points. And Konstantinov had the hit of the playoffs when he clobbered Dale Hawerchuk in Game 3 of the Finals.

After Yzerman's emotional victory lap with the Cup at the end of Game 4, he skated to owner Mike Ilitch, who raised it above his head in jubilation. It was where it went next that demonstrated how much Bowman's trades for two veteran Russians meant. The first teammate Yzerman handed the Cup to was Fetisov. He and Larionov skated their lap together, clutching the final piece of hardware missing from their hockey treasure chests.

"Stevie gives it to us, and we appreciate it very much," Fetisov said. "I have been through so many situations, winning so many gold medals, but it was unforgettable moment to carry the Stanley Cup around and have so many fans cheering."

Like so many other memorable moments in his hockey career, there was one guy Fetisov needed to share it with. "Igor is a special guy to me," Fetisov said. "I am so proud I am friends with him for so many years. We share so many different things. We win gold medals together, we fight Communism together to be able to come play over here. We have been through so much. Now we win Stanley Cup."

Fetisov and Larionov turned out to be the last missing pieces the Wings needed to end their Stanley Cup drought. That third-round pick the Wings gave New Jersey for Fetisov? David Gosselin played 13 games in the NHL. And Sheppard didn't even last a season in San Jose, serving stints with Florida and Carolina. He never scored 30 goals in a season again.

Fetisov and Larionov had been well worth those prices. They showed the Wings why it made more sense to play a puck possession game and helped foster a sense of camaraderie. They weren't the longest-serving Wings, but Yzerman's handoff celebrated their importance.

"To see them skate with it after Stevie was a special feeling for me because I am Russian and people say we don't want to win the Cup," Konstantinov said at the time. "Finally we did it, with five Russians, so now maybe everybody know Russians want to win Cup, too."

Fedorov grew sentimental. "When I just start playing hockey, I watch those guys," he said. "To see them win this is incredible feeling."

It was the last game the five played in together. Konstantinov's career ended six days later with the limousine crash. Fetisov was in the vehicle with him but sustained minor injuries. He played one more season with the Wings, helping them repeat as champions. Larionov played for the Wings until 2000, when he signed with Florida. That was a disaster, and the Wings reacquired him, leading to a second stint that lasted until 2003. Kozlov was traded to Buffalo in 2001 as part of a package for Dominik Hasek. Fedorov held out in a contract dispute to start the 1997–98 season, and left the Wings as a free agent in 2003.

As a five-man unit, they were magical to watch. Their artistry with the puck hypnotized teammates and opponents, and helped bring the Stanley Cup home to Detroit.

10

THE DROUGHT ENDS

On June 7, 1997, sitting in his owner's box at Joe Louis Arena, Mike Ilitch watched as his kids popped the cork on the bottle of 1982 Moet champagne he had bought when he purchased the Red Wings. Three floors below, everyone in the dressing room was soaked from champagne showers. Meanwhile, across the Atlantic Ocean in Sweden, Jan Erik Lidstrom opened a bottle of champagne. It wasn't even time for breakfast yet—just 5:30 AM—but he wanted to celebrate, too.

The Wings had smashed a 42-year drought and uncorked a fantastic party. They had silenced doubters and enthralled fans. The centerpiece of the celebration was the Stanley Cup, a trophy that looks good being hoisted, hugged, and chugged from. Steve Yzerman took it home with him that night, tucked away in the trunk of his silver Porsche. He had waited 14 years for this moment, had endured trade rumors and injuries, to get to this night. The Ilitches had waited 15 years, had sat in their luxury suite and watched in disappointment as one spring after another ended too soon.

Not this time. The previous years had been crushing—swept in the 1995 Stanley Cup Finals, eliminated in the 1996 Conference finals by the Colorado Avalanche and villain Claude Lemieux. But those series were also instructive. The Wings learned what it took to win in the playoffs.

The mission that was completed June 7 began April 16, when the Wings faced the Blues in the first game of the first round of the playoffs. It wasn't a great start for the Wings. They were shut out by future Hall of Fame goaltender Grant Fuhr in Game 1, and trailed 1–0 going into the third period of Game 2. The Wings were 20 minutes from going to St. Louis down two games. But then Kris Draper spotted an opportunity to score during a penalty kill and made it 1–1; three minutes later, Larry Murphy used the momentum to make it 2–1. With that, the series was tied.

Yzerman scored the winning goal in the next game to put the Wings up 2–1. But it was what he did the next game that really swayed the series and stoked Yzerman's legend. Fuhr shut them out again, the Wings falling 4–0. After the game, Yzerman stood up in the visitors' room at the Kiel Center and spoke for 10 minutes. Players were still in their uniforms.

His message was simple: we can be beaten, but we're not going to be outworked.

"We've just got to play harder," Yzerman said the next day. "Our top players have got to play harder. We've got to produce and lead the team. Everybody has a certain expectation and responsibility, and you've got to play up to them."

Yzerman spoke softly, but he led loudly. He scored 3:22 into Game 5, and capped the 5–2 victory by setting up Larry Murphy's goal. It was the first time in the playoffs coach Scotty Bowman used the Russian Five an entire game. The Wings went back to the Kiel Center and won Game 6 3–1. Next up: the Mighty Ducks of Anaheim.

The Wings would sweep their fowl opponent, but it took 18 periods of hockey to do so. Martin Lapointe one-timed a pass from Brendan Shanahan in overtime to claim Game 1 2–1. Game 2 was epic. Vyacheslav Kozlov, the quietest guy in the locker room, raised the roof at the Joe when he scored in triple overtime. The game lasted 101 minutes, 31 seconds on the ice—but 5 hours and 40 minutes for spectators. "No big deal," Kozlov said after the 3–2 final. "Not for Red Wings. We have good shape. We can play couple more overtimes. No problem."

It was, mercifully, a Sunday matinee. The Wings flew to Anaheim that evening, and Kozlov found himself the story of Game 3 as well, with two goals and one assist in the 5–3 victory at the Pond.

Kozlov proved prophetic, as the Wings did need to play a couple more overtimes in the series. It was 3:30 AM in Detroit on May 9, 1997, when the Wings secured a trip to the Western Conference finals. During intermission after the first overtime, Lapointe was the one to stand up to address his teammates, urging that someone step up and end the series that night. Fittingly, it was Lapointe himself who assisted on Brendan Shanahan's overtime goal at 17:03 of the second overtime, ending the sweep with a 3–2 victory. "We didn't want to be flying across the country anymore," Shanahan said afterward. "If we win it now, we knew we could relax and take a couple of days off."

The Avalanche polished off the Oilers on May 11. The teams that had brawled March 26 in Detroit once again were on a collision course.

The defending Stanley Cup champion Avs boasted three of the top four scorers in the playoffs in Lemieux, Joe Sakic, and Peter Forsberg. The Avalanche used home-ice advantage and won Game 1. The Wings trailed

62 AND DONE

The season was fun—and then it was forgotten. The Red Wings entered the 1995–96 season buoyed and bitter. They had distanced themselves from first-round ousters in 1993 and '94 and battled through to the '95 Stanley Cup Finals, proving something to themselves and silencing outsiders. Only then the Devils won—and won and won and won—and before the Wings could figure out how to recover, they had been swept aside.

No one could deny that the Wings had talent. Igor Larionov joined the team in the fall of 1995, acquired by Scotty Bowman, both the coach and director of player personnel at the time. The player was the last piece needed to complete what would be known as the Russian Five—Larionov, Sergei Fedorov, Vyacheslav Kozlov, Slava Fetisov, and Vladimir Konstantinov.

The Wings started the 1995–96 season 5-4-2, but by November they were rolling over opponents like a bulldozer. They lost just two games that month. In December, they went 13-1. The Wings rang in 1996 with a 3-2 victory over the Hartford Whalers. At the end of March the Wings were 58-12-5, two victories shy of the Montreal Canadiens' record-setting 60-8-12 season in 1976-77.

The Wings broke the record in their penultimate game, beating Chicago 5-3 at Joe Louis Arena on April 12, 1996. They also tied the record of 36 home victories set by the 1975-76 Philadelphia Flyers. The Wings led 4-3 in the final minute—Kris Draper scored into an empty net with 44.4 seconds remaining—and were regaled by a standing ovation from fans chanting "Sixty-*one*! Sixty-*one*!"

Steve Yzerman said afterward the Wings appreciated the milestone for about a minute. Darren McCarty was a more effusive, saying, "Obviously it's exciting. It's never been accomplished before, and we took a lot of pride in it."

Two nights later, the Wings routed Dallas 5-1. They finished the season 62-13-7, their 131 points just shy of Montreal's 132 points in '76-77. But when the Wings were eliminated in the Western Conference finals, those 62 victories could not balm the pain. "We lost a tough series to a really good team in Colorado that went on to win the Cup," Yzerman reflected in 2019. "While it was going on, it was a very exciting season. It was exciting to set the record. But once we didn't win the Cup, the regular season was forgotten about very quickly. Our hope was to win the Stanley Cup. So the regular season, while it was under way, was a lot of fun. Ultimately it was forgotten. It's not something we think or talk about."

2–1 after two periods in Game 2, then Lidstrom saved the day. Late in the third period, with the Wings ahead 3–2, he covered for goaltender Mike Vernon, sliding into the crease and stopping Eric Lacroix's point-blank shot with his stick. A minute later Darren McCarty scored. The Wings won.

Vernon stole Game 3 with a 27-save performance in a 2–1 victory. Game 4 was a 6–0 rout: Igor Larionov scored twice in the first period, and the Wings led, 5–0, after the second. The only shots the Avalanche took were cheap ones—they took six penalties in the first period, three more in the second. Colorado coach Marc Crawford became so irate in the third period that he tried to get to the Wings' bench, screaming obscenities. McCarty talked back. Yzerman stared in disbelief. Bowman toyed with Crawford, telling his younger colleague that he had known his father and that his father would be embarrassed at Crawford's hysterics. Crawford later apologized, but not before the NHL fined him $10,000.

The Wings suffered a 6–0 loss of their own in Game 5, but that meant the series swung back to Detroit. Fans at the Joe saw the Wings eliminate their archrival, two months to the day after the March 26 brawl between the teams at the Joe. Lapointe scored less than four minutes into the game, and the Wings never trailed. As players lined up for the traditional handshake after the 3–1 final, Lemieux refused to shake McCarty's hand.

The Philadelphia Flyers were waiting. Crawford had spent one of his news conferences whining nonstop about Vladimir Konstantinov, accusing the stoic Russian defenseman of playing so dirty he deserved a penalty every shift. Flyers coach Terry Murray was concerned his star player, Eric Lindros, would face Konstantinov and urged Lindros to watch his temper. Bowman had other plans. He countered Lindros with Nicklas Lidstrom. The Legion of Doom—Lindros, John LeClair, and Mikael Renberg, so named for their skill and size (each was 6'2" or taller and topped 230 pounds)—was rendered ineffective by Lidstrom and defense partner Murphy. Murphy was a trade-deadline acquisition, one Jimmy Devellano later described as the "move of moves." Murphy and Lidstrom were a finesse pairing that relied on positional excellence. Lindros and his linemates just couldn't get around them. Lindros was held to just one goal in the series.

During one of the few times when Lindros was on the ice against Konstantinov, in Game 3, Lindros raced across the ice and cross-checked

Konstantinov, drawing a penalty. The Wings capitalized during the power play. It was exactly the kind of silly antic Lindros had been urged to avoid by his coach.

The Wings claimed Games 1 and 2, both on the road, with 4–2 finals. When LeClair scored in Game 3, it was the first time in the series the Flyers had held the lead. It lasted two minutes. Yzerman converted on a power play and the Wings went on to win 6–1. The victory improved the Wings to 13–2 since Yzerman's speech in St. Louis.

Game 4 fell on a Saturday night. Lidstrom scored in the final minute of the first period to make it 1–0. At 13:02 of the second period, McCarty—already a local hero for beating up Lemieux that March—scored to make it 2–0. It was a beautiful goal: McCarty faked out Flyers defenseman Janne Niinimaa inside the offensive blue line, swooped around him, and cut to the net. Lindros scored with 15 seconds to go in the game. And with that, the Wings had their Cup.

Yzerman hoisted the Cup above his head, his gap-toothed smile a mix of relief and joy. He skated to the Wings bench so that owners Mike and Marian Ilitch could touch the Cup, then took his victory lap around the ice. "I would have preferred to go with everybody in the beginning," Yzerman said. "I wanted to go as one big group." Yzerman passed the Cup to Slava Fetisov, who held it up with Larionov. It was a very conscious, very telling choice on Yzerman's part. It revealed the respect he felt was due to the two men who had done so much to liberate Russian hockey players from Soviet red tape.

"The last couple of days I thought who I wanted to give the Cup to," Yzerman said. "I thought about Slava. He and Igor, what they stand for, are good examples for younger players.... All five Russian players were significant players and great guys."

Players took turns taking laps with the Cup. Bowman put on skates and took a lap too. "That was great," Yzerman said. "I've seen it all. He doesn't show emotion. He doesn't let us get too close to him. For a few minutes there, he was one of us."

As the night wore on, as players sprayed champagne and hugged and celebrated with the Cup, Lidstrom called his parents back home in Sweden, a six-hour time difference. "They had watched the whole game," Lidstrom said. "They sounded pretty happy."

In 1993, after the Toronto Maple Leafs eliminated the Wings in the first round, Yzerman cried in a back room at the Joe until 4:00 AM. The next spring, when his season ended with a stunning first-round upset by the San Jose Sharks, Yzerman cried until 3:00 AM. Finally, the Joe was a place for celebration.

"He tried to get it for 14 years, and now he gets it," teammate Tomas Holmstrom said. "I almost started crying."

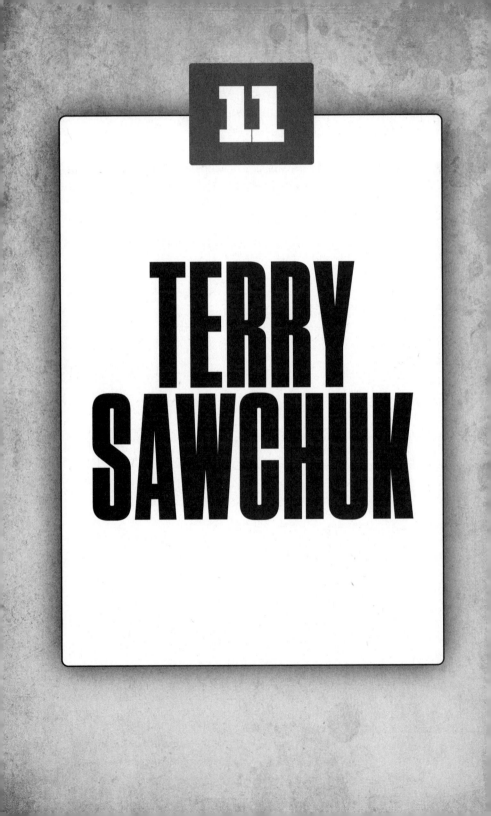

11

TERRY SAWCHUK

Terry Sawchuk's story is one of great accomplishment and tragedy, his battles off the ice vivid and consuming, his on-ice athleticism visible and dazzling.

Sawchuk won 445 games in 21 seasons, 14 of them in three stints for the Wings. He was the first goaltender to record 100 shutouts, and his 103 shutouts rank second all-time behind Martin Brodeur. He played 971 games, fourth all-time. Sawchuk was rookie of the year in the old United States Hockey League in 1948, the American Hockey League in 1949, and the NHL in 1951. He was 22 when, in 1952, he won the first of four Stanley Cups and was awarded the first of four Vezina Trophies (at that time given to the goaltender of the team allowing the fewest goals during the regular season). He was 35 when he took home his last Vezina and 37 when he celebrated his final Cup. At 40, he died in circumstances that fit his messy, pain-filled life.

Sawchuk had been dead for 24 years when the Red Wings bestowed upon him the ultimate honor in 1994, his No. 1 ascending to the rafters at Joe Louis Arena to hang in the company of Ted Lindsay's No. 7, Gordie Howe's No. 9, and Alex Delvecchio's No. 10. It was an overdue tribute to a player who set the standard by which goaltenders are measured.

Terrance Gordon Sawchuk was born December 28, 1929, in Winnipeg, Manitoba. His father had immigrated from what is now Ukraine, earning Sawchuk the nickname "The Ukey" or "The Uke" among his teammates. Two of his three brothers died before reaching adulthood. Sawchuk suffered a bad injury to his right elbow while playing rugby when he was 12 years old, but fearful of telling his parents, Sawchuk kept it from them. From lack of treatment, the joint failed to heal properly and caused Sawchuk's arm to be shorter than his left one. It caused lifelong discomfort.

His rough childhood seemed to melt away when Sawchuk was on the ice. By 14 he had drawn interest from scouts, one of them from the Wings. In 1946 he was playing junior hockey in Galt, Ontario, where Sawchuk would face future Wings teammate Red Kelly, who played for St. Michaels.

(Like Kelly, Sawchuk was a standout all-around athlete, finding success on the baseball field, too.)

His NHL career fed into the fear of many a professional athlete: beware getting hurt, because someone else may steal your job while you're healing. So it was in 1950 when Sawchuk filled in for Harry Lumley for seven games. Though Lumley had a respectable 33–16–14 record (seven shutouts) with a 2.35 goals-against average, Sawchuk impressed by going 4–3 with a 2.29 goals-against average, including recording a shutout. General manager Jack Adams saw enough; he traded Lumley to the Chicago Black Hawks even though Lumley had just backstopped the Wings to the Stanley Cup.

Sawchuk dazzled over the next five seasons. From 1950–51 to 1954–55, he led all NHL goaltenders with 195 victories (Gerry McNeil, in second place, had 112). Sawchuk's 1.93 goals-against average was the only one below 2.00 among goaltenders who'd appeared in at least 100 games. His 56 shutouts were 20 more than Lumley. Sawchuk helped the Wings to three Stanley Cups during that span, and was a first- or second-team All-Star five times his first five seasons. He went 28–15 in 43 playoff games, posting a 1.87 goals-against average. He was especially spectacular in the 1952 playoffs, going 8–0 with a 0.62 goals-against average.

Sawchuk's first five years are staggering on their own, but to put them further into perspective, he played at a time before there were backup goaltenders. The Red Wings played 350 games from 1950–51 to 1954–55. Sawchuk played 338 of them.

Jimmy Skinner, Sawchuk's coach in the mid-1950s, recalled his greatness at the March 6, 1994, jersey retirement ceremony. "There are goalies who are certain types of goalies, but Sawchuk, he had everything—reflexes, angles," he said in a *Detroit Free Press* interview. "He had it all, and he also had a lot of guts. He'd always say, 'Get me a couple and we'll win.' And he meant it. He didn't say it in a bragging way. He was just that confident."

Sawchuk was a master at crouching, posturing himself so low to the ice he could almost see the pucks coming at eye level. But beneath the exterior or self-assurance, torment tore at Sawchuk. He fought depression, which was exacerbated by heavy drinking. When team ownership passed in 1955 from Marguerite Norris to her brother Bruce, Adams took advantage of his new boss' lack of backbone and tore the team apart within weeks of winning the Stanley Cup. Believing the team had its future goaltender in Glenn Hall, Adams traded Sawchuk to the Boston Bruins. (Hall had an excellent 1955–56 season, posting 12 shutouts, winning the Calder Memorial Trophy as rookie of the year, and taking the team to the Stanley Cup Finals, but a year later he, too, was on the way out, traded to Chicago along with Ted Lindsay in another of Adams' awful deals.)

Terry Sawchuk in 1963.

The trade was a punch in the gut for Sawchuk, adding further distress to a man fighting multiple physical and personal problems. His wife, Pat, with whom he had seven children, threatened to divorce him. (She went through with it in 1969.) Years of crouching had damaged Sawchuk's posture to the extent he walked with a stoop and suffered from swayback (an abnormal bend to the back). He didn't don a protective mask until 1962, by which time he'd taken some 400 stitches to his face, including 3 to a slashed eyeball. His right arm—the one injured in childhood that had never healed properly—needed 60 bone chips removed from the elbow, further reducing his use of that arm. He was diagnosed with mononucleosis while with the Boston Bruins in 1956–57 but went back in his net after just two weeks.

He returned to the Wings in 1957 and played seven seasons, going 147–159–64 with a 2.89 goals-against average and .904 save percentage (his record reflected the damage Adams had done to the team in front of him). With Roger Crozier on the horizon, Sawchuk, at 34, was left unprotected in the 1964 waiver draft; that led to a successful interlude with the Toronto Maple Leafs, where Sawchuk teamed up with Johnny Bower to win the 1965 Vezina Trophy and the 1967 Stanley Cup. Left unprotected again in the 1967 expansion draft, Sawchuk landed with the Los Angeles Kings, as the first goalie selected. He was traded back to the Wings the next year.

Years of injuries and alcoholism had taken a toll, and Sawchuk played just 13 games for the Wings in 1968–69. His swan song came with the New York Rangers (his fourth Original Six team) in 1969–70, at 40, when he was limited to eight regular-season games and three in the playoffs. The last victory of his career was, fittingly for such a goaltending legend, a shutout: he notched 29 saves in a 6–0 victory over the Pittsburgh Penguins on February 1, 1970.

Four months later, Sawchuk was dead. On April 29, 1970, Sawchuk and Ron Stewart got into a fight over the expenses of the house they'd been sharing on Long Island. They'd been drinking. The two men pushed and shoved one another. Sawchuk fell on top of Stewart's knee, suffering damage to his gallbladder and liver. Sawchuk underwent three surgeries, including one to have his gallbladder removed. He died May 31 of a blood clot. Sawchuk had taken responsibility for the fight, and a Nassau County grand jury later absolved Stewart of blame. He had visited Sawchuk in the hospital, and even served as a pallbearer at Sawchuk's funeral.

After Stewart passed away in March 2012, the *New York Times* revisited the incident. "Recalling the Stewart-Sawchuk fight in an interview on Wednesday, [Emile] Francis said that when he visited Sawchuk in the hospital, "He said: 'It wasn't Ron Stewart's fault, don't blame him. I was the aggressor in the whole thing,'" Richard Goldstein wrote. "By Sawchuk's account, Francis said, the arguing began when Sawchuk told Stewart that he owed him $8.00 on a phone bill. But Dr. Denis F. Nicholson, a physician for a number of Rangers families, said at the time that Sawchuk had told him that he punched Stewart at the bar because he 'had been bugging him all year' and that he jumped Stewart at the house 'and I fell on his knee.'"

Sawchuk was buried in Mount Hope Cemetery in Pontiac, Michigan. The year after his death, Sawchuk, a U.S. citizen since 1959, was awarded the Lester Patrick Trophy for his contribution to hockey in the United States, and was inducted into the Hockey Hall of Fame.

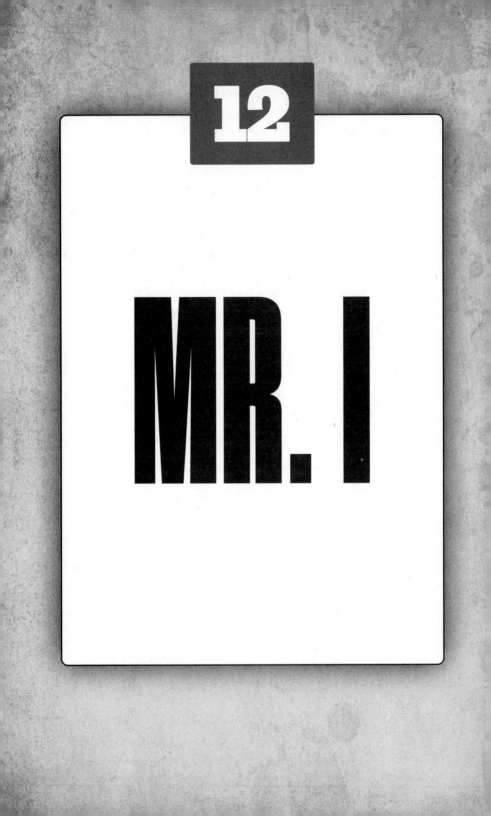

12

MR. I

When he wasn't tending to his growing pizza empire, Mike Ilitch was a hockey dad. One of his daughters played goaltender. One of his sons had such early-morning practices in winters that Ilitch would carry him across parking lots to protect the edges on the little boy's skates. Other times Ilitch could be found at Olympia Stadium cheering on the Red Wings.

He started doing his cheering from the owner's suite at Joe Louis Arena in 1982, after shelling out $8 million to buy the team from Bruce Norris, whose family had owned the Wings for 50 years. For a city and a fan base fed up with Norris' mishandling of the team, Ilitch's words elated like a nightingale's song. "I love the Red Wings," Ilitch declared at a news conference heralding his purchase. "It's a dream I had as a young boy. I remember coming to Olympia Stadium as a tot in the back of a panel truck sitting on an orange crate, parking half a mile away from Olympia so we wouldn't have to pay, running as fast as I could to get to the balcony."

Ilitch had tried to buy the Wings in the summer of 1981 but his $11 million bid was rejected. As it became increasingly clear Norris wanted to unload the team, other names surfaced in connection with the sale—former Detroit Lions linebacker Joe Schmidt and University of Michigan athletic director Don Canham. Ilitch won his bid in May 1982, taking over a franchise that had failed to make the playoffs 14 of its last 16 seasons, but when a person fulfills a childhood dream, a rosy glow envelops reality. "I expect to make the playoffs," Ilitch said when asked where he foresaw the Wings finishing in 1983.

Ilitch said the things a smart businessman embarking on a new adventure says: he wasn't going to interfere in the day-to-day running of the team because he wasn't qualified to do so, he was going to hire good people, he was going to promote an atmosphere of success. He was going to rebuild the team, restore ticket sales, reignite fan excitement, reestablish ties between the club and its storied alumni, starting with personal friends Gordie Howe and Ted Lindsay. If it seemed a Herculean task, one only had to look at Ilitch's background to believe he could accomplish it.

Ilitch was born July 20, 1929, in Detroit to Macedonian immigrants. His father, Sotir, worked in a Chrysler factory. Ilitch followed his 1947 graduation from Cooley High School with four years in the Marines, where he played shortstop. A two-year stint in the Detroit Tigers farm system ended when Ilitch suffered a knee injury.

In 1954 Ilitch met and fell in love with Marian Bayoff, herself the child of Macedonian immigrants, and took her to Wings games as part of their courtship. They married soon after and went on to have seven children. In 1959, they used Ilitch's savings from his baseball career and a job selling pots and pans to open a restaurant in a strip mall on Cherry Hill Road in Garden City, Michigan. They named it Little Caesar's Pizza Treat after Marian's nickname for Mike. A pizza cost $2.39.

As their pizza business grew (and the apostrophe disappeared), a plaque commemorated where it all began, reading in part: "The Little Caesars story starts right here. On May 8, 1959, Mike and Marian Ilitch opened this first Little Caesars store. Today Little Caesars is a household name and a favorite pizza of people around the world."

Ilitch was 29 when he opened his first pizza place, furnishing his office with a used desk he bought for a couple of bucks. Two decades later the chain introduced the "Pizza! Pizza!" catchphrase to advertise two pizzas for the price of one, a savvy selling point in a city enduring hard times.

Ilitch had first ventured into the world of owning a sports team in the 1970s, starting a local pro softball team he named the Caesars. He lost $500,000 in the first three years but persisted in bringing in good players and was rewarded with two league titles.

He was 52 when he bought the Wings. By then Little Caesars operated in nine states, had 300 stores, and was a leading television sponsor of Wings games. "Mike didn't have the skills to cut it too far in baseball, but he was ambitious and a good hustler," Tigers general manager Jim Campbell told *Detroit Free Press* reporter Joe Lapointe in 1982.

Ilitch's first choice to manage his hockey club was Minnesota general manager Lou Nanne, but the North Stars didn't give Ilitch permission to talk to him. Instead, Ilitch recruited Jimmy Devellano, who'd won three Stanley Cups with the New York Islanders, two as a scout and one as assistant general manager and director of scouting.

"I'll do whatever I have to do to have a winner," Ilitch told *Free Press* reporter Tom Henderson that month. "I'm going to spend the money and

Mike and Marian Ilitch with Sergei Fedorov and the trophy for winning the Western Conference at Joe Louis Arena, June 11, 1995. (Julian H. Gonzalez)

do whatever it takes to get myself a winner. If it takes losing money, I'll lose money, but there's a point of no return. I gotta be fair to myself and the rest of my businesses.

"I want to find my niche. If that means patting the players on the butt when they come out of the dressing room, then I'll pat butts.... If it means traveling with them on road trips, I'm going to do it. If it means keeping a distant profile to be effective, I'll do it. I'm not sure what it's going to take yet, but I'm going to do whatever it takes."

With fewer than 5,000 season ticket holders, Ilitch had to figure out how to sell the team to a fan base that had grown apathetic. His pizzas were hot, but how could he sell $15 tickets to the stale product he had on ice? "You've got to have the marketing and research and development," Ilitch said in 1982. "That's how we've gotten ahead. That's what it's all about in the '80s. You have to be an astute marketing person."

No one would counter that Ilitch wasn't astute: he'd ignored critics who told him pizza was a fad, and made his family a big part of his business. (Marian was secretary-treasurer, and four of the older children helped run things, including daughter Denise, who graduated from the University of Detroit with a law degree in 1980.) He made up for his lack of a college degree with street smarts. "If the concept gets tired, you've got to bring in new things," Ilitch said. "You just have to let your imagination go."

Unlike Bruce Norris, who ran the Wings from his homes in Chicago and Florida, Ilitch was a daily presence in Detroit. He tried new things, including flirting with the addition of a third color to the uniform. He authorized a mascot—a chicken named "The Red Winger." He took out advertisements in local newspapers heralding a new era was beginning. He got good friend Bill Bonds, a famous local TV newsman, to host the first game. On opening night, 17,343 fans treated Ilitch to a standing ovation when he was introduced on the ice before the game.

Ilitch cried. "That was too much—I was all choked up," he said. "It was a very, very touching thing."

That was October 6, 1982. Ilitch had to wait until October 23 before he could celebrate a victory. Later in his tenure, he would watch games from a walled-off section of his suite, swigging bottles of Evian water, but that night Ilitch spent the game directly behind his team's bench, ensuring players returning from a shift stared directly at the guy who paid their salaries.

Ilitch's early expectations were deflated: the Wings missed the playoffs in 1983–by 18 points. They pinned their hopes on another draft, settling for Steve Yzerman at fourth overall (after missing out on the guy they coveted, homegrown Pat LaFontaine). It was a heck of a draft for the Wings: Bob Probert in the third round, Petr Klima and Joe Kocur in the fifth.

The Wings were on the rise, and Ilitch loved it—what's more, he showed it. Yzerman had a clause in his contract that paid him a $25,000 bonus if he was voted the NHL's Rookie of the Year. Before the winner was announced, Ilitch handed Yzerman an envelope reading "You're my rookie of the year." Inside was a $25,000 check (Yzerman was a finalist, but he lost to Buffalo Sabres goaltender Tom Barasso). In 1987, Ilitch doubled his players' $13,000 playoff shares. He did the same in 1988. One Christmas, he left VCRs on every player's locker-room stool. "It's why everybody in the NHL wants to play in Detroit," Yzerman said. "He's said it to us players: 'If you play hard and work hard and do your best, you'll be rewarded.' He's done it on several occasions."

Ilitch came under criticism for his generosity when the Wings seemed to take a step back, failing to qualify for the 1990 playoffs. "I think there's some truth to that," he said. "I think sometimes I do get maybe a stronger feeling toward my players than I should. And I'm probably going to have to cut it back a little bit. I like being an owner, being with my players and my organization. And when they're performing well, it's just my nature. I want to share it with them."

Ilitch wanted to share his good fortune with the city he loved too. In 1988 he and Marian bought the iconic Fox Theatre and restored it to its former glory. They moved their corporate headquarters from Farmington Hills to the 10-story building that contains the Fox. Ilitch fulfilled another dream in 1992 when he bought the Detroit Tigers.

He was then a decade into owning the Wings. The team had made progress, no one could accuse Ilitch otherwise. Yzerman was beloved. There had been back-to-back trips to the conference finals in 1988 and 1989. The 1989 draft yielded an incredible crop in Nicklas Lidstrom, Sergei Fedorov, and Vladimir Konstantinov. But spring after spring the Wings came up short. Ilitch went back to his business philosophy: if a concept is

MRS. ILITCH

Marian Ilitch wanted her husband to be the public face of the Red Wings, but those who worked closely in the organization came to regard her as an invaluable insider. "Marian has had a bigger impact on the Red Wings than anybody would know," senior vice president Jimmy Devellano said.

Devellano was the Ilitches' first hockey employee, hired from the New York Islanders to manage the Wings. Devellano answered to Mike but found Marian indispensable. "She was a stabilizing force for the team and for her husband," Devellano said in 2019. "She was a very steadying influence on Mike. She was a great sounding board.

"A major part of her role was the business part of it. When we got here, there were 2,100 season ticket holders. Hard to believe. She rolled up her sleeves, got her family together, and they went out and pounded the pavement and sold season tickets. It was not Hockeytown back in 1982."

Marian Bayoff was born January 7, 1933, in Dearborn, Michigan. She met Mike Ilitch in 1954 and married him soon after. She started a pizza company with her husband in 1959, and in 1982, she set about to make their newly purchased NHL team a success. She manned the phones at the box office at Joe Louis Arena, and as a working mother she brought her older children with her. They would set up tables near Alumni Row and work the phones, too, trying to sell tickets.

"We wanted to emphasize to the kids that it is a business and that the bottom line is that you must get customers in the door," Marian said in a 1988 interview. "By working the box office, we talked to our customers. It's basically the same in all business. You have to know what you're selling and what the customer is telling you."

The Ilitches believed in listening to their customers and in rewarding their employees. They cut generous checks: when John Ogrodnick topped 50 goals in 1984–85, he received a $50,000 bonus. So did Steve Yzerman when he reached the plateau in 1987–88. "Mike was very generous but what people don't know is Marian was behind all of that," Devellano said. "Mike did it, I don't want to take that away, but that didn't go on without Marian's agreeing and blessing.

"She's been a rock for the franchise. Mike, of course, was the driver, but there were many, many times we would get Marian involved because we had important decisions to make and she was rock-solid. On a personal level, in the early years when I had problems—whether it be players or the media or what have you, we weren't doing very good—she really had my back. She was for stability."

Bruce Martyn, the radio voice of the Wings from 1964 to '95, recalled the impact Marian Ilitch had over the years. "She was so friendly to me, to most everybody," Martyn said in a 2019 interview. "She really nursed everything back to order. Mike would lose his temper sometimes and she would temper him."

That was in private. Publicly, Marian Ilitch was the quiet owner. "She's told me this—she felt Mike should be out front as the husband, as the man he should be out front," Devellano said. "But she was important. When things would get emotional, she would be a little more rational, and it helped. It helped us make a lot of good decisions."

Players found Marian Ilitch approachable and friendly. In the summer of 2019, Kirk Maltby sat with her at a Tigers game at Comerica Park and chatted for 20 minutes. The Ilitches had attended his wedding in July 2004. "She wanted to know how old my kids were, and we talked about how quickly they grow," Maltby said. "She's an incredibly genuine person. I wouldn't want to go up against her in a business deal or a board office, but as far as sitting beside her and watching a game, she's as nice of a person you could ask for."

Mike Ilitch died in February 2017. Marian Ilitch remained a rock for the Wings, attending games and serving as a sounding board for son Christopher Ilitch, who in 2016 was publicly announced as Mike's successor running the Wings and Detroit Tigers. Marian Ilitch had divested herself from an interest in the Tigers in 2005 when she became sole owner of MotorCity Casino upon purchasing the remaining 75 percent stake from the Mandalay Resort Group.

Her public appearances were limited, but when Yzerman was introduced as general manager on April 19, 2019, Marian Ilitch attended the news conference at Little Caesars Arena.

tired, bring in something new. In 1993 that "something new" was Scotty Bowman, who had already coached six Stanley Cup winners.

Four years later, Ilitch and his wife were on the Wings' bench. It was June 7, 1997, and the buzzer had just sounded on a 2–1 final in Game 4 of the Stanley Cup Finals against the Philadelphia Flyers. Ilitch was clad in a varsity jacket bearing a Wings emblem and a Wings hat. Marian was next to him, wearing red. They leaned over and gave the Stanley Cup a quick pat as its handlers walked past on the way to Yzerman. It had taken 15 years, but they had their championship.

"I feel fantastic," a grinning Ilitch said. "This is the hardest job I've ever had in my life. Sometimes I wondered if we'd see it through to the end. But one of my strengths is perseverance, and we hung in there."

The Ilitches celebrated with a bottle of 1982 Moet, bought, naturally, the year they bought the Wings. That $8 million investment was now valued at $146 million. That guy who was their second choice in 1983 was now like another son, a son who hoisted the Cup above his head and ended his first victory lap at the bench, where he presented the Cup to the Ilitches. Mike Ilitch believed in trusting his intuition, believed in Detroit, believed in pizza and hockey and loyalty, and this glorious silver chalice was his reward.

"I look out into the stands from my box and I see all those people throughout the arena and I say, 'These are all my children now,'" he said. "I was born in Detroit and raised here. I came from zero. This community helped make me. It's nice to give something back. I'm proud. We can say our conscience is clear. We've always tried to do what is right, and what we believed in. We had integrity and we wanted to do the things for our city."

Ilitch was inducted into the Hockey Hall of Fame in 2003. His Wings won four Stanley Cups, and his Tigers made two World Series appearances. He built a new ballpark and a new hockey arena and invigorated downtown Detroit. His father had called him a "bum" for dallying with his career after leaving the Marines, but in 2016 *Forbes* magazine listed Mike and Marian Ilitch at No. 88 on its list of richest people, with a net worth of $5.4 billion.

"We believed in the pizza," Ilitch once said.

Ilitch died at 87 on February 10, 2017. The little boy who'd run through the streets of Detroit to get to Olympia Stadium left behind a city richer for his generosity, and a hockey team richer in Stanley Cups.

13

OLD BOOT NOSE

Sid Abel would have his young linemates over to his house, where they'd feast on big dinners and listen to Abel tell hockey stories. The best one, though, would be the one the three of them wrote together.

When Tommy Ivan took over as coach of the Wings in 1947, he saw potential in putting the veteran center between the two most dynamic forwards on the team. The chemistry among Abel, right wing Gordie Howe, and left wing Ted Lindsay ignited a success story so spectacular that they became known as The Production Line.

When they became linemates, Howe was 19, Lindsay 22, and Abel 29. Abel would invite the two young men to his home, where Abel's wife, Gloria, would cook them pasta for supper. (Gloria was a secretary for Jack Adams, who'd stepped down as coach in 1947 to focus on his general manager duties.) They became like family, with Abel serving as a father figure.

"We used to sit there and listen to [Abel] for hours," Howe said in a *Free Press* interview when Abel passed away in February 2000, 14 days shy of his 82nd birthday. "He'd rehash the whole game like a coach. He helped me because he used to stir us up."

Sidney Gerald Abel was born February 22, 1918, in Melville, a small city in Saskatchewan. Budd Lynch, the team's former broadcaster and public relations director, recalled a time when Abel, then coach of the Wings, took the team to his hometown. "Across the prairies, Sid is telling everybody, 'Oh, you're going to see the most beautiful metropolitan city you've ever seen, bigger than Edmonton, bigger than Calgary,'" Lynch said in a 2000 *Free Press* interview. "Oh, he was piling it on. We get there, and you should have heard the players from the East. I don't think there was a paved sidewalk in the town."

Abel produced 49 points in 48 games in 1941–42, his second full season with the Wings. The next season he won the first of three Stanley Cups, scoring five goals among 13 points in the 10 games it took the Wings to dispatch the Toronto Maple Leafs and Boston Bruins. (By then Abel already was well versed in playing in Stanley Cup Finals, as the Wings had lost the 1941 round to the Bruins and the 1942 round to the Maple Leafs.) Abel left the Wings in 1943 to serve in the Royal Canadian Air Force, returning late in the 1945–46 season,

The following season Abel recorded 19 goals and 29 assists in 60 games. Howe was a rookie who had 22 points in 58 games. Lindsay finished second on the team with 27 goals in 59 games. They started playing together in November 1947, and finished that season as three of the team's top four scorers. In 1949–50, they were the top three scorers in the six-team NHL. The three weren't able to sustain their success in the playoffs, however, as Howe suffered a fractured skull in the first game when a checking attempt went wrong. Even with Howe sidelined, the Wings won the Stanley Cup in a seven-game series with the New York Rangers.

The Production Line was back in form in 1950–51, combining for 206 points. That grew to 208 points in 1951–52, which culminated with Abel winning a third Stanley Cup. It was during his time with the Wings that Abel gained the nickname "Old Boot Nose." "Sid told me the story," longtime broadcaster Bruce Martyn said. "They were playing Montreal back in the old days, and Maurice Richard was running the show. He took off after Gordie and gave him a shove. Gordie turned around and knocked him to the ice. Sid Abel went over and looked at him and said, 'Ha ha, what do you think of that? And all of a sudden, *wham*, Maurice Richard broke Sid's nose. He was 'Boot Nose' from then on."

Abel served as Wings captain in 1942–43, and again from 1946 until his departure in 1952.

After winning the Stanley Cup in '52, Abel bought a tavern in Detroit. He was 34, and he was preparing for his eventual retirement. He was expecting to play one more year with the Wings, but meanwhile Black Hawks players, many of whom were former Wings, had recommended to management that Abel would be an outstanding candidate to be a coach. The Black Hawks asked Adams for permission, and Abel agreed to be the coach but to also play if he deemed it necessary.

Abel's production dropped to nine points in 39 games in 1952–53, and he played just three games in what would be his last season, 1953–54.

Abel is best known for being The Production Line pivot, but he was a man of many seasons for the Wings. He was the coach. The general

ALEX DELVECCHIO

Against the New York Rangers on February 20, 1965, Alex Delvecchio scored a goal to help the Red Wings win 3–2. He scored another goal the next day to help the Wings beat the Toronto Maple Leafs 3–2.

Thus began a record that would stand for 23 years, as Delvecchio produced points in 17 consecutive games, his streak ending March 28 when he went scoreless in the last game of the 1964–65 season, a 4–0 Toronto shutout. Delvecchio scored 12 goals and recorded 19 assists, his 31 points tying Norm Ullman by a Wings player in that span. Delvecchio's record stood until Steve Yzerman obliterated it between November 25 and January 10 of the 1987–88 season, when he went on a 22-game tear that produced 20 goals and 30 assists.

Delvecchio was a durable, skilled forward who served as center on the second iteration of the Production Line, taking over Sid Abel's spot between Gordie Howe and Ted Lindsay after Abel departed for Chicago in 1952. Delvecchio spent his entire 24-year NHL career with the Wings, playing on three Stanley Cup winners.

Alexander Peter Delvecchio was born December 4, 1931, in Fort William, Ontario. He made his debut with the Wings on March 25, 1951, suiting up in their last game of the regular season. When he retired in 1973, at 41, Delvecchio had logged 1,550 games; only Howe (1,687) and Nicklas Lidstrom (1,564) played more games with one franchise. At the time of his retirement, Delvecchio ranked second in the NHL with 1,281 points, trailing only Howe's 1,809 points. Delvecchio's sportsmanlike play won him the Lady Byng Trophy in 1959, 1966, and 1969. (Delvecchio tallied only 383 penalty minutes in his career. By comparison, Lindsay tallied 1,808.) He played in the All-Star Game 13 times. He was remarkably reliable, missing only 42 games in his career, and 22 of those date to a broken ankle suffered during the 1956–57 season. He served as captain from 1962 to '73, the longest to do so until Yzerman.

In November 1973, Delvecchio retired in an arrangement to replace Ted Garvin as coach. By the spring, he also had replaced Ned Harkness as general manager. However, those were dark days. In 1973–74, the Wings failed to qualify for the playoffs for a fourth straight year and for the seventh time in eight years. The next three seasons with Delvecchio as coach and GM, although much of the time Billy Dea or Larry Wilson worked behind the bench, the Wings went 65–144–31. With 10 games left in 1976–77, owner Bruce Norris replaced Delvecchio with his old linemate, Lindsay.

Delvecchio's place in Wings history is secured by his amazing accomplishments as one of the game's most productive forwards—his 456 goals rank third and his 825 assists rank fourth. He was inducted into the Hockey Hall of Fame in 1977 and on October 10, 1991, the Wings held a ceremony to retire Delvecchio's No. 10 and Lindsay's No. 7.

manager. Color commentator. Peacemaker. Other than taking leave during World War II and a couple of years in the 1950s and in the 1970s, Abel's tenure with the Wings spanned 1938–86.

Five years after he left for Chicago, Abel returned to the Wings as coach, making the playoffs in eight of 12 seasons spanning 1958–70. Abel was known as a players' coach, but he had a rule: if he saw one of his players in a bar, he wouldn't enter the place. Conversely, if they saw him in one, neither would they.

He coached the Wings to the Stanley Cup Finals in 1961, '63, '64 and '66—only to lose in six, five, seven and six games.

General manager duties were added in 1962. One of Abel's key maneuvers was to lure Lindsay out of retirement. With the then 39-year-old in the lineup, the Wings won their first regular-season championship in eight years, in 1964–65.

Abel was replaced as general manager by Ned Harkness in January 1971. After a brief stint coaching the St. Louis Blues and two seasons as general manager of the expansion Kansas City Scouts, Abel joined Martyn in the radio booth in 1976. His passion for the game and the Wings was evident in choice commentary that connected with the blue-collar image of the city. Abel was elected to the Hockey Hall of Fame in 1969 and the Wings retired his No. 12 in 1995. Abel was older and less flashy than his Production Line wingmen, but his skill set and savvy were a perfect fit.

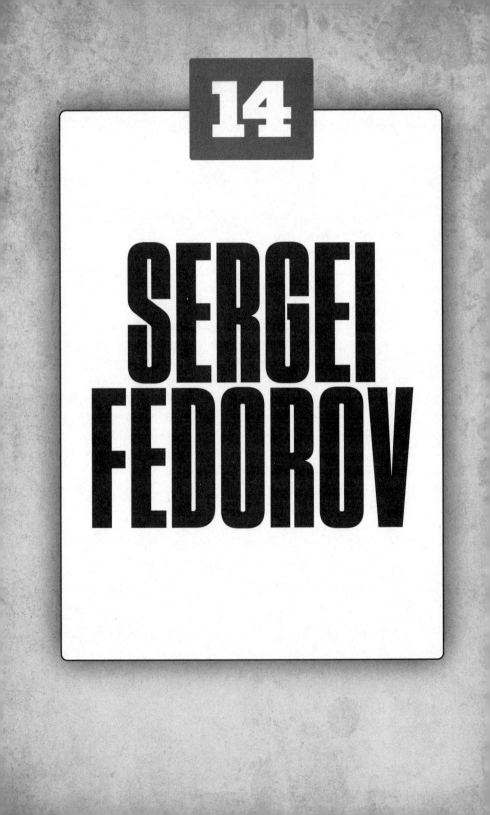

14

SERGEI FEDOROV

Such was Sergei Fedorov's skill, such was his athleticism, that he excelled at anything asked of him on the ice. Fedorov occupies a special place in Red Wings history. The first Russian to appear in a winged wheel sweater, he was an integral component in their restoration—a supernova of a player who electrified with his skill and skating. He was a key member of three Stanley Cup–winning teams, won two Selke Trophies as the NHL's best defensive forward, and captured the 1994 Hart Memorial Trophy as the most valuable player.

Scotty Bowman, who coached dozens of the most legendary and lauded players in hockey history, ranks Fedorov at the top, marveling at how he had the greatest leg strength Bowman had ever seen in a player. "He's the top skater I've had," Bowman said in a 2019 interview. "He was effortless. He was a big man, but chiseled. He had a hell of a physique. He was an unusual Soviet player because the Soviet system was built on offense and built on puck possession. They didn't have to defend very much. He was good defensively."

Bowman, who coached nine of Fedorov's 13 seasons with the Wings, was so confident in the player's ability that he used him as a defenseman at times. Even on a team that boasted Nicklas Lidstrom and Chris Chelios, Fedorov stood out on the blue line. "I'm convinced if Sergei played defense, he could have won a Norris Trophy," Brendan Shanahan said the night Fedorov was inducted into the Hockey Hall of Fame in 2015. "When he decided that it was time to end a game, he just went end to end. Regardless of what we drew up before the game, our power-play breakout and entry was give the puck to Sergei and then get out of his way. He was so talented, so strong."

The Wings never wanted to lose Fedorov. They matched a crazy offer sheet from Carolina in 1998, and when that contract expired in 2003, owner Mike Ilitch took the unusual step of intervening in contract talks to try to persuade Fedorov to stay. Twice. He was a special, special player worth taking a chance on in the 1989 draft, at a time when there was no guarantee Russian players would be able to join an NHL team. He was worth orchestrating a defection that required bribes, a private plane, and cool nerves in a hotel lobby crowded with Soviets.

Fedorov grew up skating on frozen soccer fields in his hometown Pskov, one of Russia's oldest cities, located 10 miles east of the Estonian border. As a teenager at a sports school in Minsk (the capital of Belarus, then a part of the Soviet Union), he'd lie on the ice, jump up, race to the blue line, kneel, jump up, race to the other blue line, lie back down. Repeat. That leg strength Bowman so admired? That's where it was forged.

Fedorov was a rising star on the Central Red Army team when the Wings selected him in the fourth round of the 1989 draft (one round after they drafted Lidstrom). At 74th overall, it was, at the time, the highest a Russian had been drafted. No one was sure he'd ever play for the Wings because Soviet teams didn't just release their players in those days. General manager Jimmy Devellano was willing to gamble. "When we took Sergei in the fourth round, there were snickers around the league because the Iron Curtain was up," he said. "People said that it was a wasted fourth-round pick—that Sergei was a great player, but that we would never get him. They probably weren't wrong to think that. But we thought he was the best 19-year-old player in the world. I thought, *Hell, I'm not drafting some guy who will probably end up playing in the American Hockey League when this guy is available.* So we took Sergei and we were able to get him to defect."

The Wings initiated contact with Fedorov two months after drafting him, taking advantage of an exhibition match in Helsinki to give Fedorov a letter detailing an offer for $250,000 to come play in Detroit. Intermediaries helped establish a line of communication, letting the Wings know Fedorov was interested. In July 1990, six months after Fedorov's military service had ended, Fedorov was in the United States for the Goodwill Games. Ilitch sent his private plane to Portland, Oregon, where the Soviets had an exhibition game. Wings executive vice president Jim Lites and assistant general manager Nick Polano checked in to the same hotel as the Russians. While Fedorov was playing in the game, Wings personnel retrieved Fedorov's luggage (Fedorov had slipped his room key beneath the door of Lites' room). The plan was for Fedorov to follow Lites to a waiting limousine that would whisk them to the airport, where Ilitch's jet awaited. Lites gave the driver $100 to stop asking questions.

Sergei Fedorov with the Stanley Cup, June 13, 2002. (Julian H. Gonzalez)

As Fedorov and his teammates arrived back at the hotel following the game, Lites waited in the lobby. He got up and started walking out when Fedorov was spotted by his roommate. Fedorov told him he was leaving, his nerves suppressed in quiet exhilaration. "I was excited to see nice plane," Fedorov said. "I was looking forward to landing in Detroit and getting on with a new life."

Fedorov debuted in a Wings uniform on October 4, 1990. He was 20 years old. He scored that night, the first of 31 goals and 79 points during his rookie season. The Wings supplied Fedorov with a translator. (Teammate Shawn Burr supplied him with swim trunks when Fedorov showed up for a day of boating on Lake St. Clair wearing skintight briefs.)

In December 1990, Fedorov and the Wings played an exhibition game at Joe Louis Arena against his former Red Army team. The Wings took advantage of the visit by having Fedorov meet with Vladimir Konstantinov, another of their draft picks from 1989. Fedorov led the Wings with a goal and an assist in the game. His former coach, Viktor Tikhonov, said Fedorov's performance "was nothing unusual."

Fedorov thrived in the NHL. He was runner-up to Chicago's Ed Belfour for the 1991 Calder Trophy as the top rookie. Jaromir Jagr, Mats Sundin, and Rob Blake also were rookies that season. Fedorov reached the 30-goal plateau in each of his first three seasons, and topped 80 points in his second and third seasons. Ultimately, he was joined at his metro Detroit home by his mother, father, and brother, quelling the loneliness of being so far from home.

In 1993 Bowman took over as coach. His first impression of Fedorov? "You could see his skill level was off the charts. He was so physically strong. He saw the game the right way, played offense, played defense. I just think from the get-go, he was a terrific player."

Steve Yzerman suffered a ruptured disc early in the season, sidelining him from late October until Christmas. That led to a heavier workload for Fedorov, one that appealed to a young superstar eager to shine in the absence of the captain's shadow. On New Year's Eve, near the midpoint of the season, Fedorov led the NHL with 65 points. He was a joy to watch for fans and teammates alike. "He's always had that one shift a game where you'd go, 'Wow!'" Yzerman said. "Now he's doing it every shift. He's spectacular every time he's on the ice."

When Fedorov recorded his first NHL hat trick on March 1, 1994, fans at the Joe responded with a long and loud ovation. Fedorov finished 1993–94 with his finest individual season: 56 goals, 64 assists, and 120 points. Wayne Gretzky won the scoring title with 130 points, but it was the closest margin of victory Gretzky had during his prime. "What I like most about Sergei is his unselfishness," Gretzky said. "I was taught to win and do anything for that. So the first thing I look at in a player is whether he's selfish or not."

Gretzky was not alone in his admiration: Fedorov won the 1994 Hart and Selke Trophies; the Hart was a landslide victory with 194 points to runner-up Dominik Hasek's 86. Fedorov also received the Lester B. Pearson Award, given to the most outstanding player as selected by his fellow NHL players. He was named to the NHL first All-Star team. The Wings didn't have much to like that summer after being upset in the first round by the San Jose Sharks, but Fedorov—who'd paced the team with eight playoff points—offered something to cherish: the four major honors made him the most decorated Wing in history for a single-season performance. He was 24 years old.

When a labor dispute delayed the start of the next season, Fedorov returned to his motherland for a series of charity games. The Soviet Union had collapsed, and Fedorov had been pardoned by the Russian government for defecting. By then, Fedorov had grown so used to life in North America that he signed autographs for Russian youngsters in English, not Cyrillic.

Fedorov had 50 points in 42 games during the lockout-shortened 1995 season. Then the Wings advanced to their first Stanley Cup Finals since 1966, only to be swept by the New Jersey Devils. Fedorov was the only Wing to surpass 20 points in the playoffs, setting a Wings record with 24 points in 17 games.

The Wings tore through opponents in 1995–96, eclipsing the 1976–77 Montreal Canadiens' 60 victories with a 62–13–7 season. Fedorov tore through opponents, recording two five-point performances en route to a team-leading 107 points. He recorded another five-point game on December 26, 1996, when he scored all five goals in a 5–4 overtime victory over Washington.

But 1996–97 was a strange season for Fedorov. He went from the first line to the third, from forward to defenseman. He reached 30 goals but tallied only 63 points, a 44-point drop-off from the previous season. He headed into the playoffs wondering what position he'd be playing (defense, but not for long). Whatever worries he had about his career (Was he on the downswing? What would his next contract hold?) dissipated in the playoffs. On June 5, 1997, Fedorov scored two goals and set up another two to reach a team-leading 20 playoff points. Two nights later, he was a Stanley Cup champion.

Celebrations with the Wings' first Cup in 42 years lasted six days, replaced by a vigil June 13 when Konstantinov, Slava Fetisov, and team masseur Sergei Mnatsakanov were hurt in a limousine crash. Fetisov was released from the hospital within a few days, but Konstantinov and Mnatsakanov suffered career-ending, life-altering injuries. They became a rallying point as the Wings embarked on defending their championship in the autumn of 1997.

Unfortunately for Fedorov, that fall was the beginning of a slow end to his career with the Wings. Contract talks stalled. Fedorov demanded a trade. Most players received their Stanley Cup rings at a gala ceremony in November; Fedorov received his in the office of general manager Ken Holland in January when the sides met to talk about his future. The Wings had offered long-term deals averaging $5.5 million annually; Fedorov wanted $7 million.

A week later, Fedorov practiced with the Ontario Hockey League's Whalers in Plymouth, Michigan. The team was owned by Peter Karmanos, a Detroit businessman and Ilitch rival who also owned the NHL's Carolina Hurricanes. In early February, Holland offered Fedorov a two-year deal averaging $5.5 million annually, amidst rumors the Islanders were readying a seven-year, $45 million proposal. Fedorov left for Japan to play in the 1988 Nagano Olympics. While there, he ripped into the Wings in a Russian newspaper, saying, "They don't know who they are messing with.... I won't be returning to this club. I have already fallen away from them and I can't see a place for myself there."

Midway through the Olympic Games, a tug-of-war broke out stateside. Karmanos signed off on a six-year, $38 million offer sheet ingeniously front-loaded to cost the Wings as much as $28 million if the team made a long playoff run. The first shocker was an immediate $14 million signing bonus. If the team made the conference finals (the Wings were favored to

WHAT IF HE HAD STAYED?

Sergei Fedorov was a key component of the Red Wings when they won the Stanley Cup in 1997, 1998, and 2002. Had he stayed, it's hard to imagine that there wouldn't have been more championship celebrations in Detroit.

Fedorov played in the NHL until 2008–09, and then played three more seasons of professional hockey in his native Russia. Had he played until 2011–12 with the Wings, they would have had two bona fide superstars in Fedorov and Nicklas Lidstrom (who, like Fedorov, retired in 2012). Even as they aged into their late thirties, Fedorov and Lidstrom were highly effective players. Couple that with the rise of Pavel Datsyuk and Henrik Zetterberg, who emerged as dominating players in the late 2000s, on a club that boasted Johan Franzen and Niklas Kronwall in their primes, along with Brian Rafalski and Brad Stuart. Fedorov's departure hurt the Wings, and likely cost them at least another Stanley Cup.

win the Stanley Cup, the Hurricanes to miss the playoffs), Fedorov would get another $12 million. His annual salary was $2 million. The numbers added up to Fedorov potentially being paid $28 million for the remaining 24 games of the regular season plus three playoff rounds. "I'm very excited," Fedorov said. "I'm very proud this happened."

Fedorov underestimated who he was messing with. The Wings matched. They were consumed with repeating as Stanley Cup champions, and knew they needed Fedorov. "He's a tremendous hockey player and it's all about the commitment to putting a winning hockey club on the ice," Holland said.

Fedorov was back in a Wings uniform February 27. Ilitch made a rare visit to the locker room before the game. "I told him there were no ill feelings," Fedorov said. "It was all business. It was a very good handshake. We looked into each other's eyes and everything went away."

One round into the playoffs, Fedorov had five goals. "Mr. Ilitch made the right decision," Bowman said. "He basically said, 'I'd rather have Sergei Fedorov and…not have $26 million.' A lot of owners wouldn't have said that. But when you consider what's happened with contracts since then, he looks like a bargain."

Easy for Bowman to say, since he didn't have to redden his ledgers when the Wings beat Dallas in Round 3 to advance to the Stanley Cup Finals. When the Wings repeated as champions on June 16, Fedorov was first on the team with 10 goals, second with 20 points. "I don't think we win the Cup without him," Bowman said.

Champagne expedites celebrating. It also facilitates forgetting. "Deep inside, I always wanted to stay here and play," Fedorov said, four months after saying exactly the opposite.

He was seen at Wimbledon soon after, with Anna Kournikova. The Russian tennis player first appeared in Detroit in 1997, drawing attention as she, then 16, sat next to Fedorov in his car during the Stanley Cup parade. Her presence in Fedorov's life (they would eventually marry and divorce) revealed a softer side of Bowman, which Fedorov shared at his Hall of Fame induction ceremony in 2015. "I had a little trouble with my love life and stuff," Fedorov said. "One moment I really cherished, I really got to know Scotty was when he let me figure out my life and let me off the team for a couple, three days. I really, truly finally figured out who Scotty Bowman was. After that I played even harder for him."

Fedorov played five more seasons with the Wings, helping them win another Stanley Cup as a member of the star-studded 2002 team. In 2002–03 he posted 83 points, his highest in seven seasons. It was the last year of the Carolina-authored contract.

The Wings had tried for an extension. In November 2002, Ilitch personally offered Fedorov five years and $50 million. In April 2003, their offer was four years and $40 million. The Wings' season ended with a first-round loss to Anaheim, but Fedorov remained in the Detroit metro area. He bought a $650,000 Ferrari Enzo. He said he wanted to stay "because I live here for 13 years and I play my best hockey and I love it here, but in order to stay here, it comes back to the business side."

Perhaps they teach business differently in Russia, but to the Wings, signing for five years, $40 million with Anaheim appeared insulting after Ilitch's $50 million offer. But that's exactly what Fedorov did on July 19, making good on the desire to play elsewhere he first communicated in 1997. Ilitch reached out to him days before the signing, to no avail. "I was trying to sign with Detroit and we were not able to reach some kind of agreement," Fedorov said later that year. "In order to get a deal done, both sides have to walk away happy. Our side was trying very hard; unfortunately, it did not happen. It was very hard for me to understand why."

It wasn't that hard to decipher. The 1993–94 season was Fedorov's personal benchmark for how he should be used: prominently. Signing with the Mighty Ducks (back then they still used the Mighty moniker) provided Fedorov with the Southern California lifestyle he craved and a chance to shine on a team that had just lost star player Paul Kariya.

Fedorov chose poorly. While he put up respectable numbers (30 goals and 65 points in 80 games) his average ice time under Ducks coach Mike Babcock was 21:05—six seconds less than he'd averaged the previous season in Detroit. The Ducks, Stanley Cup runners-up in 2003, missed the playoffs in 2004.

Five games into the 2005–06 season, Fedorov was part of a package that sent him to the Columbus Blue Jackets (one of the pieces going the other way was Tyler Wright, who served as the Wings' chief of amateur scouting from 2013 to '19). Fedorov logged his 1,000th NHL game on November 30, 2006, against Minnesota, playing for a team that had never known what it was like to make the playoffs.

Fedorov didn't appear in a playoff game again until 2008, after he'd been traded to the Washington Capitals. He left to play three seasons in Russia's Kontinental Hockey League in 2009, leaving the NHL with 483 goals and 696 assists (1,179 points) in 1,248 games; 400 goals and 554 assists (954 points) had come in 908 games with the Wings. Of his 176 career playoff points, 163 were with the Wings.

"It's too bad he didn't stay with Detroit, because his career didn't do as well after he left," Bowman said. "The other teams weren't as strong. He should have been playing with the Wings till the end of his career. I think people in Detroit appreciated how good a player he was, but fans didn't like that he left Detroit. That was a tough time for him. Down deep, it didn't help his career, not at the end. He had a terrific career with the Wings—just look at that part of it, it was tremendous. He won the Hart, he won the Selke, he challenged Gretzky for scoring."

Fans at the Joe held a grudge against Fedorov, treating him to choruses of boos when he returned as a visiting player. Higher-ups in the organization privately seethed that Fedorov had snubbed Ilitch in 1998 and

2003. The relationship finally thawed in the winter of 2015, after Fedorov's ascension to the Hockey Hall of Fame. He was treated to a standing ovation at Joe Louis Arena when he dropped a ceremonial puck before the Wings–Capitals game on November 10, 2015, and used the opportunity to reflect on the events of 2003. Fedorov blamed his agents for giving him bad advice in rejecting the $50 million offer. He sounded like a man who had realized too late where he was happiest.

"I am a Red Wing at heart," Fedorov said. "I had the best years of my life here."

15

FIGHT NIGHT

Three hundred and one days after Claude Lemieux's cheap shot on Kris Draper, the Red Wings punched back. Their epic, contentious night of March 26, 1997, at Joe Louis Arena, highlighted by Darren McCarty pounding Lemieux, solidified a sense of unity that inspired them into the playoffs. The Wings conquered their biggest obstacle, doubt, when they vanquished the hated Colorado Avalanche, instilling in players a confidence that would carry through to the Stanley Cup.

Thirty-nine penalties were handed out by exhausted officials, who raced from pileup to pileup like firefighters trying to contain a wildfire. The kindling had smoldered for 10 months, lit by Lemieux on May 29, 1996, when he gutlessly hit Draper from behind, breaking his jaw and nose and leaving Draper concussed. Although receiving a game misconduct, and eventually a suspension, Lemieux claimed the hit was "shoulder to shoulder. It wasn't a clear hit from behind." He suggested it was Draper's fault. "He turned to the boards right when I hit and that's why he was injured."

Adding insult to injury, Lemieux watched and then celebrated as the Avalanche eliminated the Wings from the Western Conference finals. "He's a goonish hockey player," Draper said the day after the game. "He not only had no remorse about the hit, he embarrassed the Wings by the way he was talking about our performance the past few years. He has no class whatsoever."

It wasn't even the only hit of the series that earned Lemieux a suspension; he'd been penalized one game after sucker-punching Vyacheslav Kozlov in Game 3. He received just a two-games suspension for the hit on Draper. "Is the league telling me I have to take things into my own hands?" Draper said a few days later. "Do I have free rein on Claude Lemieux next year? The league didn't even come close to taking care of it."

Lemieux was injured when the Avs made their first visit of the 1996–97 season to Joe Louis Arena. When he skated onto the ice March 26, it was to the sound of deafening boos—which soon turned to cheers. There were 10 fights in all, although officials did not consider McCarty's one of them. Jamie Pushor and Brent Severyn tangled 4:45 into the first period, although neither landed a punch. Five minutes passed. Kirk Maltby and Rene Corbet were waylaid by officials before any punches, but still received a fighting major each.

Then, a firestorm started with two of the least likely combatants: Igor Larionov and Peter Forsberg, two men more comfortable letting their handiwork show with incredible passes, not punches. As the two collided, Larionov fell backward. Forsberg took a swipe at Larionov's head, prompting Larionov to put Forsberg in a headlock as both men dropped to the ice.

While officials were busy distracted by that duo, Darren McCarty spun away and coldcocked Lemieux in the face. Lemieux made no attempt to defend himself, rolling over onto his knees and crouching like a turtle attempting to retreat into its shell as McCarty pummeled him. It was a heavyweight versus a deadweight.

Avalanche goalie Patrick Roy strode from his crease and headed for the spot. He never made it, intercepted by a leaping bear hug from Brendan Shanahan instead. "There was a little WWF from both of us there," Shanahan said. "I saw Patrick going for McCarty, and I didn't want him to sneak up on him, so I went after him. When I was three feet in the air, I was thinking, *What am I doing?* When I was five feet in the air. I said, *What am I really doing here?*"

Adam Foote grabbed Shanahan. Wings goalie Mike Vernon, who raced from his crease after Roy left his, pulled at Foote, eager to get to Roy. McCarty dragged Lemieux across the ice to the front of the Wings' bench, even as a linesman tried to restrain McCarty. Draper watched the retribution unfold intently from a front-row seat on the bench. Officials finally liberated Lemieux. Blood poured down his cheeks, his forehead. An official used his skates to try to disperse the blood that had pooled in front of Detroit's bench.

The best fight of the evening was between 5'9", 170-pound Vernon and 6'0", 192-pound Roy. Each goalie landed four blows and one big one apiece. It ended with Vernon on top of Roy, the two linesmen piled on top of them. Roy skated to his bench to wipe blood off his face. "I had a big smile on my face watching the goalies fighting and watching little Mike hold his own," Maltby said. "I was surprised it went on for as long as it did, but the emotion was so high."

There were more bouts: Shanahan and Adam Foote. Vladimir Konstantinov and Adam Deadmarsh, 15 seconds after the main event. Shanahan and Foote, four seconds into the middle period. Then 3½ minutes later, simultaneous bouts pitting Aaron Ward against Severyn and Tomas Holmstrom against Mike Keane. Four minutes later, McCarty and Deadmarsh fought. Another four minutes passed until the next—and final—on-ice fight, which matched Pushor against Uwe Krupp. After the game, the Wings contended, Colorado coach Marc Crawford elbowed Ward in the right ribs and upper hip in a hallway by the locker rooms.

McCarty hadn't received a fighting major for beating up Lemieux, but officials slapped him with double roughing minors. He wasn't done with his heroics, either: in the opening minute of overtime, McCarty strode down the left flank, took a pass from Shanahan, and buried the puck, capping a comeback with a 6–5 victory. "That was a great game," McCarty said as he sat at his locker stall afterward. "That's one to remember. We stuck together in all aspects of the game."

Vernon described it as the game that "brought the Red Wings together. We can really build on this as a team."

On the other side, Crawford fumed. "That team has no heart," he said. "They showed their true colors. Everyone is gutless on that team. I'd love to see them in the playoffs."

His wish came true. The Wings and Avalanche rivalry resumed in the 1997 Western Conference finals, and the teams traded blows again. There were 204 penalty minutes assessed in the third period of Game 4's 6–0 Wings victory, and Lemieux, ever the villain, cross-checked Konstantinov from behind into the boards in the first period. But it was the Wings who landed the last blow, taking the series in six games. Four games later, they won their first Stanley Cup in 42 years. They had silenced their own doubts and those of their fans on a raucous, revelrous night in March, igniting momentum that lasted into June.

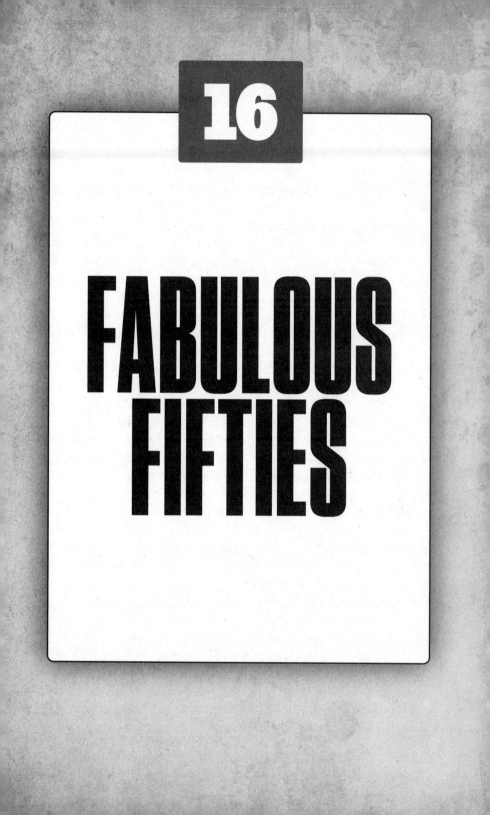

16

FABULOUS FIFTIES

The Red Wings began the 1950s with a party, defeating the New York Rangers in seven games for the Stanley Cup—on Pete Babando's goal in the second overtime.

It went on to be a successful decade for the Wings—at least the first half of it. The Wings teams of the 1950s were some of the best in franchise history. It was when many of the men whose numbers the Wings have retired—Gordie Howe, Sid Abel, Ted Lindsay, Red Kelly, Alex Delvecchio, and Terry Sawchuk—wore the winged wheel on their sweaters. The Production Line was in full swing in 1949–50, when the three claimed the top three spots in points in the NHL. Lindsay led the league with 55 assists and Howe's 35 goals were second only to Maurice Richard's 43.

The Cups kept coming. In 1950–51, Metro Prystai and Gaye Stewart were added to the team, and Sawchuk and Marcel Pronovost were promoted from the minors. Sawchuk had appeared in seven games in 1949–50, subbing for Harry Lumley, but he played all 70 games in 1950–51, when he had 11 shutouts and a 1.97 goals-against average, second lowest in the NHL. The Wings finished with a league-best 44–13–13 record to capture their third regular-season title in a row, the only team to top 100 points. The Montreal Canadiens, however, eliminated the Wings in the opening round of the playoffs.

There would be no disappointment the following season. Sawchuk posted even better numbers in 1951–52, when 12 of his 44 victories were shutouts. His 1.90 goals-against average was the best in the league, and the only one below 2.00. Howe won the league scoring title with 86 points (47 of them a league-high in goals) and Lindsay was second with 69 points. The Wings finished 44–14–12 and again were the only team to reach 100 points as they won their fourth consecutive regular-season title.

The Wings were even more dominant in the playoffs. Sawchuk shut out the Maple Leafs the first two games of the opening round and surrendered only three goals the next two games as the Wings swept Toronto. Sawchuk capped the Stanley Cup Finals with two shutouts against the Canadiens, surrendering two goals total. Lindsay scored a playoff-leading five goals, and Prystai scored twice in the 3–0 finale at Olympia Stadium. It was the first Cup sweep in history.

In December 1952, owner James E. Norris died at 73 from a heart attack and bequeathed control of the team to his daughter, Marguerite. The Production Line had come to an end before the start of 1952–53 season, when Abel, then 34, became player-coach for Chicago. But coach Tommy Ivan put second-year forward Alex Delvecchio in the middle between Howe on the right and Lindsay on the left, and a second Production Line was in business. Howe won the league scoring title with 95 points, Lindsay finished second with 71 points, and Delvecchio was tied for fourth with 59 points. The Wings won a fifth straight regular-season title when they finished 36–16–18, their 90 points 15 more than second-place Montreal. But the Wings came up short in their bid to repeat as Stanley Cup champions, losing in the opening round to the Bruins.

As the 1950s wore on, the Canadiens emerged as the top challengers to Detroit's dominance. Montreal won the Cup in 1953. In 1953–54, Richard, Bernie Geoffrion, and Bert Olmstead were among the top five scorers in the league, although Howe did win the scoring title again, with 81 points. The Wings finished 37–19–14 with 88 points to win a sixth straight title, but their margin over the Canadiens was just two victories and seven points.

The Wings toppled the Maple Leafs in five games to set up a Stanley Cup Finals against the defending champion Canadiens. The Wings took a 3–1 lead when Sawchuk came through with a shutout in Game 4, but the Canadiens took Game 5 1–0 in overtime and then claimed Game 6. Kelly scored in the second period of Game 7 to tie the game at 1. The Wings finally won the Cup at 4:29 of overtime on a goal by Tony Leswick, fired through a screen and nicking the glove of Montreal's Doug Harvey. The Canadiens immediately skated off without the traditional handshakes.

That set up another opportunity for the Wings to again win back-to-back titles (having done so in 1936 and 1937). They had a new coach in Jimmy Skinner—Ivan had left to become general manager of the Black Hawks. The Canadiens dominated the scoring race in the regular season, taking the top three spots, but the Wings won a seventh straight league title with a 42–17–11 record and 95 points, just edging Montreal (41–18–11, 93 points).

The big story going into the playoffs was Rocket Richard. On March 16, 1955, NHL president Clarence Campbell had suspended Richard for the

CITY OF CHAMPIONS

April 18 is known as "Champions Day" in Detroit. It was designated as such in 1936 by Michigan governor Frank Fitzgerald in recognition of the city's marvelous show in the world of sports.

The Wings won their first Stanley Cup championship on April 11, 1936. The Stanley Cup Finals were a best-of-five series against the Toronto Maple Leafs, and the Wings won in four games. That came on the heels of the Detroit Tigers winning the World Series in 1935, the same year the Detroit Lions won the NFL championship. All three championships were the teams' first. As the teams reveled in success, heavyweight boxer Joe Louis, whose family had moved to Detroit from rural Alabama when he was 12 years old, was heralded for his individual success. The Associated Press named him Most Outstanding Athlete of 1935.

The city celebrated its designation with a banquet at the Masonic Temple. The White House joined in the recognition, presenting the city a plaque signed by President Franklin D. Roosevelt and the 48 state governors. The plaque read: A NATION APPRECIATIVE OF THOSE QUALITIES OF CHARACTER ESSENTIAL TO SUCCESS IN COMPETITIVE ATHLETICS SALUTES DETROIT, WHICH IN THIS YEAR OF 1936 RICHLY MERITS RECOGNITION AS THE CITY OF CHAMPIONS.

The Wings repeated as champions in 1937.

final three games (two of which were against the Wings) as well as for the playoffs for punching linesman Cliff Thompson during a game against the Bruins. Thompson had intervened to stop Richard in a violent retaliatory stick attack on the Bruins' Hal Laycoe. Boston police even attempted to arrest Richard after the game.

When the Wings played the Canadiens on March 17 in Montreal, Campbell was, against advice, in attendance. Campbell had been brash enough to publicly announce he would be at the game. Fans were ready. When Campbell arrived midway through the first period, they hurled eggs, vegetables, programs—any debris they could find—at him. More rioting ensued during the first intermission. Teargas was unleashed. Montreal's fire chief declared the game had to be called off, and the Canadiens forfeited. The Wings were declared victors at 4–1, and moved into first place. Rioting moved into the streets; scores were arrested as windows were smashed and cars overturned. "This is disgraceful," said Wings general manager Jack Adams. "I have never seen anything like it. It would not have happened in Detroit."

The Wings rode that momentum into the playoffs, sweeping the Maple Leafs. The Richard-less Canadiens dispatched the Bruins to set up a Stanley Cup Finals between the best teams in the NHL. The Wings won the first two games 4–2 and 7–1. The Canadiens tied the series, but a hat trick from Howe in Game 5 put the Wings one victory away from clinching. The Canadiens pushed the series to Game 7—and the Wings won 3–1 at Olympia Stadium. Howe scored the Cup-winning goal, the last of his playoffs-leading nine goals, in the last minute of the second period of the April 14 finale.

It was a tumultuous off-season, as Marguerite Norris was ousted by her brother Bruce. Adams used the change in leadership to return to his "Trader Jack" ways, making moves involving, among others, Leswick, Sawchuk, and Lindsay. They were disastrous for the Wings, disrupting what had been a juggernaut of success. Instead, the Canadiens would go on to win five straight Stanley Cups.

Detroit's run of NHL titles came to an undignified end. The Wings finished 1955–56 at 30–24–16 with 76 points—24 fewer than the Canadiens. The Wings advanced to the Stanley Cup Finals only to lose to Montreal in five games. Howe won his fifth scoring title in 1956–57 with 89 points and the Wings recaptured the league title for the eighth time in nine seasons, but they were eliminated in the first round of the 1957 playoffs. The Wings finished third in 1957–58 with a .500 record (29–29–12) and were swept by the Canadiens in the first round of the playoffs.

The glory of the first half of the 1950s became a distant memory. At the end of the decade, in 1958–59, the Wings finished last in the league and failed to make the playoffs. They still had great players on their roster, but their great teams had been dismantled, shortchanging what could have been a decade-long dynasty.

17

THE VLADINATOR

Had his career not ended in the unfairest of ways, Vladimir Konstantinov would have been a multiple Stanley Cup champion, and very likely in the Hockey Hall of Fame.

Few players endeared themselves so quickly to Wings fans—and drew the enmity of every other team's fan base—as Konstantinov, a stoic defenseman from the far northwest of Russia. He started playing for the Wings in 1991 and earned the nicknames "Vladinator" and "Vlad the Impaler" for his open-ice hits and unforgiving play. Veterans on the team told Konstantinov, "Hey, you're a rookie. Don't run a tough guy on the fourth line, don't cross-check Wayne Gretzky, because someone will come after you." Konstantinov would nod and then go right out and cross-check Gretzky and run anyone who got in his way.

Konstantinov always was that type of player. He impressed Wings scout Neil Smith at the 1987 World Junior Championships in Piestany, in what was then Czechoslovakia, when the Soviet Union–Canada game descended into a brawl. Konstantinov broke Greg Hawgood's nose with what Brendan Shanahan later told author Gare Joyce was "the greatest headbutt I've ever seen." Brawling was part of Konstantinov's DNA. "I know him since he was 16," fellow Russian defenseman Slava Fetisov said in 1997. "Everybody call him Grandpa because he was so serious when he played, even when he was so young. He is very competitive when he plays the game. He would hit his brother."

The Wings adopted George Thorogood and the Destroyers' "Bad to the Bone" as Konstantinov's theme song. They showed a video compilation of Konstantinov's greatest hits on the Jumbotron, interspersed with cuts from *The Terminator* movies. At the end, there was a close-up of Konstantinov in sunglasses intoning, "*Hasta la vista*, baby."

It was a delightful development for an 11th-round pick. When the Wings were deciding who to pick at 221st overall, Smith campaigned for Konstantinov. Two years and multiple acts of subterfuge later, Konstantinov came to Detroit. In 1991 Konstantinov had been captain of the Central Red Army and Soviet national teams. Securing his release was daunting, but Konstantinov, initially reluctant, changed his mind after talking to Sergei Fedorov during the 1990 Super Series stopover in Detroit. Once Konstantinov was amenable, Wings front-office executive Jim Lites green-lighted an extraction plan.

That included bribing Soviet doctors to say that Konstantinov had a rare form of cancer. His wife, Irina, a civil engineer, pleaded with Red Army officials to let Konstantinov travel to the United States for treatment. Valery Matveev, a reporter who served as the Wings' facilitator in Russia, tracked Konstantinov to Burdyenko, a military hospital in Moscow. Doctors there were flummoxed by Konstantinov's original diagnosis because the form of cancer was supposedly so rare. They weren't sure if he really was sick, but they also couldn't prove that he wasn't.

Right before Konstantinov was slated to fly out of Moscow's Sheremetyevo Airport, he learned a Red Army higher-up had placed Konstantinov on a no-fly list. A decision was made to travel by train, but before that could happen, the Konstantinovs were eyewitnesses to a significant piece of Russian history. In August 1991, a group of hardline Communist officials implemented a coup against Soviet president and general secretary Mikhail Gorbachev. Tanks rolled through the streets of Moscow. Boris Yeltsin, president of Russia from 1991–99, evoked the very image of Russia as a fearsome bear as he stared down the coup d'état culprits, ending the standoff within days (and helping trigger the dissolution of the Soviet Union by the end of the year).

Had Yeltsin blinked, Konstantinov was unlikely to have made it to Detroit. The escape plan was back on—that is, until the Konstantinovs and Matveev got back to his car. During demonstrations thieves made off with Konstantinov's medical records and passport, which had been in a suitcase in Matveev's car. Back at their apartment, Konstantinov received a phone call from someone claiming they found the documents and arranged to return them. In a 1994 article in the *Detroit Free Press*, Keith Gave reported that Matveev suspected that it was the thieves who called, and that they wanted money. "The phone rang again about midnight and the caller told Matveev and Konstantinov to meet him near the Kosmos Hotel to get the documents," Gave wrote. "Armed with some hockey sticks, a helmet and some other trinkets—and the gun—they went to the hotel and made a quick exchange. The bandit/hockey fan was delighted with Konstantinov's hockey gear and an autograph, and the documents were returned."

Konstantinov and Matveev left a few days later for Budapest, Hungary. They were met by Lites and an immigration attorney, who escorted Konstantinov to Detroit. The Soviets demanded a development fee (Red Army coach Viktor Tikhonov hired a New York lawyer in an effort to wrangle money) but the Wings weren't fazed. Irina Konstantinov and the couple's two-and-a-half-year-old daughter, Anastasia, arrived in the U.S. a few days after Konstantinov. He was 24 years old.

The 1991–92 Wings were a team on the rise. There was incredible depth at center with Fedorov, Steve Yzerman, and Jimmy Carson, and a defense headlined by two rookies, Konstantinov and Nicklas Lidstrom. Konstantinov produced 34 points in 79 games, along with 172 penalty minutes. Konstantinov was remarkably durable given his aggressive style of play. His first five seasons, he missed just nine games. Konstantinov wasn't flashy, just steady and stubborn. He rarely made blunders. His bluster was the bane of opponents.

While the 1995 playoffs ended in crushing disappointment when the Devils swept the Wings in the Stanley Cup Finals, Konstantinov's performance was magnificent. He played with intensity and irritation every shift, even as he logged heavy minutes against key opposing players. When he scored in the second overtime in Game 3 of the Western Conference finals against Chicago (his only goal of the playoffs), Konstantinov shouted, "Unbelievable, guys," as teammates swarmed to congratulate him.

When the Wings traded for Igor Larionov in October 1995, it created an opportunity that would make Konstantinov part of NHL history. Coach Scotty Bowman put Larionov on a line with Fedorov and Vyacheslav Kozlov, with Konstantinov and Fetisov forming the defense. The Russian Five dazzled with their ability to control the puck. They were so fluid Bowman even used them as a power-play unit.

In 1995–96, Konstantinov scored a career-high 14 goals and his 34 points matched the career high set his rookie season. His reputation around the NHL soared as he led the league with a plus-60, the highest rating since Gretzky's plus-69 nine years earlier. Konstantinov thrived in the playoffs, agitating opponents and contributing nine points in 19 games.

During the off-season, Konstantinov tore an Achilles' tendon while playing tennis with Fedorov. Konstantinov found his form around Christmas, pumping 29 points into 45 games during the second half

Vladimir Konstantinov takes his turn with the Stanley Cup, June 7, 1997.
(Mary Schroeder)

and leading the team with a plus-20. (He finished plus-38 overall, tying for third place in the NHL.) During a March trip to California, Bowman said Konstantinov played like a Norris Trophy candidate every game. Teammates were effusive. "He really gets guys off their game," Shanahan said. "I used to really dislike him when I played against him. Playing with him, you really appreciate how he does it game after game."

"He's so competitive," Lidstrom added. "He gets in every aspect of the game. He's not afraid of anybody."

During the famous March 26, 1997, game against the Avalanche that featured 10 fights, Konstantinov squared off with Adam Deadmarsh. But there was another member of the Avalanche who wanted a bigger piece of Konstantinov. Midway through the 1997 Western Conference finals, with the Wings up 2–1, Colorado coach Marc Crawford laid into Konstantinov, berating him as a master of dirty tricks. "We've got to play very physical against Konstantinov," Crawford said. "We have to expose the fact that he's clutching and grabbing all the time. He could get a penalty every shift he's on the ice."

Crawford couldn't stop whining that May 21. "Konstantinov is very, very adept at grabbing the stick and holding it under his arm," he continued. "He's really a very, very clever player at clutching and grabbing around the net. You have to really persevere and keep your feet moving and expose the fact he does that all the time."

The accusations delighted the accused. "I just start laughing and they start complaining," Konstantinov said, his usually impenetrable face breaking into a smile.

He had been assessed one penalty in the series at that point, as teammates were quick to point out. "He's a Russian Canadian," Darren McCarty said. "He plays with a lot of heart. I'm glad he's on our team, because he would be a hell of a guy to play against. He plays with as much fire as anyone. He is part machine, I think. He just goes and goes and goes."

The Wings met the Philadelphia Flyers in the Stanley Cup Finals, pitting them against the Eric Lindros–led Legion of Doom line. When they played in Philadelphia in January, Konstantinov so aggravated Lindros that Lindros slammed Konstantinov against the boards, leaving him dazed. "He likes to get under your skin and take you off your game," Lindros said. "His

MUSH, MUSH

Vladimir Konstantinov's career-ending accident at age 30 led the Red Wings to one of their most disastrous free-agent signings and a court case involving dogsled experts and private investigators. In the summer of 1998, the Wings sized up a 6'6", 235-pound German defenseman and decided he would be an ideal fit. Uwe Krupp was 33 years old and had won a Stanley Cup with Colorado in 1996. He was considered a workhorse, adept at playing both special teams. The Wings signed Krupp for four years, $16.4 million, with a no-trade clause covering the first three years.

Both sides were excited about the deal. Krupp purchased 10 acres in the South Lyon area and had kennels built so that he could house the 28 dogs he had on his ranch outside Missoula, Montana. He raced competitively in the eight-dog class.

His job, though, was to play competitively for the Wings. Krupp lasted 22 games before complaining of back pain in December 1998. The next summer, general manager Ken Holland was at his home in Vernon, British Columbia, when a friend of Wings owner Mike Ilitch called and asked whether the team knew Krupp had been competing in sled dog races that winter. Then the faxes started coming. Holland compared the dates of the contests to the Wings' schedule.

Krupp's hobby as an amateur musher was the cover story of the Wings' official magazine, *Inside Hockeytown*, in December 1998. But when team officials found out he was racing while telling them he was in too much pain to play hockey, they were livid.

The Wings suspended Krupp without pay in August 1999 after he refused to grant them access to medical records regarding his back history. Krupp's side responded by filing a grievance in October. Nearly a year passed before a hearing was scheduled. First it was delayed because Ilitch had a health issue. Then the NHL fired the arbitrator scheduled to hear the case.

Krupp ended up sitting out two and a half years. The suspension lasted 722 days. He was not allowed to skate, work out, or use his equipment at Joe Louis Arena for most of that time. The Wings hired private investigators, one of whom sent a letter to Krupp's ex-wife in Germany asking whether she would testify against him.

After a 34-month absence, Krupp was cleared to play, forcing the Wings to end the suspension. He played eight regular-season games in 2001–02. He started the first two games of the playoffs partnered with

Nicklas Lidstrom, but after the Wings lost those games—in which Krupp had a minus-5 rating—Scotty Bowman benched Krupp. The Wings went on to win the Stanley Cup (and did not include Krupp's name among those to be inscribed on the Cup). Krupp finished his Wings career having played a total of 32 games in in four seasons.

The arbitration hearings spanned 18 months and featured testimony from professional mushers before the sides reached an undisclosed settlement.

style is to agitate and stay in your face. But you can't let that kind of player get into your head."

Flyers coach Terry Murray described Konstantinov as "one of the dirtiest defensemen in the league. Every time he hits, he leaves his feet and his elbows are always up."

On June 7, the Wings ended a 42-year Stanley Cup drought. On June 9, at a season-ticket holders rally at Joe Louis Arena, fans cheered when Konstantinov sauntered up to a podium wearing sunglasses. "You're the greatest," he told fans. "Thank you." The next day an estimated one million people showed up to celebrate with a parade down Woodward Avenue.

Konstantinov was 30 years old, in the prime of his career. He was a finalist for the Norris Trophy. He and his family had a big, beautiful home in Orchard Lake Village, a swanky suburb northwest of Detroit. The best years of his life beckoned. Until one man's selfish decision changed everything. Richard Gnida, the driver of a limousine hired by the Wings, knowingly drove on a suspended license. He later said he fell asleep at the wheel.

Six days after they celebrated on the ice at Joe Louis Arena, Konstantinov, Fetisov, and Sergei Mnatsakanov, a team masseur, were returning from a team golf outing to celebrate the Stanley Cup the evening of June 13 when their limousine crashed into a tree on Woodward Avenue in Birmingham. Konstantinov was hurled forward into the minibar, crashing headfirst into splintering glass. Doctors described Konstantinov as having "scrambled brain," a condition that can shear neurons and cause swelling.

Konstantinov was in a coma for two months at William Beaumont Hospital in Royal Oak. He was removed from a ventilator in late June, after undergoing a tracheostomy to ensure he was receiving enough oxygen. Doctors did not declare him fully conscious until mid-August. He should have been gearing up for training camp, but instead he spent four hours a day working on balance and coordination.

He was released from the hospital in November so that he could continue rehabilitation in Florida, where the warmer climate would allow him to spend time outdoors. In January 1998, he joined his teammates for their visit to the White House. "You are showing every day that you have the heart of a champion," President Bill Clinton told him.

The Konstantinov family returned to Michigan in the spring and settled into a routine. Vladimir spent eight hours a day undergoing physical, speech, and occupational therapy. His brain was severely traumatized, but hard work? That was in Konstantinov's DNA.

In June 1998, Irina gave her first compressive interview since the accident. "He is not depressed," she said. "He has the greatest attitude towards everyone. He recognizes the people he loves. I'm very happy with his progress. With this type of injury, you never say weeks, you say months. There is no absolute guarantee at all of what he will be able to do. That's the whole frustration. But every day you're just happy that there's something new—that he talks a little bit better or he can help to dress himself. That means he's not stuck."

Irina had been out to dinner with Larionov's wife, Elena, the night of the accident. Shortly after arriving home, Fetisov's wife, Lada, called. At the time, Lada didn't know who was in the limo other than her husband. Irina tried calling her Vladimir. A friend called Beaumont Hospital searching for answers.

"She was asking who was in the accident, and the woman said, we can't confirm yet who the other people are," Irina said. "The next moment she said, 'Oh, wait, oh, wait, oh, wait, we just pulled out a wallet. It is Konstantinov.'"

Half an hour later Irina was in the emergency room. A surgeon yelled at her to get out, concerned she might faint at the gruesome sight. Irina refused, believing her husband needed something no doctor could give.

"I said,, 'Don't you think I'm the only voice he knows? The only voice. I'm staying right here and talk to him.'"

Konstantinov's career was over, but his presence during the 1997–98 season was everywhere his teammates were. They wore a patch on their sweaters with his and Mnatsakanov's initials. Konstantinov's gear hung in his locker, where someone had placed a smooth stone with the word BELIEVE written on it. When the Wings won the Cup again in 1998, teammates wheeled Konstantinov onto the ice at the MCI Center in Washington, put a championship hat on his head, gave him an unlit cigar, and took him for a victory lap. Yzerman placed the Cup in Konstantinov's lap.

That was in 1998. In 2018, Konstantinov still required 24-hour assistance from a team of caregivers. Irina and Anastasia live in Florida but visit regularly at the West Bloomfield condo where Konstantinov resides.

Tragedy cut short Konstantinov's career, but in the six seasons he spent with the Wings he made an enduring and endearing impression.

18

DON'T YOU LEAVE ME

He forced himself out of his hospital bed, ignoring the pain in his ribs, and limped into the next room. It was the middle of the night, and the only people around were staff. In the other room, Slava Fetisov found Vladimir Konstantinov, his body covered in tubes and bandages, attached to monitors and IVs and a ventilator. Fetisov had been through this before. Twelve years earlier, in June 1985, Fetisov had been involved in a car accident that killed his brother, Anatoly. Fetisov couldn't face another loss.

"A nurse told me that after I was gone, Slava came to Vladdie's room," Irina Konstantinov, Vladimir's wife, said in a 1998 interview. "He could barely walk. He kind of crawled into the room, and he was sitting there in the dark next to Vladdie and he was crying and telling Vladdie, 'Don't you leave me.'"

The seven days spanning June 7 to 13, 1997, are local lore in Detroit, a stretch bookended by triumph and tragedy. On a gorgeous sunny Saturday, the city was poised to celebrate its first Stanley Cup since 1955. The joy of that night at Joe Louis Arena when Steve Yzerman raised the Cup and fans raised their hands and voices and beers lasted until the following Friday night. Revelry turned to disbelief turned to anguish.

On Friday, June 13, players and team personnel enjoyed an outing with the Cup at the Orchards Golf Club in northern Macomb County. Rides had been arranged so that no one would have to worry how many times they had sipped from the Cup. Russians Slava Fetisov, Vladimir Konstantinov, and Sergei Mnatsakanov got into one limousine, a white Lincoln Town Car. Fetisov considered Konstantinov a brother. Fetisov and Mnatsakanov had known each other since their days with rival Russian hockey clubs. Fetisov sat in the rear, with Mnatsakanov on his left and Konstantinov on the long broadside seat. Their driver, 27-year-old Richard Gnida of Westland, working for Gambino's Limousines, began the journey.

It ended with all four occupants in the hospital, two of them fighting for their lives. The vehicle was traveling south on Woodward Avenue in Birmingham about 9 PM when it veered across three lanes and crashed into a maple tree. Fetisov was hurled forward, but his trajectory was halted by the mini fridge. He was released from hospital after five days.

Konstantinov and Mnatsakanov were tossed into the minibar, shards of glass embedding in their heads. Konstantinov suffered a brain injury. Mnatsakanov was thrown so violently he suffered a fractured skull and broken spine; brain matter leaked out of fissures. Both men were comatose.

Irina Konstantinov, Vladimir's wife, found out about the accident from Fetisov's wife, Lada. Yelena Mnatsakanov, Sergei's wife, was returning from walking the family dog when she saw a strange car in their driveway. A team official was waiting for her.

Back at the golf club, cell phones started ringing. "To this day I remember that night," Kirk Maltby said in 2019. "We had no idea how bad it was at first. We thought, *Okay, they're at the hospital, they're getting treatment.* We thought it was broken bones, something like that. Like, they could rehab and that would be that."

Some players headed to William Beaumont Hospital in Royal Oak, where the men had been rushed by ambulance. Others gathered at Chris Osgood's home in Birmingham. "We just waited, which was the hardest part," Maltby said. "We didn't know it was going to be near as bad as it was. When we finally got word that in particular Vladdie was fighting for his life, it was a very nervous quiet. No one wanted to talk."

In the coming days, fans set up vigils in front of the hospital. Reporters had cameras trained to catch visiting team personnel. Hospital staff had players and coaching staff enter through side entrances to minimize disruptions. The Stanley Cup was smuggled inside stretchered beneath a sheet in an effort to bring cheer.

When the NHL glitterati gathers for their annual awards celebration, it's usually a time to celebrate the game's best players. But on June 19, 1997, Konstantinov and Mnatsakanov were in comas, fighting for their lives. It was a somber night at the Metro Toronto Convention Center. "It's pretty tough for those of us here not to have at least a part of you somewhere else," said host Ron MacLean. "And that's the William Beaumont Hospital in Detroit. Our prayers are going right to Michigan this evening."

Konstantinov and Mnatsakanov were the first people mentioned by Art Ross Trophy winner Mario Lemieux. "On behalf of the Pittsburgh

Penguins organization," he said, "I would like to send our best wishes to Sergei and Vladimir."

Dominik Hasek became the first goaltender to win a second Hart Trophy as league MVP, as well as another Vezina Trophy as the top goaltender. But his focus was on the injured Wings. "To Vladimir and Sergei, I want to wish them the chance to return to their families and enjoy happiness again," the future Wing said. "We are pulling for them."

Mnatsakanov had been with the team two years. He had come to Detroit in 1995 to see his son, Max, play in a hockey tournament. Mnatsakanov attended a Wings practice and stopped by the locker room to chat with Fetisov, an old friend. Fetisov asked him for a massage. Fetisov urged the Wings to hire Mnatsakanov, and so they did. By summer, he was a member of the staff. "He is such a good guy, everybody likes him so much," Fetisov said.

North American players delighted when Mnatsakanov introduced them to a traditional holistic treatment in Russia. "Guys get in the sauna and Sergei would soak bundles of oak leaves in hot water and then beat guys with them," said John Wharton, who was the athletic trainer at the time. "It was so funny, you would see them come out with oak leaves stuck to their bodies and they'd be beet red from being whipped. But they'd say they'd never felt better because it stimulates blood flow and eliminates toxins from the body."

The accident left Mnatsakanov paralyzed in both legs and his left arm. He hadn't suffered the extensive brain damage that impaired Konstantinov, and he remembered what life had been like before the accident. When Mnatsakanov and Konstantinov attended the May 31, 1998, Western Conference finals game between the Wings and the Dallas Stars, watching from Ilitch's suite, Konstantinov gave cheering fans a thumbs-up. Mnatsakanov waved a pom-pom with his only fully functioning arm, sobbing uncontrollably.

Gnida was released from the hospital June 15. Birmingham police initially said blood drawn from Gnida the night of the accident showed no evidence of drugs, but later amended that to say tests did show Gnida had traces of marijuana in his system. Police found a partially smoked marijuana cigarette under the driver's seat. Authorities theorized Gnida fell asleep at the wheel, causing the stretch limo to drift, jump the six-inch curb, and hit the tree. That's what Fetisov told friends—that he had shouted and pounded to get Gnida's attention after noticing Gnida appeared unresponsive. Gnida told police he blacked out. Years later, he admitted to falling asleep.

After a 15-week investigation, Oakland County prosecutor David Gorcyca said officials couldn't tell what effect, if any, the drug had on Gnida's driving. There was no evidence he was under the influence when the accident happened. However, the investigating officer, Dave Schultz, in a book written with *Free Press* columnist Charlie Vincent, said he had experts who thought Gnida had smoked pot three to six hours before the crash.

In October, Gnida admitted he knew his driver's license was suspended when he made the decision to chauffeur the limousine. He pleaded guilty to a misdemeanor second offense of driving on a suspended license. In November, Gnida was sentenced to nine months in jail and 200 hours of community service. Outrage over the law that mandated such a light sentence prompted lawmakers to pass bills that would make it a felony to cause serious injury or death while driving on a suspended or revoked license.

Gnida didn't appear to learn anything. A year later, Gnida was back before 48th District Judge Kimberly Small, who raised his bond from $10,000 to $50,000. Birmingham police had picked up Gnida, then 29, after he failed to appear at a November court hearing to answer charges of violating probation. Gnida's probation officer had filed a report saying Gnida reneged on a promise to seek counseling for substance abuse. His probation had begun in June, after Gnida served a little more than seven months of the nine-month sentence. Gnida was sentenced to 75 days in Oakland County Jail. Then in July 1999, Gnida was arrested after leaving a topless club in Inkster and running a stop sign. That incident earned him a third conviction for drunken driving and a one-year jail sentence.

Irina Konstantinov and Yelena Mnatsakanov filed a $290 million suit against Findlay Ford Lincoln Mercury, an Ohio car dealership, in 2004, alleging the limousine's seat belts were inaccessible because they had been tucked under the seats. None of the passengers had been wearing one. The dealership had sold the Lincoln Town Car to Gambino's, which was defunct by then. The trial began in 2008. Witnesses included Ted Lindsay, who in vintage Lindsay form (he was 82 at the time) suggested Gnida deserved a bullet for his actions. "People like that should be shot,"

Lindsay said. Steve Yzerman testified Konstantinov "could have played right up to now." A federal jury rejected the suit, saying evidence did not prove the dealership was to blame.

The tree on Woodward Avenue that the limo had collided with became a landmark in the days after the accident. Fans erected shrines made of jerseys, candles, flowers, and other mementos. Police removed the tributes after several accidents stemming from drivers stopping or slowing down to see the display. A storm in early July caused substantial damage and prompted the city to cut the tree down, leaving a knobby stump in the grassy median. Eventually, the stump was removed, too.

19

BELIEVE

When the Red Wings spent a gorgeous June day in 1998 celebrating with a million fans happily playing hooky to help Hockeytown relish a second straight Stanley Cup, the biggest cheers came for the men whose lives had hung in the balance 12 months earlier following a devastating limo accident.

"To see both Vladdie and Sergei in the condition they were in was heartbreaking," Steve Yzerman said in a 2019 interview. "A week after the greatest moment in all of our careers, it was one of the worst moments of our careers. It diminished the importance of the Stanley Cup. It was tough to comprehend, to wrap your head around, what had happened."

The accident on June 13, 1997—the Friday after the Wings partied with the Stanley Cup for the first time in 42 years—robbed Vladimir Konstantinov and Sergei Mnatsakanov of their way of life. When Wings personnel—players, coaches, trainers—gathered in September to begin training camp, their injured comrades were in their hearts and on their minds. "Every time you see the pictures of Vladdie holding the Stanley Cup, it really hits home," Kris Draper said. "We were watching Game 4 of the Stanley Cup Finals on the bus ride up and they showed the highlights of Vladdie's hits, and it got pretty quiet for a while, and that's when you realize how much you're really going to miss him."

Igor Larionov tried to explain that, three months after the accident, it still didn't seem real that Konstantinov never again would be milling about, would never again hop over the boards. "You start to tell yourself he's really not injured and he'll be back in a couple of days or a few weeks," Larionov said. "It's really hard to even skate. You just keep thinking about he's not with us. I miss his presence in the locker room, his jokes and his sense of humor. It's a tragedy. You can never find a guy to replace Vladdie."

It was the first year camp was held in Traverse City in northern Michigan. The location offered an opportunity to bond and enjoy a resort-like atmosphere when not on the ice. When players relocated to Joe Louis Arena, the tragedy came full face again. A stone, smooth and small enough to fit in the palm of one's hand, bearing the word BELIEVE was placed in Konstantinov's stall, next to his gear.

"I remember when we came back to start exhibition season, it really sunk in that Vladdie is not going to be here," Kirk Maltby said in 2019. "The stone was there, his equipment was there, his name tag was there, but he wasn't there. You'd go into the training room where guys would always get work done by Sergei and he wasn't there. It really set in that we needed to put the time in and work in and effort in for these guys, because we knew if they were here, they would be doing it."

It was a tumultuous autumn. Playoff MVP Mike Vernon had been traded, and superstar center Sergei Fedorov was holding out for a big contract. The Wings shut out distractions and zeroed in on their injured mates. They won 10 of their first 13 games. On New Year's Day 1998, they sat atop the NHL with a 25–9–8 record.

At the end of January, the Wings were honored for their Stanley Cup championship by President Bill Clinton at the White House. Konstantinov joined his teammates, flashing a big smile and a thumbs-up from his wheelchair. Mnatsakanov, who was partially paralyzed in the accident, was not able to travel.

The Fedorov saga ended in February. He signed a $38 million offer sheet with the Carolina Hurricanes but the Wings matched, unwilling to lose a player they viewed as crucial to their Stanley Cup prospects. Fedorov played 21 games, producing 17 points and helping the Red Wings finish third in the NHL with a 44–23–15 record.

"At the beginning of the season, everybody was being negative about the team because we were missing some key guys," Larionov said at the time. "This year was special. It was not easy to have the kind of tragedies as we had here and keep playing the way we did last year."

The defending champions went into the playoffs on a mission. "There's always, on any team during the course of what you hope is going to be a long playoffs, there's a player or something where you are, 'Let's do it for this or that,'" Maltby said. "It was about playing for them. Vladdie was such a big part of our team, and Sergei was behind the scenes."

The Wings bested the Phoenix Coyotes, St. Louis Blues, and Dallas Stars en route to a second straight Stanley Cup Finals. They won the first two games at home and won Game 3 against the Capitals at the MCI

Vladimir Konstantinov and Slava Fetisov on the ice at MCI Center after the Wings won the Cup in Washington, June 16, 1998. (Julian H. Gonzalez)

Center. On the verge of clinching another Cup, the Wings chartered an airplane and flew players' families to Washington. The passenger manifest included Konstantinov and his wife, Irina.

They watched Game 4 in Section 116—so close to Konstantinov's No. 16—behind a sign that read WE BELIEVE, YOU BELIEVE. As nearby fans figured out who was sitting there, excitement spread throughout the stands. It was Capitals territory, but everyone believed in Konstantinov. He received a standing ovation in the third period.

"The Washington organization was very classy by acknowledging Vladdie up in the stands," Maltby said. "Especially in the situation they were in, down 3–0 in the series. Both benches were up, the entire crowd was up, everybody was clapping and that was almost as emotional as winning the game and winning the Cup. You didn't know when it happened if Vladdie was even going to be around to see something like this, let alone be able to be at the arena in Washington."

When it became clear the Wings would win the game—they led 4–1 early in the third period—Irina took her husband down to ice level. As the Wings shook hands with the Capitals, Konstantinov was wheeled slowly onto the ice, where players gathered to celebrate with him. Konstantinov pulled a cigar to his mouth and raised his index finger to show he knew they were No. 1 again. Someone put a 1998 Stanley Cup hat on him. Yzerman put the Cup in Konstantinov's lap.

"During the day of the game, we had heard Vladdie was coming in," Yzerman said in 2019. "And then you are kind of wrapped up in the game and getting ready to play the game. At some point later in the game, there's a commotion in the stands and it's almost like is there a fight or something up there. We looked up and everyone was cheering and it was Vladdie sitting up there. It was emotional and very uplifting and joyful to see him there. And then 15 minutes later we've won the Cup and he's on the ice. I think everyone felt really good. Vladdie was there and had a smile on his face."

Two days later, on June 18, 1998, the sun cast glowing rays on Detroit. An estimated 1.2 million people crowded downtown as the Wings held a second straight parade down Woodward Avenue. Konstantinov and Mnatsakanov drew the loudest cheers as they rode together in the motorcade, and again when they were wheeled onto the stage at Hart Plaza. Konstantinov, with help from Fetisov and trainer John Wharton, rose and took a few steps across the stage. A year ago, Konstantinov and Mnatsakanov had almost died. Now they were where they belonged, with the team, sharing another championship celebration. "The two biggest cheers that you have, that were much deserved," Draper told the crowd, "were for Vladdie and Sergei."

The Wings received their 1998 championship rings in January 1999. The rings featured white diamonds with a red winged wheel emblem in the middle, and two large diamonds on the sides evoking the back-to-back Stanley Cups. Inscribed on the ring was a single word: BELIEVE.

20

THE GRIND LINE

A suggestion by Steve Yzerman set in motion a hire that would help the Wings end a 42-year Stanley Cup drought. It was Christmastime 1996, and the Wings were searching for the right addition to help prevent another playoff disappointment. The 1995 run had ended with the ignominy of being swept by the New Jersey Devils and the 1996 Western Conference finals loss to the Colorado Avalanche was especially embittering because led to Claude Lemieux raise the Stanley Cup.

That the Wings were talented was indisputable: the roster included Steve Yzerman, Nicklas Lidstrom, Sergei Fedorov, Brendan Shanahan, Vladimir Konstantinov, Igor Larionov, and Slava Fetisov. Darren McCarty, Marin Lapointe, and Tomas Sandstrom added toughness to the mix, but Yzerman was among those who thought the team needed to be tougher. He mentioned a former teammate to coach Scotty Bowman. Joe Kocur was well known to the organization, having formed one-half of the "Bruise Brothers" in the middle-to-late 1980s with Bob Probert. Kocur played for the New York Rangers in the early-to-mid-1990s, and had won a Cup there in 1994. After a brief stint in the International Hockey League with the San Antonio Dragons, Kocur left pro hockey. He was living in metro Detroit and fed his hockey fix playing in alumni games and in adult hockey leagues, popularly known as "beer leagues."

Then the Wings called. Kocur was 32 years old and his right hand was a mess, damaged by countless punches to opponents' faces and helmets. But the Wings loved what he brought: toughness, Cup experience, and simply knowing how to be a good fit. On January 3, 1997, Kocur was back in a Wings uniform.

"He is a really smart player," Bowman told Joe Lapointe of the *New York Times*. "He knows how to play hockey. That sounds strange, but he's really got a big sense of the game. And he's got the reputation."

Kocur finished the season with two goals, one assist, and 70 penalty minutes in 34 games. Bowman put Kocur on a line with Kris Draper at center and Kirk Maltby, hoping to create the sort of checking line that could provide a spark in the playoffs. The Wings had been thwarted in the 1995 Finals by New Jersey's "Crash Line" of Mike Peluso, Bobby Holik, and Randy McKay. But now they had a pesky combination of their own: The Grind Line.

McCarty began the playoffs on a line with Shanahan and Larionov, but with the first-round series against the St. Louis Blues at 2–2, Bowman made changes. One of them was to reunite McCarty with Draper. The Wings won Game 5 by the score of 5–2. McCarty scored the Wings' third

The Grind Line (Darren McCarty, Kirk Maltby, and Kris Draper) at Wings practice, May 30, 2008. (Julian H. Gonzalez)

goal off a pass from Draper. "It always gives the team a lot of confidence when they score goals," Bowman said. "That's the big part—they feel pretty good about themselves. They've been rewarded because they've been playing well."

The pleasure each player took in the line's success was infectious. They were having so much fun. "Playing with Shanny, sometimes you get in there and make the prettiest play, and I got away from my game," McCarty said. "Playing with these guys gets me back to that. It's basic hockey—no special plays, just bump and grind. We have a blast. Drapes is the talker out there; I just laugh. Malts will say stuff too, but Drapes is the one who talks. We all yell at each other and yell at the other guys. I just watch and laugh at those two guys."

As the playoffs went on, Kocur would sub back on to the line. In any iteration, the trio delighted. They hit. They scored. They aggravated. "It's fun, because we've got different styles," Maltby said. "We've got Drapes with the speed, and you've got the other three of us that are the more physical players. It's fun that we're able to complement each other and read each other. With our style, you get under teams' skins. You get certain guys that'll start talking to you, but I'm not great with one-liners so I keep the talk to a minimum."

Kocur was the veteran voice on the line, a guy who stressed the importance of keeping things simple. "We're not going to go out there and make pretty plays," he said. "We have to go out there and create our own chances, and the best way to do that is turnovers by their defense and by getting in and being relentless on them. I'm just out there to have a calming effect on the other players."

The Grind Line spawned T-shirts and bobbleheads. As Draper recalled in 2019, the nickname came during a group brainstorm. "We were in St. Louis in the training room," he said. "I said to Joey, you and Bob Probert were the Bruise Brothers. We need a name for our line. We were throwing names out there. I'm not sure who said 'the Grind Line,' but we were always talking about grinding. All of us perked up."

When *Sports Illustrated* ran a feature on the "Hot Wings" in its June 2, 1997, issue, it was Maltby who made the cover, depicted playing the puck while battling Avalanche captain Joe Sakic. When injuries forced Bowman to get creative with lines in January 1998 (Kocur was dealing with back spasms and Draper with a broken thumb) and Maltby started playing right wing on a line with Yzerman, Draper needled Maltby. "Can Stevie put you on the cover of *Sports Illustrated*?" Draper said. "I don't think so."

The off-ice banter between Draper and Maltby was a never-ending game of one-upmanship. After Maltby delivered a particularly physical performance in a game against the New York Islanders, Draper suggested Maltby was inspired by the AC/DC song played during warm-ups. "He thinks I'm satanic," Maltby joked.

Their chemistry was as undeniable as their effectiveness. Maltby had a knack for goading opponents into taking penalties. In Game 1 of the 1998 Western Conference finals against Dallas, Stars forward Pat Verbeek grew so irate he whacked Maltby on the chin, earning Verbeek a trip to the penalty box. The Wings converted 30 seconds later.

"The success of our team depends on everybody doing little things, and a lot of those things don't show up on the score sheet," Shanahan said. "Kirk is a great example. He's a thorn in the side of every team we play against. He finishes his checks and he doesn't care who it is—whether it's the toughest guy on the team or the leading scorer on the team. People get a little surprised when they get hit by him, how solid he is. I was when I played against him. And it angers you. You don't expect it because he doesn't look that big coming at you, but he has an ability to pop you with his shoulder with a clean, hard hit."

Yzerman's faith in the addition of Kocur paid dividends. The Grind Line helped the Wings win Cups in 1997, 1998, and, after Kocur retired in 2000, in 2002 and 2008. The Wings bought out McCarty's contract following the 2004–05 NHL lockout in order to trim the payroll under the new salary cap. With that, The Grind Line appeared to be history. But on February 25, 2008, the Wings re-signed McCarty. When McCarty was ready to play, in a March 28 home game against the St. Louis Blues, coach Mike Babcock played McCarty with Draper and Maltby. Fans gave them a standing ovation. Less than three months later, they were hoisting the Stanley Cup again.

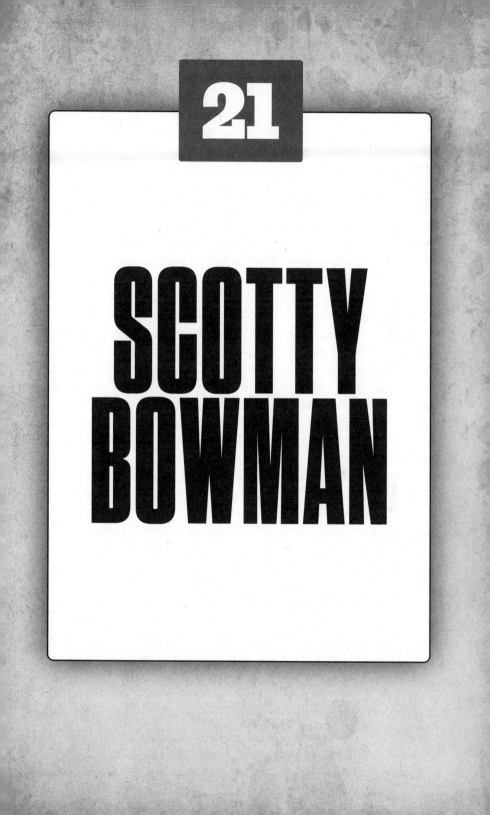

21

SCOTTY BOWMAN

Players tend to chuckle when asked what it was like to be coached by Scotty Bowman. He was quirky, demanding, baffling, sometimes aggravating, and almost always right. He called out star players, cajoled captains with threats of being traded, put power forwards on the fourth line, switched forwards to defensemen. Most of all, he won. And usually, players walked away from Bowman the better for having had him behind their bench.

"I liked playing for Scotty because Scotty challenged you," longtime goaltender Chris Osgood said in a 2019 interview. "If we were up 4–1 and I let in a goal in the last two minutes, he would let me know. He had a way of really making you pay attention to detail, which made you better—like, don't let any goals in the first five minutes of a period, the last two minutes of a period. And you think, well, if we're up 6–1, what does it matter if I let one in the last two minutes? Well, it means then it might happen another game, when it isn't a blowout, and you have to train yourself mentally to be able to play in any situation. I liked him. He was tough, but he made you better."

William Scott Bowman joined the Wings as coach in June 1993, a few months before his 60th birthday. Born September 18, 1933, in Verdun, nowadays a borough of Montreal, Bowman was a promising hockey player when a defender clubbed him over the head with his stick during a game on March 6, 1952. (The player, Jean-Guy Talbot, would go on to play for Bowman when he coached the Blues.) Contrary to popular lore, doctors did not insert a metal plate, but Bowman did undergo surgery to repair the damage from a five-inch gash to his head. "It took a piece right off my scalp," Bowman said in 2019. "It was a fracture." He continued to play hockey, but he suffered from blurred vision and headaches. He decided to switch to coaching, but had a day job selling paint to sustain an income.

His NHL head coaching career began on November 22, 1967, with the St. Louis Blues in their inaugural season after Lynn Patrick, also the general manager, resigned following a 4-10-2 start. Under Bowman, the Blues finished 23-21-14. While working for the Blues—whom he coached to the

Stanley Cup Finals their first three years—Bowman became acquainted with Jimmy Devellano, who had offered his services as a scout to the organization for free. By 1993 Devellano was senior vice president of the Wings, the first hire made when Mike Ilitch purchased the franchise in 1982.

Devellano had witnessed how the Blues jelled under Bowman. It was Ilitch himself, though, who went to see Bowman in the wake of their first-round loss to Toronto. Ilitch impressed upon Bowman how much the Wings wanted him as their coach. By that time, Bowman had coached six Stanley Cup winners, won 834 regular season games, and been inducted into the Hockey Hall of Fame. People told legends about him, like how he would ask players for matches even though he didn't smoke, because he would look at the matchbook cover to know where they hung out. Or how he would give a fan a stick to have autographed by a player returning to his hotel and make note of what time the player signed it. All of that—the success, the mystique—appealed to the Wings.

"I think it's time to win the Stanley Cup, and Scotty Bowman will give us our best opportunity," Ilitch said at Bowman's introductory news conference.

Bowman agreed to a two-year contract. The deal was worth $800,000 annually in base salary, making Bowman the highest-paid coach in the NHL. It also included an option to remain with the team when he was done coaching, as a consultant or director of player personnel.

"The one thing that stuck in my mind," Bowman said in June 1993, "was when Mike Ilitch said to me, 'We've owned the team for 11 years, and we've never won the Stanley Cup.' He said, 'We're not great losers here. These 11 years without a Cup are really starting to bother me.' That certainly triggered in my mind that that's what Mike and Marian Ilitch want so badly for the city of Detroit. They want to win. I know that. The players should know it too. These players are treated very well. It's a great place to play, and they'll be expected to win."

After Ilitch passed away in February 2017, Bowman elaborated on their relationship. "You knew how you stood with him," Bowman said. "No gray area; black or white. He wanted to win at any cost. He wanted to be informed. He always stressed if you needed something, he was just a phone call away. That was the fact of it. You just made a phone call and said, 'This is what I think we should do, this is what it's going to take,' and he was 100 percent backing of the people that worked for him."

Bowman was Steve Yzerman's sixth coach in 10 years with the Wings. "I think he can make a difference, but the bottom line is the players have to go out and do it," Yzerman said at training camp.

The Wings had a talented roster—Yzerman, Nicklas Lidstrom, Sergei Fedorov, and Vladimir Konstantinov were among the headliners—but their first playoff run under Bowman ended after one round, when the Wings were upset by the eight-seeded San Jose Sharks. In the off-season, Ilitch fired general manager Bryan Murray and gave Bowman the authority to make trades. In Bowman's second year the Wings advanced to the Stanley Cup Finals, but were swept by the New Jersey Devils.

With a new contract and his title as director of player personnel, Bowman set about tinkering. He explored trading Yzerman, but when those rumors became public knowledge—and Yzerman eviscerated the organization in October 1995, saying he deserved to be told in person rather than by reporters—Bowman quickly found out he was operating in dangerous territory. At the 1995 home opener, fans let Bowman have it; when he was introduced, it was to a chorus of boos so thoroughly deafening Bowman couldn't ignore the reaction. He showed fans he heard them but that he couldn't be cowed. He pretended to stomp off the bench—only to come back smiling. He told reporters afterward he thought there was "just a sprinkling of boos," drawing laughter. "Well," Bowman quipped, "I looked up and saw my wife and kids clapping."

That was the last time Yzerman's name came up in trade talks. But Bowman wasn't about to try another playoff run with the same team. He wanted Igor Larionov on the team, and when the Sharks asked for Ray Sheppard, Bowman didn't hesitate. He didn't care about the optics, about having to explain why an undersized forward about to turn 35 was a better fit for the team than a 50-goal-scoring winger.

"We're much stronger at a position we have to be strong in," Bowman said, pointing to the nine centers on the roster. Plus, as Bowman would demonstrate, Larionov was the missing piece to the Russian Five. Fedorov, Konstantinov, and Vyacheslav Kozlov were mainstays on the team, and Bowman had traded for Slava Fetisov in April 1995. Back then, pundits still questioned whether non–North Americans had what it took to win the Stanley Cup. Bowman scoffed at such xenophobia. "I'm not a bigot," Bowman said. "I don't care what nationality they are. I'm only interested in the best players for a team."

Scotty Bowman hoists the Stanley Cup in Washington, June 16, 1998.
(Julian H. Gonzalez)

In the spring of 1996, Bowman acquired Kirk Maltby from the Edmonton Oilers. The Wings were well on their way to a record 62 victories and Maltby—a scrapper who had suffered an eye injury that January—wasn't sure what to expect. By the time he retired, Maltby had won three Stanley Cups with Bowman as his coach.

"Scotty was interesting," Maltby said in 2019. "He kept you on your toes and it didn't matter who you were. It didn't matter if you were a first-liner or a fourth-liner. Scotty did whatever he felt was the best for the team, whatever was going to give the team the best chance to win on any given night. As a player, you didn't have to agree with it, but looking back, it's hard to argue with the decisions he made. You didn't understand Scotty's decisions sometimes, but they worked out a lot more than not."

Bowman didn't hesitate to demote Brendan Shanahan to the fourth line or take him off the power play. He put Kris Draper on a line with Sergei Fedorov. He asked Fedorov to play as a defenseman for a stretch. He moved Mathieu Dandenault from forward to defense.

Bowman mixed and tinkered until he found a way to get the most out of his players. He pushed their buttons. After a loss in Calgary in December 2001, Bowman called out Shanahan and Fedorov, saying they had been outplayed. Fedorov took it in stride. "I'm not really disagreeing with what Coach said but overall, I don't feel that my line got outplayed," he said. "It's not sort of my concern."

It bothered Shanahan, though. "I'm surprised because no one said anything to me," he said when told by reporters. "I'm surprised I have to get the coaching from you guys. These types of things shouldn't be played out in the press. They should be played out in the coach's room between two men. But it's nothing new."

Bowman needled his players, but he also stood up for them. When he perceived that NHL referees—Bowman named Terry Gregson in particular—were biased against the Wings' Russian players, he risked the ire of the NHL and complained about officials in January 1997. "Some of them have a better rapport with the Russians," Bowman said. "Gregson has none at all. He just buries them—especially Konstantinov. They don't get many calls. Maybe they can't verbalize as much as the other guys. When in doubt, penalize them. I don't understand it. The Canada-Russia series has been over since 1972. It makes it tough." When the NHL levied a $10,000 fine, Bowman joked he was going to demand $1,000 from each of his

Russian players "because I was trying to help them. So it's going to end up costing me five."

A month later, Bowman had other things on his mind. On February 8, he recorded his 1,000th regular season victory. He came into the season needing to win 25 games to get there, and it had taken longer than he anticipated. "It's nice it's over," he said. The 6–5 overtime victory in Pittsburgh put Bowman's regular season coaching record at 1,000–442–255 and also spanned jobs with the Blues, Canadiens, Sabres, and Penguins.

Players really noticed what an advantage it was to have a legend like Bowman behind their bench when they were in the playoffs. When Bowman started, he was a brilliant young coach going against brilliant veterans such as Montreal's Toe Blake and Toronto's Punch Imlach. Three decades later, Bowman was the brilliant veteran who had reached 11 Stanley Cup Finals in 1997. "Scotty has such an aura about him that the other coach is at a disadvantage before the game even starts," defenseman Larry Murphy said during the 1997 playoffs. "Everybody talks about what a great bench coach he is, and he plays that to his advantage. He's got that coach reeling."

Bowman described his coaching style as always looking for an edge. "I was always trying to pattern our play after what the other team does best," he said in 2019.

Bowman did exactly what Ilitch hired him to do on June 7, 1997. The Wings swept their way through the Finals to hoist the Stanley Cup, ending a 42-year drought. Bowman put on a pair of skates and took a lap with the Cup, remembering the teenager whose playing career sputtered after injury. "I always wanted to be a player in the NHL and skate with the Cup," Bowman said. "How many chances to you get to do that? I said if we win, I'll go for it. I have always dreamt about doing that."

There had been conjecture that Bowman would retire after winning the Cup in '97. He was turning 64 that September, and had just hoisted the Stanley Cup for the seventh time. But then Bowman started thinking about what else he would do, and decided he wanted to come back. The Wings re-signed Bowman for two years, gave him a raise, but made him relinquish his role as director of player personnel. Ilitch promoted Ken Holland from assistant to general manager. There was some internal squabbling before a deal was worked out. "I really didn't do that much

MIKE BABCOCK

Following a legend is hard, and the Red Wings' first choice to succeed Scotty Bowman lasted only two seasons.

Minutes after the Wings won the Stanley Cup in 2002, Bowman announced that he was done coaching. The Wings promoted assistant coach Dave Lewis, who had been with the organization for 16 years.

Lewis guided the Wings to two straight 48-victory seasons. In 2003–04, the Detroit won the Presidents' Trophy. But by then the Wings were used to Stanley Cup success, and Lewis' 6–10 record in the playoffs did not impress franchise higher-ups. When a labor dispute scrapped the 2004–05 season, the Wings let Lewis' contract expire and offered him a job as a scout.

At the same time, they courted Mike Babcock, who had coached the seventh-seeded Anaheim Ducks to a 15–6 record in the 2003 playoffs. Babcock rode goaltender Sebastien Giguere all the way to the Stanley Cup Finals—including a first-round sweep of the Wings—where the Ducks lost in seven games to the New Jersey Devils. Babcock declined contract extension overtures from the Ducks, knowing that, among other NHL teams, the Wings would have an opening.

It wasn't just Babcock's NHL success that appealed. In 2004, Wings assistant general manager Jim Nill was in charge of the Team Canada for the World Championships. When coach Joel Quenneville fell ill, Nill selected Babcock as the replacement. Babcock guided Canada—which included Wings forwards Kris Draper and Kirk Maltby—to the gold medal.

Babcock was introduced as the Wings' coach in July 2005. He was heralded as a gruff, no-nonsense taskmaster who demanded accountability. In his first season, he guided the Wings to the Presidents' Trophy with a 58–16–8 record, but they fared no better in the playoffs, losing in six games in Round 1 to the Edmonton Oilers. During the off-season, Steve Yzerman announced his retirement.

In 2006–07, Babcock coached the Wings to a 50–19–13 record, the first time in franchise history the team won 50 games back-to-back (the streak would eventually grow to four consecutive seasons of at least 50 victories). The Wings advanced to the Western Conference finals, losing to Babcock's former team in six games.

The groundwork had been laid for another championship. The Wings finished 2007–08 in first place in the NHL. Babcock was named a finalist for the Jack Adams award as coach of the year (he finished third behind Washington's Bruce Boudreau and and Montreal's Guy Carbonneau). The Wings defeated Nashville in six games in Round 1 of the playoffs, swept Colorado, and ousted Dallas in six games to set up the Stanley Cup Finals against Sidney Crosby and the Pittsburgh Penguins. As they worked their way through the rounds, players credited Babcock for reinstilling a culture of accountability.

"I think since the first year he was here, we're definitely a tougher and a harder team to play against," goaltender Chris Osgood said. "Since the Edmonton series, we realized we had to get stronger, tougher—not necessarily fighting-wise, but by getting pucks deep and grinding down teams."

Babcock had put his mark on the Wings, and it was paying off. "First year, it was more like a culture shock because of the way he was with practice and everything," Tomas Holmstrom said. "For sure he knows what he is doing, and he prepares really good, and he's done a good job."

Players grew used to Babcock's way of talking. He would talk about needing to show "stick-toitiveness" in games. Players' minutes came on "an as-earned basis." Faced with a tough situation, Babcock would talk about how he wanted to be the guy who defused the bomb.

He had a situation to defuse on June 3, 2008, during the Stanley Cup Finals. The Wings had a three-games-to-one lead in the series; Game 5 was at Joe Louis Arena; the Stanley Cup was in the building. Families, friends, and fans were poised to erupt the second the buzzer sounded on a Wings victory. The first overtime came and went. So did the second. Finally, midway through the third OT, Petr Sykora doused the hopes of another Cup party in Detroit and forced the series back to Pittsburgh.

Babcock pushed for normalcy as he prepared for Game 6. He broke down film, showed his players what they did well, what they needed to do better. One game later, Babcock hoisted the Stanley Cup. Within a few days, he signed a three-year contract with the Wings.

Babcock coached the Wings back to the Stanley Cup Finals in 2009 in a rematch with the Penguins. There would be no more Cups for Babcock in Detroit, but on April 8, 2014, he earned his 414th victory behind the Wings' bench, surpassing Jack Adams as the winningest coach in franchise history.

before as far as what a manager would do," Bowman said at the time. "I made some trades to bring in some veterans, but we really didn't make too many trades because we wanted to keep our young players. Ken has done most of the managerial stuff. It's not a big change for him."

Bowman coached the Wings to a second straight Stanley Cup in June 1998. He underwent angioplasty in July and had his left knee replaced in August. Still, Bowman couldn't think of anything he would rather do. Two years turned into nine. Bowman came to the Wings with six Stanley Cup championships and left with nine.

On the night of June 13, 2002, the Wings had just won the Stanley Cup after a five-game series with Carolina. Bowman, now 68, had made up his mind, and he told everyone within earshot: "That was my last game."... "I coached my last game."... "I'm done. That was my last game."

"I had a great conversation with the coach, finally," Fedorov said. "I said, 'It wasn't an easy road, but it was fun playing for you.' At times it was very, very hard, but as long as we stick with the winning, that was the main goal."

22

A LIT
PIECE OF
DYNAMITE

A hit ignited the rivalry, and two teams mirroring one another in talent fueled it. From the middle-'90s to the early aughts, no matchup captivated the hockey world as much as the Detroit Red Wings and Colorado Avalanche. They battled in the playoffs and they fought in the regular season; they celebrated Stanley Cups, often after having faced one another in some of the most competitive hockey of the playoffs. Heroes were anointed and villains were reviled when two of the best teams in the NHL met, and it made for incredible entertainment.

"Everybody talks about the fights, and it was a great rivalry," Steve Yzerman reflected in 2019. "I can only speak from my perspective, but I had tremendous respect for how good they were—Joe Sakic, Peter Forsberg, Adam Foote, Patrick Roy. They were a really good team. They beat us in '96 and we came back in '97 and beat them. That was a great series. We felt really good because we played really, really well to beat them in six games. They had Hall of Famers and were every bit as good as us. There were side stories to it all, but ultimately it made for really good hockey."

The Wings rolled into the 1996 playoffs with an NHL-record 62 victories, the only team to go through the entire season without being shut out. They bested the Winnipeg Jets in Round 1, and won Round 2 against the St. Louis Blues when Yzerman scored on a 55-foot slap shot in double overtime in Game 7. Then it was on to the Western Conference finals, against the Avalanche.

Leading up to the series, the focus was on the captains. Yzerman and Joe Sakic were highly respected leaders, renowned for their quiet excellence. (In fact, they almost were teammates—at the 1987 draft, Wings management debated whether to select Sakic or defenseman Yves Racine at 11th overall. The Wings picked Racine, and Sakic went four spots later to the Quebec Nordiques. That franchise relocated to Denver in May 1995 and was renamed the Colorado Avalanche.) Both wore No. 19—and when an eye injury prevented Yzerman from playing in the 2004 World Cup of

Hockey, Sakic declined to wear No. 19 for Team Canada out of respect for Yzerman.

In 1997, Yzerman was the better all-around player, while Sakic was coming off a 51-goal season. "It'll be really fun to watch," Wings defenseman Marc Bergevin said on the eve of the series. "Both are highly skilled offensively. And for as much skill as they have, they both take a lot of punishment. They both do everything."

Six games later the Wings' dream season died in Denver—but a rivalry was born. During the first period of Game 6, Claude Lemieux slammed into Kris Draper from behind. Draper's face shattered as it hit the dasher. The impact broke a cheekbone, his jaw, and his nose. He needed 30 stitches that night to curtail the damage. "I was sitting on the bench, and it happened right in front of me," Darren McCarty told Bill Dow for the *Free Press* in 2017. "I saw Lemieux coming at Kris, and it was like seeing a car crash in slow motion. I could literally hear the bones break in Drapes' face. It was difficult for us to process. Lemieux was an agitator and a cheap-shot guy. But he was one of the best playoff performers ever."

Lemieux's villainy wasn't selective: while playing for New Jersey in 1992, he was sitting on the bench during a game against the Rangers when referee Kerry Fraser skated by and heard Lemieux telling teammates to slash Rangers captain Mark Messier and break his wrists. Fraser penalized Lemieux 10 minutes for inciting an infraction.

Draper was still wiping blood from his mouth as he left McNichols Arena with his teammates. "I'm out there playing," he said. "All of a sudden, I'm there lying on a table getting fixed by four doctors."

The Wings vowed to avenge Lemieux's cheap shot. "He did something we're not going to forget," Chris Osgood said. "None of the players are going to forget it. When he comes back to play the Red Wings next year, we'll be waiting for him, and he'd better be ready. He can say what he wants about going to the Finals. We know we're not going. We can deal with our situation. He'd better be ready to deal with what he's going to have to face next season. It's not a threat; it's just something that's going to happen."

Lemieux was recovering from abdominal surgery when the Avalanche made their first visit of the 1996–97 season to Joe Louis Arena in November and when the Wings went to Denver in December. On March 16 in Denver, Draper and Lemieux received 10-minute misconduct for jawing at each other but little else materialized. Lemieux's appearance on March 26 at the Joe was greeted with deafening boos from fans. But boos turned to cheers near the end of the first period. There already had been two fights in the game before a collision between Igor Larionov and Peter Forsberg distracted officials. McCarty seized the moment, spinning away from a linesman to coldcock Lemieux. It was only the beginning. Lemieux crumbled to the ice, holding his bloodied face. McCarty held him by the neck and hit him again. Finally, he dragged Lemieux to the Wings' bench, where officials separated the two. By that time, Patrick Roy was on his way to defend Lemieux, but Brendan Shanahan took a flying leap to intercept Roy and send him splaying. Adam Foote went after Shanahan; goaltender Mike Vernon attempted to intervene there only to get tangled up with Roy. There were nine fights total in the game (McCarty's pummeling of Lemieux did not officially count as one), and the Wings capped the night with McCarty's overtime goal to win their first game that season against their rival.

When the Western Conference finals once again took them to Colorado, the Wings were better prepared than they had been the previous season. That March 26 game sparked something within them, made them closer, stoked their belief that this was their year.

Both sides, though, played it cool going into the series. "I know the fans would like to see a bloodbath again," Martin Lapointe said, "but you can't afford to be stupid like that by taking penalties and jeopardizing our team."

In a game of one-upmanship, Bowman and Marc Crawford heaped praise on one another's team. Still, the series crackled with electricity before it even began, only to be upstaged by a power outage at McNichols Arena. The ice was mushy during the first two periods. Fans couldn't see much—concession stands and restrooms were in the dark. Wings announcers Ken Kal and Paul Woods broadcast the game by phone.

Shanahan scored first, but the Avs took Game 1 2–1. Lemieux, ever the villain in this rivalry, cross-checked Vladimir Konstantinov from behind into the boards in the first period.

Lemieux finished Game 2 breaking his stick on his net, embodying the Avalanche's frustration as the Wings scored four unanswered goals to claim Game 2 4–2. The Wings won Game 3. Then the fun began.

The Wings humiliated Colorado in Game 4, winning 6–0 at the Joe. Igor Larionov scored the first two goals and Kirk Maltby the last two. The third period degenerated into a farce as the Avs lost composure, culminating with a shouting match between Crawford and Bowman with two minutes left. Crawford climbed the glass partition to the well that separated the benches and screamed at Bowman. A linesman jumped between the coaches. Crawford said afterward it was nothing. Bowman told Crawford the game was over. Bowman put Crawford in his place, telling him, "I knew your father before you did, and I don't think he'd be too proud of what you're doing right now."

"His eyes were coming out of his head," Bowman said later. "So he was pretty excited."

SPARKING A TRADE

The Russian Five tormented many a rival during their time together, but one night in particular led to one of the biggest trades in Montreal Canadiens history—and one that would greatly impact the Red Wings.

On December 2, 1995, the Wings played the Canadiens at the Montreal Forum, and the Russians feasted, combining for 15 points as the Wings handed the Canadiens a franchise-worst 11–1 home loss.

A dozen of those points came at the expense of Patrick Roy, who had backstopped the Canadiens to Stanley Cups in 1986 and 1993. Igor Larionov scored the first goal on a power play at 3:10 of the first period, with Sergei Fedorov drawing an assist. Vyacheslav Kozlov scored twice in two minutes and again three minutes into the second period. It wasn't until Fedorov scored to make it 9–1 at 11:57 of the second period that Montreal coach Mario Tremblay finally relented and pulled Roy. By then, Fedorov had piled up four points, Kozlov and Larionov each had three, and Vladimir Konstantinov and Slava Fetisov each had an assist. (Kozlov scored the last of his four goals late in the second period, assisted by Fedorov and Larionov.)

Roy was so furious at not being pulled earlier he stormed to the bench and shouted to Canadiens president Ronald Corey that it would be his last game in Montreal. Four days later, Roy was a member of the Colorado Avalanche. That spring, Roy was a key reason the Wings were eliminated in the Western Conference finals en route to his third Stanley Cup.

The NHL fined Crawford $10,000. He woke up a contrite man. "I embarrassed the league, and more important I embarrassed my team," he said. "And for that, I am sorry. There's no way you can justify anything like that. If you try to, it's wrong. I was wrong."

Crawford and Bowman never came to blows, but the players did that night. There were eight fighting majors, 12 misconducts, four roughings, two game misconducts, two instigating penalties, and one goalie interference among 204 penalty minutes—and that was just in the third period.

The Wings lost Game 5 6-0, but closed out the series two days later, on home ice. They had vanquished their nemesis, and a Cup party was on the horizon.

The rivalry flared up again that autumn, when the Avalanche played at the Joe on November 11, 1997. Lemieux tried to distance himself from how he had cowed in the March 26 game and lined up against McCarty on the opening faceoff. Lemieux threw a punch, catching McCarty in the chest. McCarty soon gained the upper hand, and the fight fizzled. "I did well until his arm came out and his shirt came out," Lemieux said afterward.

The next meeting at the Joe, on April 1, 1998, was much more entertaining. The Wings reflected on the March 26 game as the first anniversary passed. "A huge game," Draper said. "It was a fun night. I don't think the anniversary is going to be a repeat of that, but on April Fools' Day, you never know what's going to happen."

It turned out to be another great installment in the rivalry. Referees assessed 45 penalties totaling 218 minutes. The third period was a blast for fans: Fedorov scored two goals, and then Roy beckoned Chris Osgood to fight.

Over on the Wings' bench, associate coach Dave Lewis wondered whether Osgood could fight. "I guess we'll find out," Draper replied.

Draper delighted in seeing his good friend hold his own. "Ozzy stood up for himself and did a great job," Draper said. "But he was also standing up for our team. And he was doing it for the rivalry and to keep things going."

The Wings defended their Stanley Cup championship in 1998 but were eliminated in two quiet series by the Avalanche in 1999 and 2000. Then the Avs traded Lemieux to New Jersey in November 1999, robbing the rivalry of its primary villain.

In March 2002, Dominik Hasek was determined to join the brotherhood of Wings goaltenders who had fought Roy, but he never made it. Hasek skated the length of the ice only to trip over Roy's discarded stick. Two months later the Wings rallied to win another Western Conference finals against the Avalanche, scoring six goals on Roy in Game 7. In 2008, the Wings swept the Avalanche in Round 2 en route to another Stanley Cup championship. The rivalry had died down by then—most of the principal participants had been traded or had retired—but in their heyday, the Wings and Avalanche enraptured the hockey world.

"Once it got sparked, the great thing about the rivalry was the skill level on both teams," Maltby said. "It was skill mixed with toughness—it wasn't just goon hockey. We had to respect them, too. The entire hockey community [was] watching those games because the hockey was fantastic. It was a lit piece of dynamite."

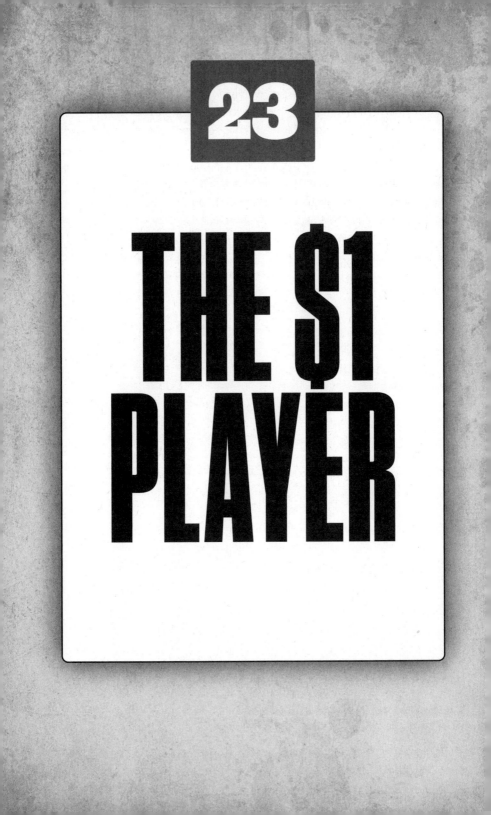

23

THE $1 PLAYER

On January 24, 1994, Kris Draper was at the front desk at the Ponchartrain Hotel in Detroit, his bags hastily packed after he was called up by the Red Wings. Draper had just arrived from the Wings' farm in upstate New York. He gave his name. The clerk looked at the reservations and said, "Oh, yes, Mr. Draper, with the Detroit Red Wings." That had a nice sound to it, Draper thought. The clerk continued. "We have you checking in today and checking out tomorrow." That was less encouraging.

As it turned out, Draper stayed two nights at the hotel, and only checked out because the Wings headed on the road, to Chicago. Draper went with them—and stayed for more than 1,000 games. He recorded his first NHL point, an assist, during the game in Chicago.

"I went to see him when he was with Adirondack," Scotty Bowman recalled in a 2019 interview. "For some reason, we weren't doing well on faceoffs. I went to watch him play on a Sunday. We were looking for someone to come up and play for a little bit. We brought him up for the weekend. He never went back."

Arguably no player in Wings history has paid better dividends than Draper, whose career spanned four Stanley Cups. He came to the organization in 1993, acquired by Adirondack general manager Doug MacLean from the Winnipeg Jets for $1. "Who knows if that dollar was ever even paid?" Draper wondered 10 years later.

Draper wasn't laughing when the trade occurred, though. How could he? In his three years with Winnipeg he'd never played more than 10 games in a season. The Jets had selected him at 62nd overall in 1989 and had given up on Draper after 20 games. (That draft is legendary in Wings history for reaping Nicklas Lidstrom, Sergei Fedorov, and Vladimir Konstantinov.) In 1993, the Jets weren't that good, but the Wings were on the rise—they had Steve Yzerman, they had Lidstrom, they had Fedorov. "You're excited to get a fresh start, but kind of wonder, like, *If I couldn't make it with the Winnipeg Jets, how am I going to make it with the Detroit Red Wings?*" Draper recalled.

Draper spent the rest of the 1993–94 season with the Wings, scoring five goals. He had just two goals in 36 games in the 1994–95 season, which was shortened to 48 games because of a labor dispute. He was more prolific in the playoffs, producing four goals in 18 games. It was the first of six Stanley Cup Finals Draper would play in, though it ended with a resounding dud as the New Jersey Devils swept the Wings.

While Draper endured a disappointing finish to the 1995 season, 1996 ended with a different kind of pain. On May 29, 1996, during Game 6 of the Western Conference finals against the Colorado Avalanche, Claude Lemieux slammed Draper from behind, sending him into the boards. Lemieux was ejected from the game in Denver. Draper flew home with the team and underwent surgery to repair a broken jaw. He also had a concussion, a broken nose, a handful of displaced teeth, and cuts around his nose and right eye. Draper needed 30 stitches in his mouth alone.

John Wharton, in his sixth year as team trainer, said the next day that "I'd be hard pressed to find and add together three or four head and facial injuries that would accumulate to the damage that this one injury has caused."

Draper spent weeks recovering—and seething. "I got absolutely blindsided," Draper said. "I had no chance of protecting myself; I was absolutely defenseless. A couple friends I have from the Avalanche said it was a dirty hit—and that's coming from his teammates. They couldn't believe he did something like that."

Draper's jaw was wired shut for two weeks. He missed a retirement party for defenseman Mike Ramsey. He missed a vacation he had planned with roommate Chris Osgood. He missed eating—instead of steak and salad, Draper subsisted on milkshakes. "I don't think I'll ever have [shakes] again," Draper said two months after the hit. "I was mixing all kinds of fruit together and it tasted okay, but I'd have my fifth one and then Ozzy would come home and he'd look all happy because he just had a big steak dinner."

When Osgood went on the trip, Wharton stepped in to help. "I got my daily workout just carrying his mail over to him every day," Wharton said. "It was like two or three sacks of cards, collages, flowers."

Draper lost 10 pounds. When the wires came off, he realized he didn't have feeling in three teeth. He was hungry, though, so he adopted

Kris Draper at a Red Wings Alumni Association game in 2012.

the motto "You gotta eat hurt." For the first time in years, he indulged in desserts.

The NHL suspended Lemieux for all of two games for the hit. Then he went on to celebrate a second straight Stanley Cup after the Avalanche swept Florida.

Draper's mother, Mary Lynn Draper, was so angered by Lemieux's light sentence she wrote a petition to send to NHL commissioner Gary Bettman, a letter asking people to sign if they disagreed with the punishment. It drew 700 signatures (and this was before the Internet; had it been 2017, it would no doubt have gone viral).

Lemieux never apologized to Draper. The two didn't speak for 19 years, until meeting in a Miami hotel after the 2015 draft. The Wings had just drafted a player in the fourth round, Joren van Pottelberghe, who

Lemieux represented. Lemieux approached Draper, who was with his wife, Julie, and their three children in the lobby. "My wife and kids, they obviously know everything about it, and they weren't quite sure," Draper said in 2016. "My son was just looking—his eyes were bugging out. He wasn't sure what was going to happen. Julie wasn't quite sure. She went through the whole process with me. We sat there and talked. He said it was great meeting everybody. He walked away, and I was just like, 'Wow.'

"It was probably a four- to five-minute conversation. Nothing was mentioned about the game, the hit, the rivalry. It was just basically an agent talking to someone in management, and that was it. That's the extent of the interaction that I've had with him."

After the pain of 1995 and 1996, 1997 brought Draper vindication *and* victory. Lemieux was sidelined by abdominal surgery when the Avalanche visited Detroit in November 1996, making for an anticlimactic first meeting since the playoffs. March 26, 1997 made up for it: during the first period McCarty laid into Lemieux with a right hook. Lemieux didn't even try to fight back. He dropped to the ice and turtled, content to let the officials deal with McCarty.

Pandemonium ensued. By the time it was over, officials had handed out 148 penalty minutes. The game unified the Wings and carried them into the playoffs. Draper anchored The Grind Line between Kirk Maltby and either McCarty or Joe Kocur.

On June 7, the Wings completed a sweep of the Philadelphia Flyers with a 2–1 victory at the Joe. A year after he'd spent the month of June getting by on soup and milkshakes, Draper was sipping champagne from the Cup, smoking cigars, and grinning so hard he boasted he didn't even remember the previous year's plight.

The next season was pretty great too. Bowman promoted Draper to play with Fedorov and Shanahan and Draper responded with personal highs of 13 goals and 10 assists. In Game 2 of the Stanley Cup Finals against the Washington Capitals, Draper scored the goal kids dream about, securing a 5–4 overtime victory on home ice.

Another Cup followed in 2002. Draper enjoyed his most successful year statistically in 2003–04, when he scored 24 goals among 40 points in 67 games. Draper was recognized with the Selke Trophy as the NHL's best defensive forward.

Draper was made an alternative captain in 2006–07, and he won another Cup in 2008. By the time he retired in July 2011, he'd played 1,137 regular season games in a Wings uniform, plus 220 playoff games. He immediately was added to the front office, gaining the title of assistant to the general manager—Dwight Schrute from *The Office* would have approved—under Ken Holland. When Steve Yzerman took over as general manager in 2019, Draper was promoted to director of amateur scouting.

That hotel clerk may have had a short reservation for Draper, but Draper made a home in Detroit, raised his family there, celebrated four Stanley Cups there. He was known for his speed—and inability to convert on breakaways—his smile, his work ethic, and his loquaciousness.

There was one evening, however, when Draper found himself short on words. He was driving home from the Fox Theatre on a November 2002 evening. His wife was next to him. They glanced at the Stanley Cup ring, his third, that he'd just received. "You're just kind of like, 'Holy geez,' how fortunate am I considering where I came from," Draper said. "That's when you think how thankful you are."

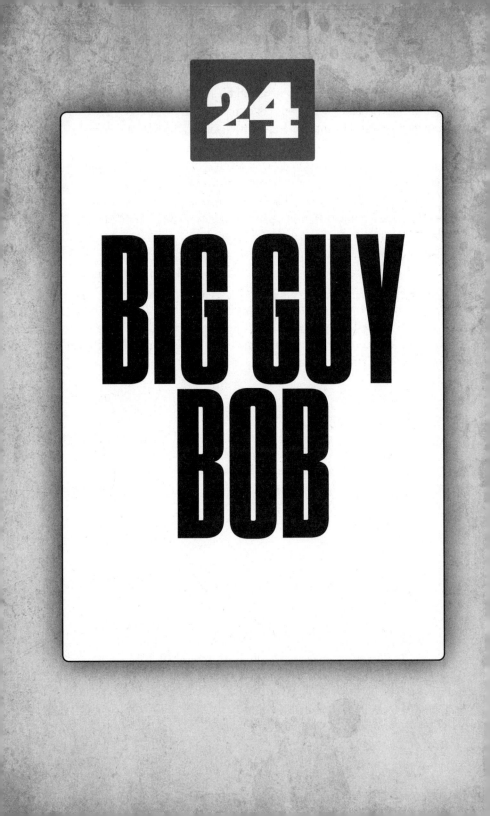

24

BIG GUY BOB

I n nine turbulent seasons with the Red Wings, Bob Probert broke records and hearts, made headlines for fights with enforcers and officers, was an NHL All-Star and a federal prisoner. He crashed nets and vehicles. He thrilled and exasperated, he amazed and angered. He was a fearsome bruiser and a family man with an endearing bedtime routine. He was proud of his high IQ but too proud to ask for help fighting booze and cocaine.

Probert's career with the Wings was marked by talent and tumult. When he was selected for the NHL All-Star Game in February 1988, Probert already had been in alcohol-related trouble with authorities four times. He battled addiction at a time when there was still enough misunderstanding or just mere disregard that some teammates and some friends would urge him to have "just one drink," even though one would never be enough.

"He has me worried every day I live," general manager Jimmy Devellano said in 1988. "Not a day goes by when I don't think about him. I think about him when I'm sleeping. I have deep feelings for him."

Probert had soft hands around the net but iron fists beneath his gloves. He made sure no one messed with Steve Yzerman. Probert had legendary fights with Tie Domi, Stu Grimson, Marty McSorley, Donald Brashear, and good friend Joe Kocur—and with police officers from Canada to Florida. He seemed invincible, but he died at just 45.

Robert Alan Probert was born June 5, 1965, in Windsor, Ontario. His relationship with the Wings began at the 1983 draft, a day when the Wings also culled Yzerman, Petr Klima, and Joe Kocur. The Wings selected Probert in the third round, 46th overall. He was 18 years old and already 6'3", 206 pounds, and had racked up 133 penalty minutes as well as 28 points with Brantford in the Ontario Hockey League. By the time he left for his first year of junior hockey he had buried his dad, lost to a stroke at only 52 years old. Had the Wings looked closely, they would have seen a troubled teenager who readily, regularly outdrank everyone around him.

Devellano, running his first draft since being appointed general manager by new owner Mike Ilitch, said he hoped Probert would turn into a "Clark Gillies–type player." Gillies was a four-time Stanley Cup champion with the New York Islanders who had matched offensive prowess with physical presence.

Probert delivered both. He became the game's measuring stick for fighters, recording 246 fights in 16 seasons with the Wings and Chicago Blackhawks. He received at least 200 penalty minutes in a season nine times and finished with 3,300, the fifth-highest total in NHL history. His first fight came in his third game, on November 11, 1985, in Vancouver, when he fought 6'4", 210-pound Craig Coxe, a former rival from the OHL and a Wings fourth-rounder in 1982. The two went blow for blow for more than 40 seconds—until a Probert right to the top of the helmet sent Coxe to the ice.

The Wings put up with Probert's problematic behavior for so long because in between the bouts with law enforcement he was a powerhouse forward, a Herculean hero whose labors pulled the team from decades of decrepitude. He worked his way onto the first line, playing next to Yzerman and Klima. In 1987–88, his second full season, Probert scored 29 goals, reached 62 points, and led the NHL with a staggering 398 penalty minutes, sixth-highest in NHL history for a single season. Fans revered him; opponents respected him. It made it easier to overlook that by the time Probert played in the February 1988 All-Star Game, he already had been busted twice for driving under the influence.

Probert was 20 years old in April 1986 when he was arrested on drunken driving and speeding charges in Windsor, spending several hours in jail after refusing to submit to a Breathalyzer. He'd been clocked going more than 100 kilometers an hour (60ish mph) in a 50-kilometer zone. A Windsor police sergeant told the *Free Press* that Probert "got very snarky and snotty and made a real jackass of himself."

Wings management noted there had been indications of that kind of behavior before. It was only the beginning.

Probert, whose father had been a Windsor police officer, was arrested again in July 1986 after another an altercation with an off-duty policeman at a Windsor tavern. For a while Probert acted as if he got the message, enough so that coach Jacques Demers heaped praise on him in mid-December, calling him "a winner."

Within days Probert was in trouble with Windsor police again over another drunken driving incident. On December 19, 1986, after leaving a tavern, Probert crashed his car into a utility pole. Probert suffered separated cartilage in his ribs and cuts on his face. His 1986 Monte Carlo SS was totaled. Probert was arraigned on charges of driving while impaired and violating probation. "This has ruined everything he worked for," Yzerman said at the time. "He had cleaned up his act, got himself in good shape. And now he's ruined it with this one stupid incident."

Some teammates tried to look out for Probert, but Yzerman wondered about the people who had gone drinking with him. "They know he is an alcoholic," he said. "They should have watched out for him."

The Wings suspended Probert but lifted the suspension four days later. Demers, whose father was an alcoholic, swore that if Probert had another alcohol-related incident "he's gone." Demers pleaded with Probert to stop his bad habits. He was often met with a wink and a smirk. One time, when Demers implored Probert not to smoke, Probert responded by lighting a cigarette with a butane blowtorch players used to shape their sticks.

A Windsor court revoked Probert's driver's license for a year, fined him $1,000, and ordered him to continue treatment for alcoholism. In February 1987, he spent two weeks in a treatment facility in Windsor.

There's a revealing interview with former Wings assistant coach Colin Campbell (who had been tasked by the team to serve essentially as Probert's warden) in the documentary *Tough Guy: The Bob Probert Story*. Campbell reveals why the Wings kept giving Probert chance after chance. "We were selfish too," he said. "We knew how good Bob was and how he could help us. We didn't fix it the way we really had to fix it. We wanted him cleaned up in two weeks. He spent a lifetime getting the way he did and we thought we could fix it up in 7-to-10 days."

In the mid-1980s the team was just beginning to emerge from the Dead Wings era. The Wings won 34 games in 1986–87, their 78 points a 38-point improvement over the previous season. They advanced to the conference finals, overcoming a 3–1 deficit against Toronto in Round 2 before falling to eventual Stanley Cup champion Edmonton in five games. Probert was a pivotal part of the revival. Probert, Yzerman, and Gerard Gallant were the Wings' most effective line in the 1987 playoffs. Fans were excited. Yzerman endeared with his skill and soft voice, while Probert captivated with his bravado.

Bob Probert at a Red Wings alumni game, January 27, 2007. (Julian H. Gonzalez)

In the fourth game of the following season, Probert scored a goal, hit Maple Leafs goaltender Ken Wregget, and fought Chris Kotsopoulos. When the teams met again the next day in Toronto, Probert's stat line was identical: one goal, seven penalty minutes. It seemed so promising. It sounded so, too. "I want to put all my problems in my past and start new," Probert said.

He starred in another fight with Coxe on November 19, 1987, in Detroit. Again the two went blow for blow for 45 seconds before Probert KO'd Coxe with two right hooks. Fans were on their feet. At the time, Probert was second on the team with 18 points (and first, of course, with 72 penalty minutes).

December brought a dose of unease. Probert spent a night in jail for violating probation after missing appointments with his probation officer and skipping Alcoholics Anonymous meetings. January brought joy: Probert, along with Yzerman, was named to the All-Star Game. Probert, at 22, had 22 goals and 21 assists and led the league with 253 penalty minutes. He also had the shortest fight of his career, in a January 13 game when he schooled Michel Petit for cheap-shotting Yzerman into the end boards, using two big right hooks to knock Petit out in two seconds.

At the All-Star Game in St. Louis on February 9, Probert shared a locker room with Wayne Gretzky, Mark Messier, Jari Kurri, Denis Savard, and Grant Fuhr. Edmonton coach Glen Sather personally picked Probert to represent the Campbell Conference, citing his toughness and talent— and troubled past. "He's beat a problem that millions of Canadians and Americans suffer from," Sather said. "Whether he's going to beat it permanently or not, I don't know. But I thought this would be a great chance for him to get some recognition." At the time, Probert claimed he had been sober almost a year.

The Wings rewarded him with a three-year contract extension in March. It was Probert's third year in the NHL, he was putting up career numbers, and he appeared to have gotten a handle on his alcoholism. The only downer that month was losing Yzerman to a knee injury.

April was awesome for Probert. The Wings hosted Toronto in Round 1, and Probert finished the six-game series on a five-game, 10-point streak. He added six points in the Round 2 against the Blues. The Wings advanced to a Western Conference finals rematch with the Oilers. The Wings lost the first two games, but with Yzerman back for Game 3, managed to edge within 2–1. Game 4 deflated: the Wings lost 4–3 in overtime, overshadowing a history-making performance by Probert. He scored twice to reach 21 points, eclipsing Gordie Howe's club record of 20 points in the 1955 playoffs.

Then Probert poured his promising spring into a shot glass and downed one drink after another. On the eve of Game 5, Probert and a handful of teammates including Klima and Kocur went to an Edmonton nightclub named Goose Loonies. Probert—by then an admitted alcoholic— drank heavily. When Campbell and chief scout Neil Smith discovered some players weren't in their rooms, they headed to Goose Loonies, paid the $3 cover charge, and searched for the curfew culprits. When they didn't see them they headed for the exit, only to be tipped off by the doorman that there were hockey players from Detroit in the back room. It was three hours past the 11:00 PM curfew.

Demers didn't hold back his disappointment. "It's breaking my heart thinking about it," he told the *Free Press'* Keith Gave. "They're a bunch of idiots. They're fools for doing that." Reports singled out Klima (who was sidelined by a broken thumb at the time) as being the one who encouraged Probert to party. Klima and Probert initially denied they had gone out at all.

Probert looked listless in Game 5. The Wings lost 8–4.

Fallout over the Goose Loonies episode lasted for days. Demers said two of the culprits (John Chabot and Darren Eliot) were remorseful but "I don't think Probie is. I don't think Klima is. Darren Veitch is not, and I question Kocur."

It emerged Probert had stopped taking Antabuse, a medication that makes people sick if they consume alcohol. (Probert had snuck into Campbell's office and replaced the pills with aspirin.) He had been prescribed the stuff at the start of the season, after completing his fourth stay at a treatment center. The Wings tried to persuade Probert to enter the prestigious Betty Ford Center in Rancho Mirage, California. Instead, he bought a boat and spent the summer sailing.

Probert arrived at training camp in fall 1988 out of shape and overweight. During the exhibition season, he missed a team flight home after showing up at the wrong Chicago airport. The Wings assigned him to their AHL affiliate in upstate New York. When they recalled him, Probert missed the flight. The Wings suspended him without pay and started the 1988–89 season without him.

Devellano explored trading Probert and Klima, but their antics had sullied their value. The talks at least rattled Probert enough to enter the Betty Ford Center in October 1988. He bailed within two weeks, going home to Windsor and checking into a hotel under an assumed name. Probert was unable to go to Detroit, denied entry at the border because his suspension from the Wings affected his immigration visa status.

The Wings reinstated Probert in November (they had gone 4–4–3 in October) but his availability was delayed because he weighed in at 227 pounds, a good 12 pounds heavier than deemed ideal. He finally appeared in his first game of the season on November 27 at Joe Louis Arena, when he was welcomed by fans chanting "Pro-*bie*, Pro-*bie*." He had missed 22 games. Devellano continued to explore trading Probert, as much for his off-ice problems as his paltry contributions on ice (three goals, two assists in his first 20 games).

"My conscience is very clear, extremely clear when it comes to him," Devellano said. "People don't know the half of it, what we've attempted to do to get the boy to play." Devellano suspended Probert again in January after he showed up late for a game for the second time in two weeks.

In his memoir *Tough Guy* (which formed the basis for the documentary), Probert revealed just how bad things had been off the ice. He started boozing when he was 14 years old and recognized he had a problem by 16. He first tried cocaine after helping the Wings' minor-league affiliate capture the American Hockey League's Calder Cup in 1986. Probert estimated that in one year he spent $42,000 on his cocaine habit.

His drug dependency took center stage March 2, 1989, when Probert was busted by U.S. customs agents at the Detroit-Windsor Tunnel at 5:15 AM. One of the three passengers in the 1988 GMC Jimmy was Dani Wood, Probert's future wife. Agents spotted alcoholic beverage containers in the vehicle. Probert, who was behind the wheel, was disoriented and ordered to undergo a strip search. Agents found a mill used to grind cocaine in one pocket and 14.3 grams of cocaine when Probert pulled down his underwear. In his book, Probert revealed that he went into a restroom and snorted cocaine after first dumping it in the toilet. He described himself as looking like someone who had just inhaled a powdered donut, white particles frosting his face.

Probert was charged with drug smuggling and faced up to 20 years in prison, $1 million in fines and deportation. He was 23 years old. He had been to five rehabilitation centers at that point.

"I guess this ends our Bob Probert problem," Yzerman told reporters, "in the wrong way."

The NHL expelled Probert indefinitely. The Wings stopped paying him his $200,000 annual salary for breach of contract. Federal officials asked a judge to revoke Probert's $5,000 cash bond, claiming he had violated conditions when he left a treatment facility to go drinking with teenage patients. The judge cut Probert's privileges, denying him visitors and access to a telephone.

Probert pleaded guilty to cocaine importation. He remained at a treatment facility while awaiting sentencing. "I pleaded guilty because

THE PROBLEMS WITH PETR

Bob Probert patrolled the Red Wings' domain as one half of the Bruise Brothers (along with teammate Joe Kocur) in the 1980s, but he and Petr Klima were booze brothers, a duo so tempted by trouble it exasperated management. The two appeared on score sheets and police sheets, their drinking escapades an eternal thorn in the side of coach Jacques Demers, general manager Jimmy Devellano, and the franchise at large.

"I can't believe two players can have such a negative impact," Demers said in October 1988, when Klima had just made the news for his second drunken driving incident. Klima and Probert had been suspended without pay after breaking several team rules, including skipping practices and missing flights.

As with Probert, Klima intrigued for his immense talents. A fifth-round pick in 1983 (40 spots after Probert), the Wings engineered Klima's defection from what was then Soviet-controlled Czechoslovakia in 1985. It was such a momentous event in Klima's life, he wore the No. 85 in tribute. Klima, billed as one of Europe's best players, went from making $7,000 in his homeland to more than $200,000 annually in his new country. He bought a house in the affluent Detroit suburb Birmingham and a black Camaro. He owned two Great Danes and a German shepherd. He was joined by his fiancée, Irena Zelenak.

On opening night that October, fans gave Klima a five-minute standing ovation. Klima went on to score 32 goals as a rookie, although the 1985–86 season was an embarrassment for the Wings. They won just 17 games, 10 fewer than the previous season.

The Wings put up with Klima because he kept giving them reason to hope that he, along with Probert, would lead them to the Stanley Cup. Klima hit the 30-goal benchmark in each of his first three seasons, but a career-high 62 points in 1987–88 were tarnished by an incredibly selfish and stupid decision in Edmonton on the eve of Game 5 of the Western Conference finals. Klima and Probert were among half a dozen players who went out boozing, even with the Wings on the verge of losing the series. Klima wasn't playing because he was injured, but his willingness to drink with Probert—a known alcoholic—angered team officials.

Klima tried denying he was at Goose Loonies, then fought the Wings' attempts to get him to enter a treatment facility for alcohol abuse. He said he stopped drinking on his own in the summer of 1988. The Wings didn't believe him and were running thin on patience. At training camp, Demers told the rest of the team not to count on having Klima—or Probert—back on the team. The Wings listened to offers for Probert, but didn't hear any they liked. Klima drew little interest.

Teams were right to be wary. In October 1988, Klima, then 23, was arrested and charged with operating a vehicle under the influence of alcohol. After leaving a bar in Royal Oak, Michigan, he backed his GMC Jimmy into another car and drove away. When police stopped him, Klima was caught trying to switch places with one of two women inside his vehicle. He was still on probation from his first drunken driving arrest in May 1987.

Klima convinced the Wings he was contrite and agreed to a conditioning stint in the minors. His court case was delayed while he recovered from post-concussion symptoms stemming from being hit in the left ear with the stick of Flyers goalie Ron Hextall during a game in Philadelphia. On December 2, a judge revoked Klima's driver's license for six months and extended his probation to two years. Klima was also ordered to live at Children's Hospital of Michigan for nine days, eating, sleeping, and working with disadvantaged children.

Klima at least seemed to have gotten straight. He scored 25 goals in 51 games in 1988–89, earning praise from an ever hopeful Demers. "He has turned his game and his life around," his coach declared.

He hadn't. Klima was arrested for a third drunken driving offense on Memorial Day 1989. He served a 35-day sentence in Oakland County Jail for violating terms of probation. On November 2, 1989, the Wings sent Klima to the Oilers in a blockbuster deal with Joe Murphy and Adam Graves, essentially for Jimmy Carson.

"They had no right to trade me," Klima said three weeks later. "They took me from my home once. Then they took me away again. I defected for this team."

Klima's time in Detroit was marked by promise and problems and Probert, their off-ice woes stealing headlines from the team's on-ice successes. Klima resented being traded, but he won a Cup with the Oilers in 1990, and then played for Tampa Bay, Los Angeles, and Pittsburgh. In January 1999, at age 34, Klima attempted a comeback with the Wings, appearing in 13 games in his final NHL season.

"Since I left Detroit," he said, "I'm always trying to come back."

of what I did," Probert said. "I realized I was wrong in what I did and it was foolish. Right now my concern is to try to get my life back in order and that's what I'm working on."

Probert was sentenced to three months in prison in October. Wings owner Mike Ilitch, Devellano, and Demers appeared on Probert's behalf at the sentencing. Probert began serving the sentence November 7 at a medium-security federal prison in Rochester, Minnesota, that was famously home to televangelist Jim Bakker.

While he was in prison, an immigration judge ordered Probert to be deported after finishing his sentence February 5, 1990.

"I'm not really sure what to expect right now," Probert said as he left prison. "It's real scary at the moment."

When he visited the Wings' dressing room on February 16, it was the first time he had been there since his last game, March 1, 1989, the day before his arrest. Probert, Yzerman noted, "looked great."

As part of his plea deal, Probert segued from prison to a 90-day residency at a Detroit-area halfway house. He granted his first in-depth interview in early March, telling the *Free Press*' Keith Gave that the night he was arrested for smuggling cocaine "it was like I didn't care. It was over. When I look back, I think it's the best thing that ever happened to me. I've had low self-esteem in the past. And from what I've been taught, recovery equals change."

Demers and Devellano, who had been through so much with Probert, were hopeful this time there would be real change. Allowed to remain in the U.S. while his immigration appeal dragged on, Probert was welcomed back to the team and scored a goal in his first game in more than a year when he suited up March 22, 1990. He scored in each of his next two games to end the season with three goals in four games.

The Wings missed the playoffs in 1990 (the last time before their historic 25-season streak that spanned 1991 to 2016) but Probert's seemingly phoenixlike emergence from years of substance abuse and legal troubles balmed the disappointing finish to the season. Probert sounded as if he fully grasped his situation. "I've come to the conclusion that every time I've been in trouble, gone to institutions or jail, it's been because of substances— alcohol or whatever," he told the *Free Press*' Mitch Albom in April. "It's been hard for me to ask for help. I always thought, *I'm Bob, Big Guy Bob, I don't need anybody's help. I'm strong enough.* But I was wrong."

Probert used his time at the halfway house to pass the GED, earning the equivalent of a high school diploma. His daughter Tierney remembered years later how proud Probert had been he had scored 146 on an IQ test.

Probert was serious about living a clean and productive life. "I know I can't afford any slips," he said. "One slip and I could be finished. I've taxed everybody's patience. I'm out of chances."

He and Dani moved in together in 1990. Probert took a summer job at Birmingham Tanning Club, where he had been a customer. It would keep him busy. As the summer cooled toward fall, there were whispers that Probert was drinking again. Wings personnel denied it, saying Probert was tested twice a week for alcohol and other substances.

In the 1990–91 season opener, Probert elbowed Claude Lemieux in the face, pounded Al Stewart, and fought Troy Crowder. Crowder bloodied Probert, opening a cut around his right eye that required 13 stitches. Probert looked stunned at the outcome.

Six days later Probert scored in overtime in the home opener. Fans gave him the loudest ovation of the night. Between travel restrictions (his immigration status was not resolved until December 1992) and injuries, Probert was limited to 55 games in 1990–91. He collected 39 points and 315 penalty minutes. He restored his reputation as the NHL's heavyweight champion with a series of bouts: Probert twice knocked down Chicago's Bob McGill in November and fought the first of 13 career fights with Chicago's Stu Grimson on New Year's Eve. Probert wrestled Grimson to the ground, but Grimson got back up and the two exchanged blows for 40 seconds. Probert avenged the loss to Crowder in January, bringing him to his knees with two big punches.

More importantly, Probert restored trust with teammates and personnel, including Bryan Murray, who had taken over as coach and general manager in 1990. The reward was a stint as an alternate captain. "I think he was proud of it, and he should be, the way he has turned his life around," Murray said.

Probert began the 1991 playoffs with three points in his first two games, but after he decked St. Louis goaltender Vincent Riendeau in Game 2, Probert was suspended for Game 4. The Wings lost the last three games of the seven-game series. It was another disappointing finish, but Probert was a bright spot, and the Wings gave him a three-year contract.

Murray signed Crowder during the off-season, admitting it was "so our tough guy wouldn't have to fight him every game." The Devils asked for

BRUISE BROTHERS

At home, they used to fight over who should clean their apartment. At work, they would study the game roster and figure out who should fight which opponent. Bob Probert and Joe Kocur were Bruise Brothers until they were bloodied brothers, separated after six gory-filled seasons together with the Red Wings.

The Wings traded Kocur to the Rangers in March 1991. On December 17, 1993, Probert and Kocur fought one another, their bout cheered by the 19,875 fans at Joe Louis Arena who scrambled to their feet when a melee broke out during the first-period scuffle. Kocur and Probert said that at first, neither one realized who he was punching.

"It came in the heat of battle, and we'll laugh the next time we talk," Kocur said. "He swung at someone on our team, and I went over to stop him. The next thing I know, he hit me a couple times in the chops. It was fun."

Probert said he didn't realize it was Kocur until he was already swinging away. "At that point," he said, "you can't stop."

Kocur gave Probert a bloody nose but Probert slammed Kocur into the boards, knocking off Kocur's helmet. Linesmen broke up the fight just as Probert got his helmet off. "It was more weird afterward," Kocur said. "It wasn't that weird while we fought."

The Wings drafted Kocur in 1983 in the fifth round, attracted by the physicality he had shown racking up 289 penalty minutes in junior hockey with Saskatoon of the Western Hockey League. "He likes to get the dukes up and fight a little," general manager Jimmy Devellano said.

Kocur played 59 games with the Wings in 1985–86, and was a regular by next season. So was Probert. The Wings weren't winning much in those days, but when Kocur and Probert dropped their gloves, fans got to their feet and cheered. In 1985–86, Kocur amassed 377 penalty minutes, becoming the Wings' all-time single-season leader in penalty minutes. (Probert grabbed the record two years later after his breakout 1987–88 season, when he racked up 398 penalty minutes.)

Kocur began the 1987–88 season in coach Jacques Demers' doghouse after insulting assistant coach Colin Campbell during an annual photograph session. Steve Yzerman noted it meshed with the front office's message that no player was bigger than the team. Kocur, then 22, had just signed a four-year contract in the off-season. He was coming off a nine-goal, 276-penalty minute season in 1986–87. He wasn't the hardest worker on the team, but he was certainly one of the NHL's hardest hitters. The Wings wanted to send a message, but they knew they needed him as part of their revival.

The fights eventually took a toll on Kocur's right hand. In January 1990, he pounded Minnesota's Link Gaetz and the next game fought Winnipeg's Peter Taglianetti. Doctors feared he had injured a tendon. Off the ice, Kocur had been fighting suits by two separate women who had accused him of assault. Both cases were settled out of court.

The Wings dealt Kocur at the 1991 trade deadline in a five-player swap. Teammates lamented the departure of one half of the Bruise Brothers. "Joey literally fought for guys like me and Shawn Burr, always there for this whole team," Steve Yzerman said. "I'll always be grateful for that part of it. I know Joey went through a lot of soreness and problems in his hands just to give us some room on the ice."

It was Yzerman who, in December 1996, suggested to Scotty Bowman that Kocur would add the toughness the team needed after being manhandled in the 1996 Conference finals by Colorado, and the 1995 Stanley Cup Finals by New Jersey. He was in the lineup on January 3, 1997, fought Probert to a lengthy draw and bloodied Cam Russell two days later in Chicago, and helped the Wings win the Stanley Cup that spring.

Probert as compensation, but an arbitrator nixed that exchange. (Another guy who had felt the fury of Probert's fists became a teammate in October 1991, when the Wings acquired Riendeau from the Blues.)

The Probert the team needed and the fans loved was back. Probert reached 20 goals in 1991–92, and his 44 points were the second highest of his career. He picked up 276 penalty minutes. One of the most illustrious rivalries of his fighting career began February 9, 1992, when a New York Rangers scrapper named Tie Domi challenged Probert. Domi, who at 5'8" was dwarfed by Probert, traded punches with him for 45 seconds—Probert nailing Domi with a couple big rights while Domi answered with lefts. As he skated away, Domi derided Probert's heavyweight status, delighting fans at Madison Square Garden by motioning with his hands across his waist, mimicking buckling a belt. Domi happily explained afterward that it was a World Wrestling Federation move. "When I saw the blood," he said, "I was kind of happy."

Probert called Domi "a little dummy." Anticipation built for a rematch at the Joe in March (tickets were going for as much as $125), but Domi missed the game because of a knee injury.

Never mind; by then the Wings were focused on the playoffs. In 1991–92 they had five 30-goal scorers and a rookie defenseman named Nicklas Lidstrom. They won 43 games and finished first in their conference. The Wings rallied from a 3–1 deficit to beat Minnesota in the first round of the playoffs but were swept by Chicago in Round 2. Probert did his part: seven points, 28 penalty minutes in 11 playoff games.

His slow start to the 1992–93 season was brushed aside as hype greeted a December 2 rematch with Domi. Probert wanted to get it out of the way and goaded Domi on the opening shift at Madison Square Garden. Domi dropped his gloves but landed few blows, unable to do much as Probert grabbed Domi and pounded him. When Probert tired of using his right fist, he switched to his left. Domi played to the crowd as he skated to the penalty box, but Yzerman played it to the hilt from the Wings' bench, mocking Domi by mimicking his championship belt taunt.

The Garden party was a highlight during an otherwise forgettable season for Probert. He didn't play with the same energy, the same confidence. During a game late in the season at Chicago, he turned the other cheek when Chris Chelios cross-checked and slashed him. Probert was quiet in the seven-game, first-round loss to Toronto, offering a mere three assists. By fall he found himself playing under a new Wings coach in Scotty Bowman.

The hard miles Probert had put on his body were catching up. There was a broken tailbone. Then a sprained knee. The points didn't come. Probert had only 7 seven goals and 10 assists in 1993–94. But he had one of his more memorable bouts when he traded punches with Pittsburgh's Marty McSorley on February 4, 1994. About 35 seconds into their marathon melee, McSorley's jersey came off. A minute in, the two were still throwing haymakers. Officials tried to intervene, but the blows kept coming. "It's the best fight I've ever seen," teammate Ray Sheppard said afterward. "They were throwing punches to kill each other."

The pugilists clocked in around 1 minute, 40 seconds. "It's one of the longest ones I've ever had," Probert said that night. "It was the most tired I've ever been after a fight."

He was fighting a different fight off the ice. In April it emerged that Probert was drinking again when he was spotted at a gathering in downtown Detroit that included his wife, Dani, who was expecting their first child.

In what would be the last chapter in his Wings career, Probert sputtered through the seven games it took the San Jose Sharks to upset the Wings in the first round of the 1994 playoffs. Alcohol once again had a hold of him. On July 15, Probert got drunk, hopped on his Harley-Davidson motorcycle, crashed into a car, and catapulted through an intersection, landing on its one slice of grass. He suffered cuts, bruises, and a separated shoulder. Witnesses told police that Probert was speeding and weaving through traffic when he hit another car. At North Oakland General Hospital, doctors called police. A blood sample was taken. A report released in August revealed that Probert had a blood-alcohol content three times the legal limit, and that he had threatened police and hospital emergency room workers, yelling, "When I get out of here, I'm going to hunt you down and kill you." He also tested positive for cocaine.

Probert was 29 years old and the Wings had had enough. After countless treatment centers and coddling and encouragement, they severed ties with Probert on July 19. "Through both adversity and favorable times, we have done our utmost to help Bob and to do what we felt was in his and the team's best interests," Devellano, now senior vice president, said in a statement. "This is another of those times. We appreciate his contributions to the Detroit Red Wings. We wish him the best."

In an interview from his home in Florida, Devellano told Keith Gave that "in my 12 years with the Red Wings organization, myself, the coaches, the ownership, we've never spent more time on one player and his issues and problems than we have on Bob Probert.'

The *Free Press* headline read: PARTY'S OVER. At least it was in Detroit. Three days after the Wings washed their hands of him, Probert was in Chicago, inking a four-year, $6.6 million deal. Later in the summer Probert faced trial in Dallas on charges he assaulted a woman in a bar the previous December and resisted arrest. A police report stated Probert had been drinking when the altercation took place around 2:30 AM on December 27. Police ended up resorting to Mace to subdue him. Teammate Darren McCarty posted Probert's $200 bond.

The NHL forced Probert to sit out an entire season because of substance abuse. He then spent seven seasons with the Blackhawks. Desperate to prolong his career, he turned to steroids. There were more incidents with police after he retired in 2002: resisting arrest in Delray Beach, Florida, in June 2004. "He was so combative in our jail we didn't take a booking photo because we didn't want to struggle with him again and out of handcuffs," a police spokesman said at the time. Probert listed his alias as "The Bad One" on booking documents. That was the day before his 39th birthday. A few weeks after his 40th birthday, Probert was charged with assaulting an officer after his wife called police to their lakefront house. He had been drinking all night.

Through it all, he remained beloved in Detroit. When he appeared at Steve Yzerman's retirement ceremony on January 2, 2007, at Joe Louis Arena, fans gave Probert a thunderous ovation. "It just shows they're just true fans here," Probert said.

When he was clean, Probert showed what a good person he wanted to be, what a doting father he was. One of the most touching scenes in the *Tough Guy* documentary is near the end, when Dani details her husband's nighttime routine. Probert would go room to room saying goodnight to daughters Brogan, Tierney, and Declyn and son Jack. "Goodnight Brog-ita Chiquita banana, and he'd give her a kiss," Dani said. "Then he would go to T-rose, or Tee-tee-lee, I love you and a kiss goodnight. And then into Declyn's room with his duck call. 'I love you.' The last one would always be, 'Jack, my boy, I love you and good night.'"

Probert died of a heart attack July 5, 2010, one month after his 45th birthday and four days after his and Dani's 17th wedding anniversary. He was posthumously diagnosed with an enlarged heart and with chronic traumatic encephalopathy (CTE), a degenerative disease caused by repeated blows to the head. On April 9, 2017, Probert's family, with assistance from Kocur and Chelios, spread some his ashes in the penalty box after the final game at the Joe. Probert had made the arena, named after one of the greatest heavyweight boxers, his home, electrifying fans through thrilling, turbulent times.

25

OZZY

Nearly four years had passed since he left—years he later recognized were significant to his growth as a person and as a goaltender. But as he approached the meeting with his longtime friend and former boss, all Chris Osgood cared about was his heart.

Osgood spent the first, best, and last parts of his 17-season NHL career with the Red Wings. He won his first Stanley Cup backing up Mike Vernon in 1997, his second Cup as the team's starter in 1998, and his third as reliever-turned-starter in 2008. He missed out on the Wings' 2002 Stanley Cup because they had jettisoned him the summer before, putting him on waivers because he was expendable after general manager Ken Holland traded for Dominik Hasek.

"It was crushing when I had to leave," Osgood said in a 2019 interview. "I was always conflicted because I thought I could stay there with Dom. I wished I could have stayed, but looking back it was better I left. It made me better. But having a personal relationship with Kenny and knowing in the back of my mind that I would be back one day helped with that."

That day came in the summer of 2005, as the NHL prepared to emerge from a labor dispute that had wiped out an entire season. The two men, 17 years apart in age but with a relationship that stretched back before the Wings drafted Osgood at 54th overall in 1991, shared the same intention. "I met Ken at this restaurant or lounge on Haggerty Road and he wrote down some numbers," Osgood remembered. "The salary cap, we knew it was coming. Basically he wrote out a contract on a napkin. It didn't matter to me how much I would be making or how many years, I just wanted to come back to Detroit."

It was where his heart was—where he had met his wife, Jenna, where he had celebrated the greatest moments of his career. The Cups. Scoring a goal. Fighting Patrick Roy—which, back in the late 1990s and early aughts, was pretty much mandatory for a Wings goaltender. It was where Osgood had built lifelong friendships, where he had the most fun, where he faked ticket requests for teammates and tinkered with helmets and tied one assistant coach's shoelaces to a stool—in front of Scotty Bowman.

"Dave Lewis always wore running shoes on the bench, but he wouldn't do up the laces," Kirk Maltby said in a 2019 interview. "There was one game, Ozzy was sitting there and he tied the laces around the base of the stool. So when Lewie went to walk away, he was dragging the stool. And he had Scotty Bowman right behind him."

Osgood won 23 games as rookie in 1993–94, but the lasting memory of that season came in Game 7 of the first-round playoff series against the San Jose Sharks. The score was 2–2 late in the third period when Osgood skated from his crease to chase a loose puck. He tried to clear the puck—only to have it land on the stick of Sharks forward Jamie Baker. Baker scored, the Wings lost, and Osgood, 21 at the time, wept as he spoke to reporters afterward at his stall.

The Wings brought in Mike Vernon, a veteran goaltender who had won a Cup, but Osgood remained a significant asset and retained his status as the guy who ultimately would be a big part of their future. After the Wings were swept in the 1995 Stanley Cup Finals—with Vernon in goal—Osgood started 47 games in 1995–96. He led the NHL with 39 victories and a 2.17 goals-against average, and was runner-up to Jim Carey for the 1996 Vezina Trophy. On March 6, 1996, he became just the second goaltender in NHL history to score a goal, in a game against the Hartford Whalers. Osgood played 15 games in the playoffs, including the Western Conference finals against Colorado. Osgood finished 8–7 with a 2.12 goals-against average and .898 save percentage.

Osgood played 47 games in 1996–97, but Scotty Bowman opted to go with Vernon in the playoffs. The Wings won the Cup, and Vernon was awarded the Conn Smythe Trophy as MVP of the playoffs. Holland, however, had seen enough in Osgood to risk trading Vernon in the summer of 1997.

It was an emotional time for the team and the city, as the exultation over ending a 42-year Stanley Cup drought had ended six days later when a limousine carrying defensemen Vladimir Konstantinov and Slava Fetisov and masseur Sergei Mnatsakanov crashed into a tree on Woodward Avenue in Birmingham. The accident ended Konstantinov's and Mnatsakanov's careers.

The Wings entered the 1997–98 season under intense scrutiny. They were the defending champions, one of their top defensemen had been struck by tragedy, and their playoff MVP had been traded. They managed to emerge with a 44–23–15 record, finishing third in the NHL behind Dallas and New Jersey. Osgood started 64 games and went 33–20–11 with a 2.21 GAA and .913 save percentage. Well entrenched in the Colorado rivalry, Osgood fought Roy on April 1, 1998, and afterward he took a good-natured jab at his predecessor. Roy, Osgood said, "is a lot weaker than Vernie said he was."

Roy, who had fought Vernon in the infamous March 26, 1997, game, challenged Osgood with just over seven minutes to play. "I had no intention to fight with Osgood, but when he came to the middle of the ice, what the heck," Roy said. "My glove was already on the net before I went, because I didn't want to make the same mistake I did last year."

Osgood shook off his gloves, unsnapped his helmet, and put up his fists as deafening cheers of "Ozzy! Ozzy! Ozzy!" reverberated from the stands. Roy landed the first punch, a nice right, but Osgood responded with several left hooks, and, once rid of his jersey, battered Roy until he lost his balance by the Detroit bench.

"It was Roy trying to show up Ozzy," Kris Draper said. "I think he underestimated Ozzy. Ozzy stood up for himself and did a great job."

The Wings rolled into the playoffs. Osgood relied on the experience he had gained from the Sharks series in '94 and from the 15 playoff games he had played in '96.

"There was a lot of pressure," he said in 2019. "Vernie had won the Conn Smythe. I was grateful that Ken Holland gave me the opportunity to play. There's not a lot of times you trade the Conn Smythe [recipient] the year he wins it. So that was a responsibility I took real seriously. I was never nervous because I had played in the playoffs. I had had big wins and tough defeats. I was just trying to make the most of a great opportunity."

The Phoenix Coyotes were dispatched in six games in Round 1. The Blues were gone after six games in Round 2. The Wings led three games to one going into Game 5 of the Western Conference finals against Dallas. The Wings were minutes from clinching when Guy Carbonneau scored with 1:25 to play in regulation. Forty seconds into overtime, Osgood let in a terrible goal. Jamie Langenbrunner fired a shot from the red line that slid past Nicklas Lidstrom and bounced off Osgood's stick. Game over.

Outsiders wondered whether Osgood could recover. Insiders didn't give it a thought. "In my career, I don't think I've played with anyone that could let something bad roll off his back so quickly," Kirk Maltby said in

2019. "Like the Langenbrunner goal in the playoffs in Dallas—he came back and pitched a shutout the next game back at the Joe to close it out. Ozzy never lost track of enjoying playing the game. I think that's why he could let go of a bad goal or bad game, because he didn't get caught up in that moment. And it makes a difference to a team—when you know you have a goalie back there that if he gives up a bad goal, there's a real good chance he is going to shut the door after that—that's a big advantage."

The Wings closed out the series with a 2–0 victory in Game 6, then swept their way to another Stanley Cup, this time against the Washington Capitals. On the eve of Game 4, Steve Yzerman was asked who would have his vote as the MVP. His answer was Osgood. "He has had so much attention focused on him," Yzerman explained.

Instead, it was Yzerman who ended up with the Conn Smythe Trophy. But Osgood had silenced doubters, had come through with 30 saves as the Capitals tried to stave off elimination only to see the Wings win Game 4 4–1. His dad, John Osgood, was among those cheering on Osgood at the MCI Center. "He called me almost every single night of the playoffs and he talked and I mostly listened," John Osgood said. "He got out a lot of frustration."

Osgood was 28 when the Wings put him on waivers after numerous attempts to trade him went nowhere. Osgood spent nearly two seasons with the New York Islanders before being traded to St. Louis on March 11, 2003. By the summer of 2005, he was a free agent. The Wings, meanwhile, needed a veteran goaltender; the only guy they had in the fold was Manny Legace. Nikolai Khabibulin was the biggest name on the free-agent market, but the Wings were wary after the Curtis Joseph experiment had gone so poorly. (Joseph had been brought in to replace Hasek after he retired in 2002; even before Hasek decided to come back a year later, the Wings had soured on Joseph.)

The next summer, the Wings re-signed Osgood—and Hasek. The two worked together for a pair of seasons. The same temperament that served Osgood so well when he let in a bad goal made him an ideal fit with Hasek. In 2007–08, coach Mike Babcock alternated the two in starts. Hasek described his relationship with Osgood, whom he had known since he was a teenager, as "the best I have had with another goalie."

Hasek went into Round 1 against Nashville as the starter, but it was Osgood who emerged from the series as the starter, replacing Hasek in

Game 4 after Hasek had allowed three through one and a half periods. On June 4, Osgood hoisted the Stanley Cup for the third time.

"I wasn't supposed to play," he said. "But I never doubted myself, I never looked on myself as the backup, because I knew behind the scenes what I was doing to get better. I'll never give up until I'm done with my last game in Detroit. I'll always give it my all and that's the way I approach it. I always try to get better and I never give up, and that's why I'm here."

Osgood recorded his 400th career victory on December 27, 2010, in a game against Colorado. He was the 10th goaltender in NHL history to reach the milestone. In January he underwent sports hernia surgery that ended his season. In the summer, he announced his retirement. He worked briefly for the Wings as a mentor to their goaltending prospects, but in 2013 started working as a studio analyst for Fox Sports Detroit.

Osgood had grown up near Edmonton, Alberta, watching the Oilers. He played junior hockey in Medicine Hat, Alberta. It was Holland who scouted Osgood, but their relationship went beyond scout and player. They played for the same ball-hockey team in the off-season. Osgood was a forward, Holland played defense.

"He was a competitive ball-hockey player," Holland recalled. "He was competitive with everything. Laid back, but very, very driven."

The name of the ball-hockey team was—of course—the Red Wings.

26

SANTA HOMER

Few players in Red Wings history have delighted and surprised quite like Tomas Holmstrom. He and Nicklas Lidstrom were best friends, their careers with the Wings overlapping by 15 seasons, but the two Swedes were hockey's odd couple. Lidstrom was a calm superstar who made everything look effortless; Holmstrom was an emotional grinder who scrapped every shift.

To his North American teammates, Holmstrom was an inventor of language, a conduit to Santa Claus, and the rare player who could score more often with his back to the net than facing it; to referees he was a rule straddler; to opponents he was frustration wrapped in tenacity.

In 1994, the NHL entry draft dragged on for 11 rounds (it dropped to seven rounds in 2005), and as the 10th round drew to a close, the Wings selected Holmstrom at 257th overall. He was nothing more than a footnote after the June 28–29 event at the Hartford Civic Center in Connecticut, relegated to a "who knows" behind the excitement team management bestowed upon Russian defenseman Yan Golubovsky, who was drafted at 23rd overall, and forward Mathieu Dandenault, who was picked at 49th. The Wings left the draft with 10 players; only Golubovsky, Dandenault, and, yes, Holmstrom made it to the NHL. Golubovsky turned out to be a dud; he appeared in 56 games over four seasons before washing out of the league. Dandenault was converted to a defenseman by Scotty Bowman and helped the Wings win three Stanley Cups before joining Montreal, finishing with 868 career games.

Holmstrom's arc was memorable from the start. He came to the Wings in 1996 with two reputations: One, he was known as "Demolition Man" for his ability to agitate opponents, and two, he was apparently the only player out of Sweden who couldn't skate. His stride was awkward and he had no acceleration. Years later, Kris Draper would say, "I hated his skating. He hated his skating."

Holmstrom wore No. 15 his first season, 1996–97, but gave it up a year later when the Wings acquired veteran Dmitri Mironov. As Holmstrom searched for a new number, Bowman joked he should wear No. 98 because it'd be the year he'd return to Sweden. That was an astronomical mistake.

Holmstrom played in the NHL for 15 seasons. When he returned to Sweden in 2013, he'd been a part of four Stanley Cups, including the 2002 team, on which he was a part of one of the best fourth lines ever, skating next to future Hockey Hall of Fame members Igor Lariornov and Luc Robitaille. Holmstrom posted 530 points in 1,026 games. He scored 243 goals, many of them deflections that showcased his hand-eye coordination. He posted 97 points in 180 playoff games, the latter ranking fourth in team history.

Bowman, whose No. 98 joke is part of Wings lore, lavished praise upon his former player. "He never complained," Bowman said. "He was a terrific player because he accepted his role. That's why he's going to go down as such a solid player. There weren't many guys tougher than him that I ever had that could play. If he missed a game, I knew he was really badly injured."

Holmstrom wore extra padding to offset the hacks and whacks of angry opponents; notable ones who tried to dismember him included goaltender Ed Belfour and defenseman Chris Pronger. By the end of his career, Holmstrom didn't have any ligament left in in one of his knees. It was Bowman who encouraged Holmstrom, a thickly built six-footer, to be a pest without taking penalties.

There were others who played in front of the net but none more masterfully during Holmstrom's tenure. He was so good at corralling or tipping pucks that Lidstrom would purposely shoot just wide at home games to take advantage of the Joe's famously giving end boards, knowing Holmstrom would be there to finish the play. "He scored the tough goals, learned how to play in the crease and just outside the crease, and didn't lose many goals that way," Bowman said.

Officials would grow exasperated trying to determine whether Holmstrom violated a goaltender's space (this was before video replay). Lidstrom joked he'd have a lot more goals were it not for Holmstrom "stealing them" with his penchant for tip-ins. Were the NHL to track goals scored by a player with his back to the net, Holmstrom would be among the leaders.

"He basically created a role in this league standing in front of the net and just taking a beating, night in and night out, and he became really good at it," Henrik Zetterberg said. The two were also Olympic teammates in 2002 and 2006, winning gold at the Turin Games. Holmstrom was selected again in 2010, but was unable to play because of a knee injury.

Wherever he played, opponents shoved and poked him without getting anywhere. Holmstrom heeded Bowman's advice: aggravate, but do not retaliate. "As a hockey player, he was a hard worker, worked

Tomas Holmstrom screens Nashville goaltender Chris Mason, November 7, 2007. (Julian H. Gonzalez)

harder than anybody," Niklas Kronwall said. "The beating he took over the years—it's pretty unbelievable what he's been able to accomplish. He basically made sure that there was a new role on everybody's team with what he did in front of the net on the power play, and even in five-on-five situations, it really created more jobs for more people."

On February 10, 2011, Holmstrom played his 1,000th game in a Wings uniform, joining an elite group that included Gordie Howe, Alex Delvecchio, Steve Yzerman, Lidstrom, and Draper. A couple days later, teammates surprised Holmstrom after a practice with a snowmobile. It was a nod to Holmstrom's hometown of Pitea, located in the northernmost county of Sweden. Teammates, especially Draper, used to figure it was close enough to ask whether Holmstrom could pass Christmas lists on to Santa Claus. Holmstrom gleefully took the snowmobile for a spin around the ice on Joe Louis Arena.

How much better could his story get? After all, he was a Swedish forward who had been drafted even though he wasn't a scorer, playmaker, defender, or skater. "The interesting thing for me, with Homer, is—not a very good skater, but he was the quickest guy from the net front to the corner, back to the net front, that I've ever coached," coach Mike Babcock said. "He competed to get to his spot. A great, great, great teammate, great man. Very, very ultracompetitive."

When Babcock needed a winger to play with Zetterberg and Pavel Datsyuk, Holmstrom got the nod because he'd track down the puck, get it to one of his standout linemates (just as he once had for Robitaille and Larionov), and go to the net. Mission accomplished.

Holmstrom's last season was 2011–12, the same as Lidstrom, though Holmstrom did not officially announce his retirement until January 2013, following the labor dispute that lasted through the fall of 2012. His news conference at the Joe spanned 15 of the funniest minutes ever spoken by a player who'd gained a reputation for speaking "Swenglish," delighting Swedish and North American teammates alike.

Holmstrom thanked his dad for building him a rink when he was six because, as Holmstrom recalled his dad saying, "we need to work on your skating." There was a shout-out to scout Hakan Andersson for recommending him to management at the 1994 draft: "Good job, Hakan, for doing that." There was a deep appreciation for Lidstrom and the carpooling the two shared: "I didn't know he was going to be such a good friend. All the car rides we took over 15 years, I can't remember how much we talked. Maybe I was doing all the talking. He is a good listener, for sure." On and on Holmstrom cracked, suggesting teammate Johan Franzen ate too much on planes. Current and former teammates watched and laughed. The farewell, Kirk Maltby noted, "summed up the kind of person Homer is. He's a very funny guy. Even though [it's been] 15 years and he still doesn't have the English language down, that's part of his character."

"Homer didn't even realize that he'd throw something out there and loosen up the whole atmosphere," Draper said. "That's the beauty of it. Every day, sometimes twice a day, you'd get it in the morning and at the game. That's why he was so popular with his teammates."

The humor, the ability to laugh at himself, was what charmed those around Holmstrom just as much as how a 10th-round pick surprised everyone by sticking around for 1,000 games.

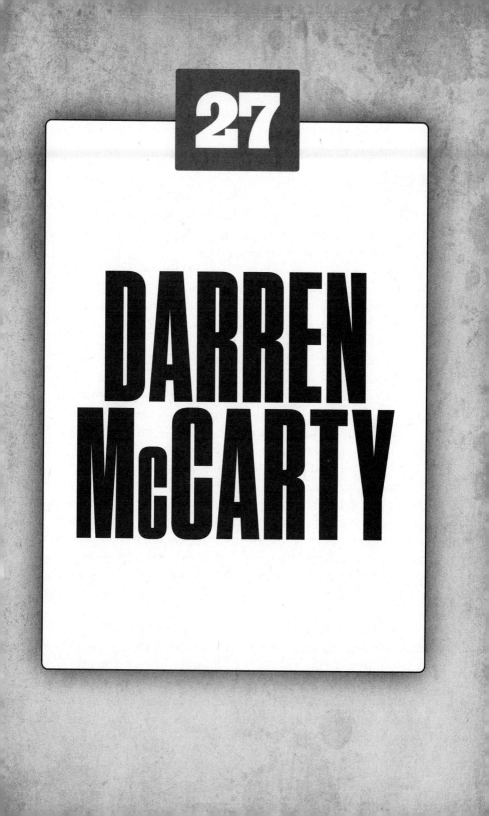

27

DARREN McCARTY

Teammates used to joke Darren McCarty never met a mike he didn't like. Chris Osgood once suggested McCarty purchased a karaoke machine just so he could hear the sound of his voice. McCarty's outsize personality was an attention grabber that was matched by the performances he turned in on the ice.

"He was a guy that made himself a player by persevering," Scotty Bowman said in 2019. "Those kind of guys are worth their weight in gold. For a big man he had a very good amount of hockey sense. It sounds corny, but some guys know how to play. He had a high IQ, because he was not a good skater."

The Wings drafted McCarty at 46th overall in 1992. He spent 1992–93 with the Adirondack Red Wings in the American Hockey League. He played 67 games with the Wings in 1993–94, in what was Bob Probert's final season in Detroit.. When the Wings parted ways with Probert that summer (he crashed his motorcycle while under the influence in July), McCarty knew he had an opening to grab a bigger role.

"A lot of people think it's a tough onus, trying to fill his shoes," McCarty told the *Detroit Free Press* in 1994. "But if I can stick a few toes in those shoes, I'll be doing my job. I can only play 100 percent and try my best as a hockey player and make sure no one gets taken advantage of. I take pride in my game. My main thing is to go out and play physical and take the body and make some plays and maybe bang some in the net. But obviously, I know that if something happens to anybody on our team that somebody has to step in. I'm fortunate to be blessed to be able to handle myself."

McCarty handled himself all right, but also he cut easily. By the end of his third NHL season, his face was a mess of scars and stitches. He liked to tell the story of how, when he was 11, he was hit between the eyes with a baseball bat. His buddy puked, but McCarty just stuck one of his fingers into the bloody mess. "I could feel the bone," he would say. "It didn't knock me out or anything."

McCarty was tough, but during the 1996 off-season, he faced a battle that even a swift punch couldn't knock out. McCarty spent part of the summer as an outpatient at Maplegrove Center for Chemical Dependency in West Bloomfield, Michigan. "If I didn't pass out, I wouldn't stop drinking," McCarty said that September. "I realized I've had a problem for the past few years.... But I wasn't willing to accept it."

McCarty's decision to take charge of his life came after the birth of his son, Griffin, and as McCarty came to terms with his father, Craig, who was battling multiple myeloma, an incurable form of cancer. Darren established the McCarty Cancer Foundation in his father's honor, raising money for cancer research. Craig McCarty passed away in 1999.

Just 24 years old in fall 1996, Darren had made strides in his personal life, and professionally, he was going off a career-best season of 15 goals. He was respected for his physicality and his perseverance. "He had the rare combination of someone could be extremely physical and go to the hard areas and fight, and he could score," Kirk Maltby said of his former Grind Line mate in 2019. "Mac didn't have to fight, but he could and would stand up for his teammates. And at the end of the day he'd be out on the ice in a game where he'd get the big goal.

"I remember talking to him soon after I got traded there. When he broke into pros, he had really worked on a lot of things—his hands and puck handling and skating—to make his skill set better. He was a hard worker and had a great deal of determination to make it in the NHL and be effective."

McCarty enjoyed a career season in 1996–97, scoring 19 goals and tallying 49 points. The other side of him—the protector—stepped forward on March 26, 1997, and stepped straight into local folklore.

Ten months had passed since Claude Lemieux hit Kris Draper from behind in Game 6 of the Western Conference finals, leaving Draper with a shattered, bloodied face. When the Avalanche came to Joe Louis Arena, McCarty took advantage of Igor Larionov and Peter Forsberg jostling and went after Lemieux. As McCarty pulled away from a linesman, fans jumped their feet. McCarty coldcocked Lemieux and pummeled him as he cowered on the ice. Fans cheered and hollered.

They jumped to their feet again in overtime when McCarty ripped a slap shot that sank into defending champion Colorado's net. "I don't think it could happen to a better guy," Draper said afterward.

It was the start of one of the best springs of McCarty's life. On April 1, 1997, he turned 25. The parking lot crew at Joe Louis Arena sent him a birthday cake decorated with a pair of boxing gloves. While McCarty admired it, Martin Lapointe and Joe Kocur blindsided him with towels full of shaving cream. Osgood got in his shot from his locker. "You know what he bought himself for his birthday?" Osgood said to a reporter. "One of those karaoke machines and a recorder thing—so he can interview himself."

Teammates loved ribbing McCarty. "We'd always say he never met a mike he didn't like," Maltby said. "He was great with fans, he was great with guys who had kids around. He wasn't a showboat but he had fun with it. He lived in the moment."

McCarty didn't lack for microphones during the '97 playoffs. His line with Draper and Maltby, the Grind Line, was a huge hit. They scored timely goals and aggravated opponents. They were so popular they spawned T-shirts and bobbleheads. "Mac and I did a commercial for the bobbleheads when they were the big thing coming out," Maltby recalled in 2019. "There was one time we were supposed to have a bite of pizza and I think Mac ate a whole pizza by himself—after take after take after take. He never spit it out. He just kept eating pizza. We were like, 'Mac, you're not going to be able to move.'"

McCarty showed off a sweet move during the highlight goal of his career in the 1997 Stanley Cup Finals against the Philadelphia Flyers. Team personnel delighted when McCarty took a pass from Tomas Sandstrom during the second period of Game 4, strode across the blue line, turned Flyers defenseman Janne Niinimaa inside out, and drove up ice. McCarty cut to the net with the puck on his forehand, drew the Flyers goaltender from the crease, pulled the puck to his backhand, and tucked it behind Ron Hextall. A period later, the Wings celebrated their first Stanley Cup in 42 years.

"He's scored huge goals for us in the playoffs, and now this is the icing on the cake," Draper said. "It's good to see a guy like that get a big goal in a big game. Everyone loves him in the dressing room. You can tell by the reaction when he scored."

Osgood was joking about the karaoke machine, but McCarty really did love a mike. He was the lead singer of a band he named Grinder, and during an October 1998 game at Dallas—not in Detroit, but on the road—its

Darren McCarty, with his son, Griffin, on his shoulders, raises the Stanley Cup, June 13, 2002. (Julian H. Gonzalez)

song "Step Outside" played during warm-ups at Reunion Arena. "That was the most shocking thing I ever heard," Osgood said. "I don't even know where they would get it from."

Teammates crowded around McCarty. "The guys were like, 'What the hell! Is that you?' And I was like, 'Um, well, yeah.' Of course, I took some heat for it," McCarty said.

Grinder was formed to raise money for the medical treatment of Vladimir Konstantinov and Sergei Mnatsakanov. But fans wanted more, and so McCarty became a local rock star, performing in sold-out shows in the metro Detroit. McCarty likened being on stage to being on ice. "It's like scoring a big goal or winning the game," he said. "It's a huge rush. You do something that you've never done before, and it's a huge adrenaline rush that way."

McCarty added a second Cup in 1998. Then in 2002, he experienced one of the biggest adrenaline rushes of his career. On May 18, McCarty recorded his first and only hat trick. It was a natural one, and it came in the playoffs during the third period of Game 1 of the Western Conference finals against Colorado. McCarty scored on Patrick Roy to pull the Wings ahead 3–2 at 1:18 in the third period. When he buried a slap shot at 12:44, fans jumped up and cheered. A lone octopus landed on the ice. When McCarty converted Maltby's rebound at 15:55, fans erupted in a frenzy. Hats flew. Octopi flew.

"It's a wonderful effort from a guy that gives his all every game," Bowman said afterward. "They were all great goals against one of the greatest goaltenders who ever played the game. There wasn't anything lucky about any of them."

McCarty had scored only five goals all season, and none to that point in the playoffs. Suddenly he had an armful of hats, if he wanted them. "You've all read the Bible and heard of the apocalypse?'" McCarty asked, grinning. "It's my first hat trick. It's huge. But the bottom line is, you take the win first."

McCarty was limited to 43 games in 2003–04 and tallied just 11 points. When the NHL emerged from an ugly labor dispute in 2005 with a salary cap, the Wings bought out McCarty's contract, rendering him an unrestricted free agent. McCarty signed with the Calgary Flames, but endured a tough couple years—divorce, bankruptcy. His NHL career appeared over after he failed to score a point in 32 games with the Flames in 2006–07. McCarty reached out to Draper, who pledged to help his old friend. He offered him a chance to play for the Flint Generals, then an International Hockey League team partially owned by Draper. McCarty played 11 games for the Generals.

While McCarty tried to reboot his hockey career, the Wings tried to boost their Stanley Cup chances. A string of disappointments followed the 2002 title—it wasn't until 2007 the Wings made it out of the second round again. McCarty's battles with alcohol, marijuana, gambling, money problems, and marriage problems (McCarty had remarried while in Calgary) were well known, but the Wings also knew McCarty as a key member of three Stanley Cup titles. General manager Ken Holland decided McCarty was worth a flier and signed him in February 2008. Injuries kept him from playing until the last three games of the regular season.

McCarty celebrated his 36th birthday on April 1. On June 4, he celebrated his fourth Stanley Cup. He played 17 games in the playoffs, providing grit and experience. He earned a one-year contract with the Wings and split his last season of professional hockey between the Wings and their AHL team in Grand Rapids. McCarty retired in December 2009.

"It meant a lot when he came back," Osgood said in 2019. "He knew what it took to win the Cup."

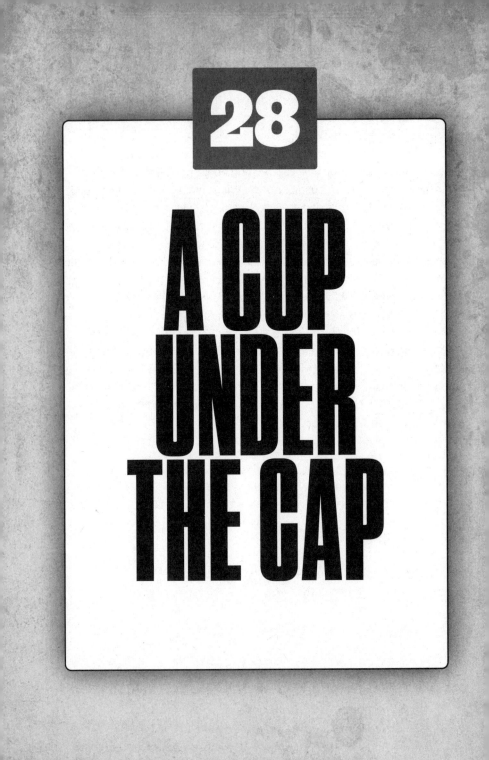

28

A CUP UNDER THE CAP

Chris Osgood remembered Dallas Drake being too rattled to even watch. He had waited his whole career for this moment, and the Red Wings already had squandered one opportunity to close out the Stanley Cup Finals against the Pittsburgh Penguins.

The final round of the NHL playoffs tends to feature really awesome goal highlights, such as Darren McCarty's in 1997, when he spun around a Philadelphia defender and deked Ron Hextall into history. This 2008 edition was notable for its penalty kills, the Wings' resolve on full display.

There were questions whether a club that relied on a generous owner to assemble superstar rosters with a payroll to match could win in the salary cap era. Steve Yzerman had retired, and Brendan Shanahan, Brett Hull, and Luc Robitaille were also gone. The Wings still had Nicklas Lidstrom, though, along with fellow three-Cup champions Kris Draper, Tomas Holmstrom, and Kirk Maltby. Darren McCarty joined the team in the spring. Pavel Datsyuk had been part of the '02 team, and he and Henrik Zetterberg were entering their primes.

The Wings had made it to the Western Conference finals the previous season, and received a significant boost to their 2008 hopes at the trade deadline. On February 26, 2008, general manager Ken Holland acquired defenseman Brad Stuart from the Los Angeles Kings for two draft picks. That gave the Wings Stuart, Lidstrom, Niklas Kronwall, and Brian Rafalski on the back end. Lidstrom and Rafalski formed a finesse pairing: two positionally sound defenders with tremendous offensive punch. Lidstrom led all NHL defensemen with 70 points in 2007–08, and Rafalski was eighth with 55 points.

Stuart and Kronwall were the team's demolition duo. Kronwall was one of the game's fiercest open-ice hitters, and Stuart was a thick-bodied defenseman who made opponents pay for being in the Wings' zone. "They're both big guys, and they like to hit," Chris Osgood said as the Wings embarked on the 2008 playoffs. "They're aggressive and give us something we didn't have last year in the playoffs. Nick and Rafi are very good, but they're not physical, while those two are. So we have a nice mix of defensive pairings."

The Wings entered the playoffs having allowed only 184 goals, the lowest in the league. With Cup champions Osgood and Dominik Hasek in net, goaltending was considered one of the team's biggest strengths.

It didn't look that good four games into the Round 1 series against Nashville. Hasek had allowed 10 goals, and was pulled in Game 4. It ended up being the last playoff game of his Hall of Fame career. From there, Osgood took over. The Wings won Game 5 on an overtime goal from Johan Franzen, then Osgood made 20 saves as the team won the series with a 3–0 victory in Game 6. Lidstrom—whose goal from the red line in Game 3 of the first round in 2002 against Vancouver had turned that

A SQUANDERED OPPORTUNITY

Those who were on the team still carried the disappointment a decade later. In 2009 the Red Wings were within one victory of repeating as Stanley Cup champions. They blew two shots at getting there. "It's something you'll never forget," Kris Draper said in 2019. "The opportunity was right there. We put ourselves up 3–2 in the Stanley Cup Finals and just couldn't find a way to get that one win."

The Wings strutted into Game 6 in Pittsburgh after walloping the Penguins 5–0 at Joe Louis Arena. They weren't the powerhouse team of the previous season, but they still had Nicklas Lidstrom on the back end, had Henrik Zetterberg and Pavel Datsyuk in the lineup, and had Stanley Cup veterans in Draper, Kirk Maltby, and Tomas Holmstrom.

They slunk home after losing 2–1. Chris Osgood pointed to the goaltending of Marc-Andre Fleury, saying "that was the game he stole in the series."

The Wings still had Game 7 at home. But the offense that had scored 15 goals the first five games sputtered. They couldn't score. In fact, their only goal came from one of the least likely sources, defenseman Jonathan Ericsson. The Penguins took the game 2–1 and took away Detroit's Cup.

"You have Game 7 at home, and we couldn't find a way," Draper said. "You never forget how close it was for our team to go back to back. For myself, Malts, Homer, Nick, it was an opportunity to have five Stanley Cup rings. It would be so, so special for us. But in the end, you tip your hat to the Pittsburgh Penguins. They found a way."

series—scored shorthanded midway through the second period on a long-distance shot that bounced into Nashville's net.

The Wings advanced to meet their old nemesis in Round 2, but the rivalry with the Colorado Avalanche was at little more than a simmer by then since the principals were gone. The Wings swept their way through the series, burying the Avalanche 8–2 in Game 4. Johan Franzen tallied his second hat trick in three games to net nine goals for the series, topping Gordie Howe's record of eight goals in a playoff series, set over seven games against Montreal in 1949. "They kind of gave up, I think, after 4–1," Franzen said afterward. "We got a couple of freebies there."

The Wings won the first three games of the Western Conference finals against the Stars. It was Datsyuk's turn to tally a hat trick in Game 3, in Dallas. Zetterberg and Datsyuk combined for six points. "We didn't have much answer for them," Dallas coach Dave Tippett said. "Those two are a rare breed, because they're a line that you look at that you should be checking, but in actual fact they're a checking line."

Datsyuk and Zetterberg scored again in Game 6, but it was Draper who netted the first goal and Drake who helped push the Wings to a 4–1 victory. Drake was part of the Wings' amazing 1989 draft, selected at 116th overall. (Lidstrom was selected at 53, Sergei Fedorov at 74 and Vladimir Konstantinov at 221. Lidstrom, Fedorov, Drake, and Mike Sillinger, selected 11th, all topped 1,000 NHL games.) Drake played 1½ seasons with the Wings before being traded; he spent most of his career with the Arizona franchise and the Blues.

With the salary cap imposed after the 2004–05 lockout, the Wings were looking for inexpensive help in the summer of 2007 and signed Drake to a one-year deal. He was 38 years old and hoping for one last shot at the Stanley Cup. The Wings knew what Drake could do, and saw him as a low-risk, potentially high-reward addition. "He's a good penalty killer, he blocks a ton of shots," said Osgood, who had been teammates with Drake in St. Louis. "He'll put guys in line when he has to—he's not afraid to make a big hit or fight somebody. I've seen him run over quite a few guys pretty hard that came after one of our guys. And he'll do it right away—he doesn't hesitate. He's been suspended a few times for big hits and that's not a bad thing sometimes, to have a guy like that."

The Wings secured a spot in the Stanley Cup Finals on May 19, 2008, besting the Stars in six games. They won two of the first three games against the Penguins headed into Game 4 at Pittsburgh. Jiri Hudler broke a 1–1 tie early in the third period. Then the Wings staged a penalty kill that was the talk of the game. Maltby was called for hooking Adam Hall at 9:36, and while the Wings were killing off that penalty, Andreas Lilja was penalized for interference on Sidney Crosby at 10:10. That gave the Penguins 1:26 with two extra skaters.

Zetterberg shadowed Crosby like a high-noon sun, staying so close to his adversary Crosby was left frustrated and scoreless. At one point, Zetterberg put his stick on Crosby's stick to prevent him getting a shot off. The Wings won 2–1.

The Penguins used a power play during the third overtime in Game 5 to stave off elimination, and the Wings headed back to Pittsburgh. The first period of Game 6 forced another big penalty kill, when the Wings were short two men after Draper ran into Sergei Gonchar from behind 27 seconds after Drake was called for charging. Zetterberg, Lidstrom, and Kronwall—the same trio that killed off the 86-second, two-man Penguins power play in the last minutes of Game 4—limited the Penguins to two slap shots by Evgeni Malkin.

In a 2019 interview, Draper recalled what that moment was like. "We couldn't breathe," he said. "We couldn't talk. Dallas Drake and I, we couldn't believe that both of us were in the penalty box for a 5-on-3. And Henrik Zetterberg goes stick on puck with Sidney Crosby and basically stops a wide-open net that could have put them up early in the game, and who knows what happens after that. That's something I'll never forget."

Draper, Maltby, McCarty, Holmstrom, and Lidstrom hoisted the Stanley Cup for the fourth time that night. Lidstrom, the captain, after the initial lap, passed the Cup to Drake. "Dallas was so nervous the last couple games in the Finals," Osgood said in 2019. "We lost in triple overtime to Pittsburgh and he was retiring that year. The last four or five minutes of the last game, he had his head on the bench. That's when you understand how much it means to people. It was a great feeling to win it. People wondered if we could, but we had a bunch of great guys in the dressing room."

It took 15 seasons and more than 1,000 games, but Drake finally got that Cup. It was a fitting end for a player who began and ended his career with Detroit. And the Cup proved the Wings could win it all despite a salary cap.

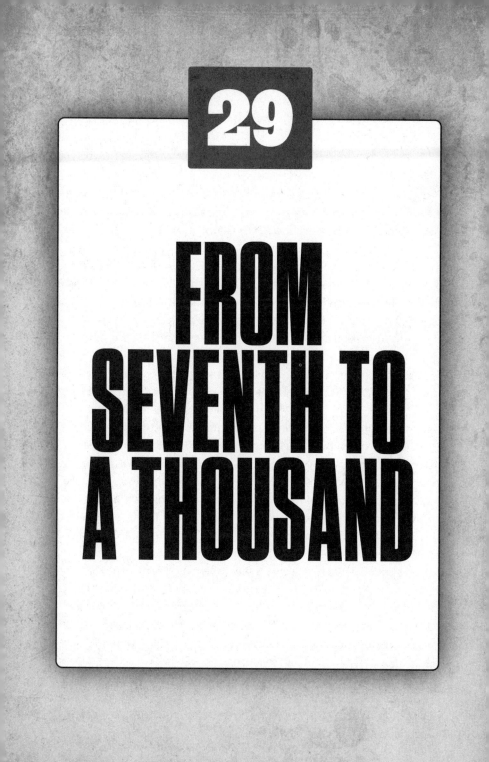

29

FROM SEVENTH TO A THOUSAND

Steve Yzerman noticed the young forward in blue and yellow and knew his name meant something to the Red Wings. The player for Sweden made a nice move on his backhand on a two-on-one. *This guy is good*, Yzerman remembered thinking.

Henrik Zetterberg rose through the Red Wings organization from a seventh-round pick in 1999 to 1,000 games in 2017. A few months after Yzerman noticed Zetterberg at the 2002 Salt Lake Olympics, the Wings invited Zetterberg and fellow Swedish draft pick Niklas Kronwall to Detroit to watch the playoffs. The gist of it was for the prospects to see what it took to succeed in the NHL. Zetterberg took note of the pace, of the physicality, and spent the summer in the gym.

He returned for training camp in September. On October 10, 2002, the day after his 22nd birthday, Zetterberg debuted with the defending Stanley Cup champion Wings in a 6–3 victory in San Jose. Zetterberg had an assist that game, and scored in his third game, on October 13 in Anaheim. He finished sixth on the Wings in scoring with 44 points in his rookie season, holding his own on a team that included Sergei Fedorov, Brett Hull, Brendan Shanahan, Pavel Datsyuk, Igor Larionov, and Luc Robitaille (knee surgery limited Yzerman to 16 games that season). Zetterberg was runner-up to St. Louis' Barret Jackman for the Calder Trophy—and he had good company on the team: Yzerman was runner-up in 1984, Chris Chelios in 1985, Fedorov in 1991, and Lidstrom in 1992.

Zetterberg was a rookie who played with the poise of a veteran. "The thing you could see with Z right away was the way he carried himself," Kris Draper said in a 2019 interview. "The confidence he had when he walked into a room, that was his personality. On the ice, you could really see Z's competitiveness because he was never a great skater, but you could never get the puck off him. That had so much to do with hockey sense and will and determination."

It was Draper who dubbed Zetterberg and Datsyuk the "Euro Twins." They sizzled on ice and clicked off it. Within a couple of seasons, it was clear they were the future of the team.

Zetterberg spent the 2004–05 lockout season playing for his old club in Sweden. The Wings named him an alternate captain in 2005, and he went on to produce career highs with 39 goals and 85 points in 2005–06, almost double the 43 points he produced in 2003–04. Zetterberg returned from the Turin Olympics with a gold medal and also won gold at the 2006 World Championships. Zetterberg was 25 years old. He impressed with his consistency, his work ethic, and his quiet leadership.

Yzerman retired after the 2005–06 season, further pushing Zetterberg and Datsyuk into prominence. Zetterberg led the Wings with 33 goals in '06–07, and his 68 points were second to Datsyuk's 87—though injuries limited Zetterberg to 63 games. Zetterberg contributed 14 points in 18 playoff games in 2007, the first time he advanced to the Western Conference finals.

Zetterberg set a franchise record with a 17-game point streak (13 goals, 14 assists) to open the 2007–08 season. He scored his second career hat trick on December 7 in a 5–0 victory against the Minnesota Wild. He missed five games in December with a lower back injury, an ailment that became an undercurrent for the remainder of his career. By the end of the season, Zetterberg netted a team-high and career-best 43 goals and was second on the team with 92 points—five fewer than Datsyuk. The two were finalists for the Frank J. Selke Trophy for the league's top defensive forward. (Datsyuk won it for the first of three straight years.)

The 2008 playoffs brought the will and determination that made Zetterberg such a standout player to the forefront. That was when those who didn't watch him on a regular basis fully realized his full talent. "He is a Hall of Fame player," Scotty Bowman said in 2017. "He is such a good two-way player. It's so reliable as a coach to have a guy like him, because you could play him against anybody. In 2008, he was going head-to-head against Sidney Crosby. Z was able to neutralize him."

Some of Zetterberg's finest work came in Game 4 of the Finals, when the Penguins had 86 seconds with a two-man advantage. He shadowed Crosby with such relentlessness that Crosby failed to score. The Wings won 2–1. Then Zetterberg did the same during a 93-second two-man Penguins power play in Game 6. "I think the greatest display of Z's will and determination—and I had a great view of it—was in 2008 on the penalty kills against Sidney Crosby," Draper said in 2019. "He was not going to let Sidney Crosby score."

Henrik Zetterberg and Pavel Datsyuk, October 1, 2007. (Julian H. Gonzalez)

Zetterberg scored his 13th goal of the playoffs at 7:36 of the third period of Game 6. It would stand as the championship goal in a 3–2 victory. That night, June 4, 2008, Zetterberg carried the Stanley Cup and the Conn Smythe Trophy, awarded to the MVP of the playoffs, on the strength of a superstar performance that included 27 points, a club record in a single postseason. It was an enormously satisfying moment for Zetterberg, for the franchise, and for the men responsible for making Zetterberg a Wing.

Those men were assistant general manager Jim Nill and chief of European scouting Hakan Andersson, who were in Finland to scout a player named Mattias Weinhandl when Zetterberg caught their attention. "He was always working," Nill said the night of the 2008 championship. "He was real weak, real small, but he was catching our eye, so we marked him down. The rest is history."

On January 28, 2009, the Wings signed Zetterberg to a 12-year, $73 million extension. Before signing, Zetterberg sat down with Yzerman, who gave his young successor sage advice. "I had some understanding of what he was going through and what his feelings were and what not," Yzerman said at the time. "What I just wanted to stress with him was that I thought was important for him—he's that type of player and has that stature—that he should play for one organization his entire career. Actually there were two that I mentioned, the Detroit Red Wings and the Swedish national team. Those are the two jerseys you'll see Henrik play in now. It really creates an incredible legacy for him."

Zetterberg led the Wings back to the Stanley Cup Finals in 2009 with a team-high 24 points in 23 playoff games, but the Wings squandered two chances to close out the series against the Penguins and lost in seven games.

In the prime of his career, Zetterberg was coach Mike Babcock's go-to guy. If a winger was in a slump, Babcock played him with Zetterberg. Zetterberg made Jiri Hudler a better player, made Gustav Nyquist a better player, made Tomas Tatar a better player. In 2015–16, he played with a rookie, Dylan Larkin, and helped him score 23 goals. "He controls the pace of play and, a lot of times, he controls the game itself," Larkin said.

When Lidstrom retired at the end of the 2011–12 season, Zetterberg was the clear choice to become the next captain. The announcement was delayed until January 2013 because of a labor dispute, but the line of

HOW SWEDE IT WAS

The Red Wings famously fielded the Russian Five in the 1990s, when Sergei Fedorov, Igor Larionov, Vyacheslav Kozlov, Slava Fetisov, and Vladimir Konstantinov dazzled with their puck possession game. A decade later, Swedish was the second language in the locker room.

Nicklas Lidstrom, Henrik Zetterberg, Johan Franzen, Niklas Kronwall, Mikael Samuelsson, Andreas Lilja, and Tomas Holmstrom manned the squad that won the Stanley Cup in 2008. It was the fourth championship for Lidstrom and Holmstrom. Zetterberg paced his teammates with 27 points, and he and Franzen tied for the team lead with 13 goals, setting a franchise record for most goals in a single playoff year.

Franzen was in his third season with the Wings, who drafted him at 97th overall in 2004. Teammates called him "Mule" ever since fall 2005, when Franzen, who was 6'4", 220 pounds, caught the attention of Steve Yzerman. "He just skated by me one day during practice in Los Angeles," Yzerman said, "and he was just so big and powerful and I just thought, *That guy is a mule.*" (When Kris Draper played on a line with Franzen and Kirk Maltby in 2007–08, Draper dubbed the big Swede "Shrek." Maltby was "Donkey" and Draper was the self-anointed "Lord Farquaad.")

Franzen's career was derailed by repeated blows to the head that caused him to suffer from post-concussion syndrome, but in his prime, he was a beast. On March 30, 2008, he scored his sixth game-winning goal of the month, breaking Zetterberg and Gordie Howe's record of five. Howe was at the game against Nashville at Joe Louis Arena, the day before his 80th birthday. In a 2008 second-round series against Colorado, Franzen recorded two hat tricks en route to nine goals total, topping Howe's record of eight goals in a single series.

While Franzen was a force to deal with up front, Kronwall patrolled the back end. His knack for open-ice hits became known as a player being "Kronwall-ed." They were all the more remarkable for how unimposing Kronwall looked at 6'0", 190 pounds and a run of injuries that included missing the entire 2007 playoffs because of a fractured sacrum; he broke a leg in 2004 and tore up a knee in 2005. His left knee was in such bad shape he tried stem cell therapy in 2017.

The Wings drafted Kronwall at 29th overall in 2000. He caught the attention of Swedish scout Hakan Andersson while playing for Djurgardens in Sweden's top league. Even as a teenager, Kronwall rattled opponents with monster hits. "Kronwall came in and was still a junior player, and he would hit guys and they would have to be carried off the ice," Andersson said in 2008. "Some of them woke up and said, 'Who did that?' and they'd say, 'Oh, it was that little junior kid over there.' And that was embarrassing for a lot of guys, that a little junior guy could level them. He's always played that way."

Kronwall played 68 games for the team in 2006–07. The 2007–08 season was a spectacular one for Kronwall, who gained Brad Stuart as a partner at the trade deadline and paced all defensemen with 15 points in the playoffs. Teammates razzed Kronwall for his small feet (he wore size 6 skates) and head (they pilfered his favorite Tigers baseball cap during the 2008 run).

Kronwall and Franzen were especially close, rooming together on the road in the '08 playoffs. "He says I like to sleep a lot, but maybe that tells you a little bit about how boring he is to live with," Franzen joked at the time. "He usually tries to read a book or something to build up his image, his smart-guy image."

Kronwall played his first game for the Wings on December 10, 2003, and his 953rd and last on April 6, 2019. He tallied 83 career goals and 349 assists. For 15 seasons Kronwall smote opponents and scored points, his fierceness on ice in contrast with a personality amiable and humble.

succession had been clear for half a decade. "As Stevie's career started coming to an end, Henrik started taking his game to the next level, you knew the transition of the Detroit Red Wings was right there," Draper said in 2019. "You knew Nick was going to be the next captain and then you knew Henrik was going to be the next captain."

Zetterberg led the Wings with 12 points in the 2013 playoffs, when they pushed eventual Stanley Cup champion Chicago to a Game 7 overtime in Round 2. Back problems limited him to 45 games in 2013–14, and he departed the Sochi Olympics after one game because of debilitating pain. Zetterberg flew home on an NHL charter that departed mid-tournament with players who had been eliminated. When Zdeno Chara, a Slovakian defenseman for the Boston Bruins, saw Zetterberg carrying a backpack as he made his way to the airplane, Chara grabbed the bag and carried it for him.

Zetterberg underwent surgery in February 2014 to repair what general manager Ken Holland described as a "floating piece of a disc lodged in a nerve in his back." He returned in time for the tail end of the first-round playoffs, but the Wings lost to Chara's Bruins in five games. Zetterberg had a goal and an assist.

"Many players would have said, wait till next year," Holland said. "Z did what he could to help our team in the playoffs. There is a reason he has accomplished what he has. He's competitive, leads by example. He's got a burning desire for success."

Zetterberg matched a career high with 49 assists in 2014–15, rebounding from back surgery to play in 77 games. On November 6, 2015, he became the eighth player in franchise history to reach 300 goals. He was also the fifth player in Wings history to record 300 goals and 800 points, joining Gordie Howe, Alex Delvecchio, Yzerman, and Fedorov.

On April 9, 2017, Zetterberg became the 54th player in NHL history to log 1,000 games with one franchise. His milestone coincided with the Wings' farewell game at Joe Louis Arena. Zetterberg, then 36 years old, led the team with 68 points in 82 games.

The Wings missed the playoffs in 2017—the first time in 26 seasons—but Zetterberg's accomplishment made the finale at the Joe one to celebrate. The Wings held a ceremony to commemorate the event before the game against the New Jersey Devils, a 4–1 victory. Fittingly, Zetterberg had a goal and an assist.

"From the day that he came into the organization, he was very mature and professional in the way he conducted himself on a daily basis," Yzerman said. "He has special qualities as a leader. He is a tremendous all-around player. From day one, he had all those abilities, which I really admire, because a lot of us had to learn all that stuff. And he knew it as a young man. He has just been a fantastic leader for the team."

The Wings' first season at Little Caesars Arena was Zetterberg's last. He played a third straight 82-game season in 2017–18, producing 56 points. He had figured out how to train after back surgery in 2014, but those 1,000-plus games had taken a toll. Zetterberg announced he was done with his playing career on September 14, 2018, during training camp in Traverse City, Michigan.

Zetterberg was on vacation in Cyprus on June 26, 1999, the day the Wings called his name in the draft with the 210th selection. His parents called him and told him about it. Zetterberg celebrated with his friends, who made him pay for dinner.

"When you come into the league like I did, you don't have that much expectation," Zetterberg said years later. "You are just happy to be here, to get a chance to play. I hoped I'd last for a bit, but I didn't have a thousand games in mind."

His 1,082 games ranked third most among 1999 draft picks, behind Henrik Sedin's 1,330 and Daniel Sedin's 1,306. However, Daniel Sedin was drafted second overall and his brother Henrik third. Zetterberg's 960 career points also ranked third in the '99 draft class behind the Sedin brothers. Zetterberg topped all 1999 draft picks with 120 playoff points and 137 playoff games.

"I've been through all the good things, and some low things, during my career," Zetterberg said. "Being in one organization for the whole time, being named the captain for this organization, I think that's something special."

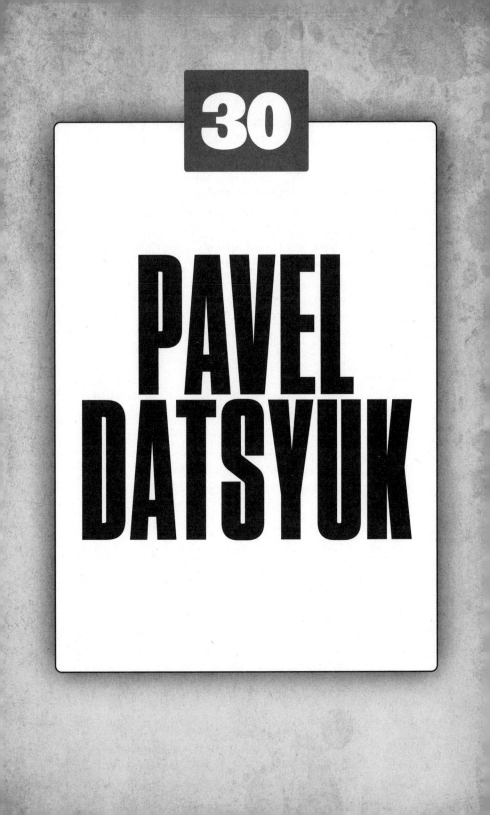

30

PAVEL DATSYUK

Pavel Datsyuk played like an artist—and sometimes spoke like one too. He was 23 years old when he won his first Stanley Cup, capping off an incredible rookie season with one of the greatest hockey teams ever assembled. His joy the night the Wings clinched the 2002 championship was indescribable. He celebrated with teammates and with his then-wife, Svetlana, who was pregnant with a daughter. Datsyuk grabbed his friend, teammate, and translator Max Kuznetsov to convey his emotion.

"He says it is a feeling you cannot explain, like seeing the sun coming up in the morning. He says it's wonderful," Kuznetsov said.

There was no greater compliment to young Datsyuk than the fact Brett Hull wanted him as a linemate. Hull was 37 when he signed with the Wings in the summer of 2001. Given his prowess at scoring goals, Hull figured he'd be on a line with one of the world-class centers the Wings had that year in Steve Yzerman, Sergei Fedorov, and Igor Larionov. "Instead it ended up being one of the greatest kids on Earth," Hull said.

It worked because if Hull was open, Datsyuk would find a way to get him the puck regardless of how many defenders were between them. The third guy on the line—23-year-old Boyd Devereaux—was an ideal fit because he had the speed to chase down the puck. Hull self-effacingly dubbed the trio "Two Kids and a Goat."

All teammates knew about Datsyuk when he arrived in the fall of 2001 was that he was supposed to be a gem for a guy drafted 171st overall. As the amplitude of Datsyuk's talent grew clearer, his NHL genesis story became legend: Hakan Andersson, the Wings' director of European scouting, had noticed Datsyuk while scouting another player in eastern Russia in the summer of 1997. Datsyuk wasn't on anyone's NHL radar. "I was going to a city called Yekaterinburg, where the czar was killed in the early 1900s," Andersson said. "I was going to see a defenseman, Dmitri Kalinin. His team was playing at Yekaterinburg, and there was Pavel—shifty, creative. As the game went on, I saw he was pretty good."

Andersson returned home but couldn't stop thinking about Datsyuk. The Wings caught a break when he didn't make the Russian World Junior team, which greatly limited Datsyuk's exposure to other scouts. It helped, too, that Datsyuk played for a remote team, as travel within Russia in those days was cumbersome.

The Wings had two picks in the sixth round on June 27, 1998, in Buffalo, New York. They used the first one, at 151, on a guy named Adam DeLeeuw. Andersson argued for Datsyuk next. The choice was a credit to Andersson, and a crowning achievement for the Wings. Of the 11 players the team drafted in 1998, the only other player to become a regular in the NHL was defenseman Jiri Fischer (25th overall), whose career ended after he suffered a cardiac episode in November 2005. Datsyuk ranks third all time among 1998 draft picks with 918 points in 953 games; his 0.96 points-per-game average ranks first.

It wasn't just hockey that made Datsyuk so endearing as a rookie. He made up for his lack of English by smiling a lot and relying on Russian teammates as translators. He had an early penchant for fast food and Mountain Dew, *Tom and Jerry* cartoons, and Martin Lawrence movies. "We could tell even before he could speak English that he had a lot of personality," Brendan Shanahan said. "He was a funny kid. You could tell he had a good sense of humor."

His second season began a beautiful friendship as Henrik Zetterberg, a late-round Swedish gem from the 1999 draft, joined the Wings. The two showed such chemistry on and off the ice Kris Draper dubbed them the "Euro Twins."

Datsyuk's role grew even bigger after Fedorov departed in the summer of 2003, leading to a spot in the 2004 All-Star Game. The playoffs were less fun, as the Wings were eliminated in the second round by the Calgary Flames.

After spending the 2004–05 season in the Kontinental Hockey League with Dynamo Moscow while a labor dispute scuttled the entire NHL season, Datsyuk returned to the Wings in September 2005 armed with a two-year deal worth $7.8 million. Datsyuk recorded 87 points in each of those two seasons, and collected two straight Lady Byng Trophies recognizing the gentlemanly style that went hand in hand with his on-ice wizardry.

Datsyuk's importance to the Wings was cemented in April 2007, when he was signed to a seven-year, $46.9 million contract. By the start of the 2007–08 season, many of the superstars from the 2002 team were gone. Hull had left in 2004. Yzerman had retired in 2006 and taken a front-office job. Shanahan was playing for the New York Rangers. Datsyuk and Zetterberg were the new headliners.

"Those two kids can do a lot of magic together," Tomas Holmstrom said.

Datsyuk finished 2007–08 setting a high with 97 points in 82 games, joining Yzerman, Gordie Howe, and Ted Lindsay as the only players in history to lead the Wings in scoring in three straight seasons. Two months later Datsyuk celebrated his second Stanley Cup, producing 23 points in 22 playoff games, including two points in the Cup-clinching game. Later that June, Datsyuk took home a third straight Lady Byng, plus the Selke Trophy.

He matched his 97-point output in 2008–09 and picked up another Lady Byng and the second of three straight Selke trophies, but the playoffs disappointed. The Wings had the chance to become the first team since the 1998 Wings to repeat as Stanley Cup champions, but instead watched the Penguins capture the Cup after a seven-game Finals.

While the four Lady Byng Trophies prove how cleanly Datsyuk played, even as he faced top defenders every game, he delighted teammates with a decidedly un–Lady Byng move on opening night of the 2010–11 season. During a game against Anaheim, Datsyuk held his own as he fought Ducks forward Corey Perry, who had roughly four inches and 15 pounds on him. The Wings played the next night in Chicago, prompting Blackhawks forward Marian Hossa, who'd played for the Wings in 2008–09, to jokingly text Datsyuk not to fight in that game. Datsyuk also scored a goal and had an assist in that opener against the Ducks, earning a Gordie Howe hat trick.

Datsyuk battled injuries for a couple seasons, but he finished the lockout-shortened 2013 season with a team-high 49 points in 47 games. That spring the Wings upset Anaheim in a seven-game series and pushed the Blackhawks to overtime in a second straight Game 7. During the off-season, Datsyuk agreed to a three-year, $22.5 million extension. "He's got tremendous will and determination," general manager Ken Holland said. "I think it's great for the Detroit Red Wings to know we have him in the fold for four more years."

Holland would turn out to be off by one year. The 2013–14 season was a painful one: Datsyuk and Zetterberg battled injuries, each limited to 45 games. Datsyuk played one game in January, two before going to play in the Sochi Olympics (where his Russian hockey team placed fifth), none in March, and six in April leading into the playoffs. The 2014 playoffs run lasted five games before the Bruins eliminated Detroit—though it began promisingly enough when Datsyuk scored in a 1–0 victory to claim Game 1 in Boston. (Datsyuk had five points; no teammate had more than two.) He became a father for the second time between Games 3 and 4 as his second wife, Maria, gave birth to a daughter, Vasilisa, on April 23.

In February 2016 Datsyuk reached 900 career points, only the sixth player in franchise history to do so. He finished the season 47 games shy of 1,000. But that milestone didn't dissuade Datsyuk from deciding he wanted to go home.

Holland tried to convince Datsyuk to play out the year remaining on his contract, but on June 18, 2016, Datsyuk made his decision public. He was a month from his 38th birthday, and he missed the baby girl he'd welcomed in 2002, Elizabeth, who had lived in Russia since he and Svetlana divorced in 2010.

Datsyuk signed a two-year deal to play with SKA St. Petersburg in the Kontinental Hockey League. His first season mirrored his rookie season with the Wings: He and his wife welcomed a child, son Pavel Jr., in February 2017, and that spring Datsyuk helped St. Petersburg win the Gagarin Cup. Moving home enabled Datsyuk to participate in the 2018 Winter Olympics, where Russia won the gold medal in a tournament in which NHL players did not participate. That medal gave Datsyuk membership in the Triple Gold Club, signifying he'd won the Stanley Cup and gold medals at the Olympic Games and World Championships.

Had Datsyuk honored his contract and played for the Wings in 2016–17, he'd almost certainly have been back the following season to see his jersey retired in what would have been the first such ceremony at Little Caesars Arena. There's no question No. 13 belongs in the rafters. Datsyuk earned a place among Red Wings greats, expressing himself to dazzling effect even as a shy rookie.

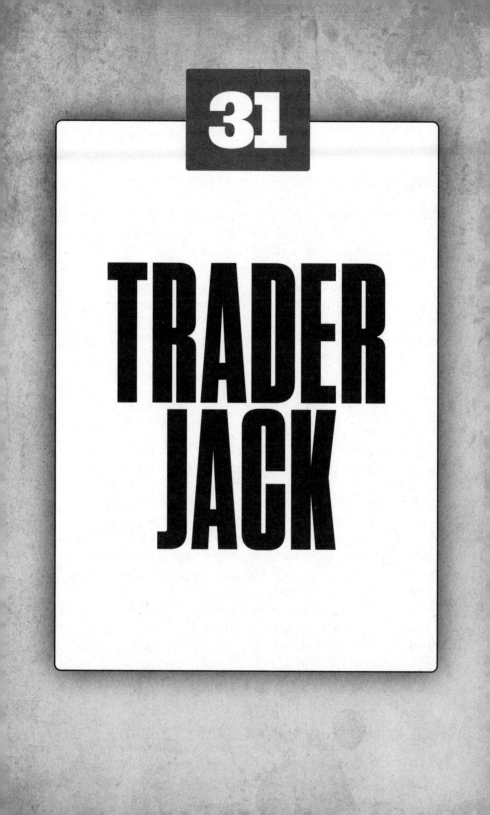

31

TRADER JACK

Jack Adams was revered and reviled during his 35 years with the Red Wings, lauded for crafting championship rosters, lambasted for tearing apart a contender. He was with the franchise in its infancy as the Detroit Cougars, prospered under James E. Norris, answered to Marguerite Norris, and was fired by Bruce Norris.

Adams coached the Wings to their first Stanley Cup in 1936, four years after the Norris family purchased the club. He won two more Cups before stepping down in 1947 to concentrate on his management duties. During his last season behind the bench, Adams coached a rookie who would become the greatest player in franchise history. Gordie Howe was 18 when he made his debut on October 16, 1946.

"Dad was just a farm boy," son Mark Howe said. "Jack as nicely as he could kind of took him under his wing. He knew what he had in Dad. Dad was very impressed. Whenever he had something to say about him, it was always a positive thing."

That would change later in Howe's life, but during his reign with the Wings, few dared point a finger at Adams. He was a 5'9" scrapper who had played 173 NHL games over a 10-year pro career with Toronto and Ottawa—a career that began and ended with winning the Stanley Cup.

Born June 14, 1894, in Fort William, Ontario, John James "Jack" Adams' early hockey days included a stint for the Calumet Miners, a team based in Michigan's Upper Peninsula. His NHL playing career began in 1917 with the Toronto Arenas—the league's inaugural season—and ended in 1927 with the Ottawa Senators. He won a scoring title in 1922–23 (66 points in 23 games) and was inducted as a player into the Hockey Hall of Fame in 1959. Adams was hired to coach and manage the Detroit Cougars for 1927–28, their second season. In 1930, the Cougars were renamed the Falcons. It wasn't until Norris bought the team in 1932 and rechristened it the Red Wings that Adams had the means to succeed.

After failing to make the playoffs three of his first four years with the franchise, the Wings only missed the playoffs twice (in 1935 and 1938) while Adams was coach, and won the Cup again in 1937 and 1943. Adams served as coach from 1927 to 1947, recording 413 victories, 390 losses, and 161 ties. Adams' last season as coach, 1946–47, was Howe's rookie season. The team finished 22–27–11, just good enough to make the four-team playoffs.

Adams was succeeded by Tommy Ivan, who led the Wings to three Cups before being replaced by Jimmy Skinner in 1954. Skinner was a protege of Adams who would go on to serve in multiple roles with the Wings, including as a scout, director of player personnel, and assistant general manager. As general manager, Skinner hung a large oil painting of Adams in his office at Joe Louis Arena. When things were going badly, Skinner would talk to the portrait. (Unfortunately, one of the imprints Adams left on Skinner was the impulse to trade. In December 1981 Skinner sent three former first-round picks in Mike Foligno, Dale McCourt, and Brent Peterson to the Buffalo Sabres for veterans Danny Gare, Jim Schoenfeld, and Derek Smith. Skinner also swapped first-round picks with the Minnesota North Stars, costing the Wings a chance to draft second overall in 1982. Instead the Wings picked 17th.)

Adams won four Cups as general manager, in 1950, '52, '54, and '55. James E. Norris bequeathed control of the team to daughter Marguerite upon his death on December 4, 1952, but she was ousted by her brother Bruce after the 1954–55 season. That benefited Adams, but not the Wings. Marguerite kept Adams' penchant for trading in check; Bruce let Adams have free rein.

Tony Leswick, who had scored the Game 7 overtime goal in the 1954 Cup Finals, was traded with Johnny Wilson, Benny Whoit, and Glen Skov to the Chicago Black Hawks, where James D. Norris (another son of James E. Norris) was in charge. In his book *Mr. Hockey: My Story*, Gordie Howe called the trade "a real Norris brothers special."

There was worse to come. Adams traded Terry Sawchuk—the great goaltender who had backstopped the team to the Cup in 1952, 1954, and 1955—to the Boston Bruins with Vic Stasiuk, who would go on to have a prolific career with the Bruins. The Wings received three players who combined for three goals in 42 games, a goalie who went 0–3, and Warren Godfrey, a steady but unspectacular defenseman.

"To this day, his reasons for blowing up our championship squad defy explanation," Howe wrote. "By the time the smoke cleared, Trader Jack had dealt away half our team."

That included Ted Lindsay, whom Norris wanted gone because of Lindsay's efforts to form a labor association. The last thing Norris wanted was for players to have a unified voice, so Adams traded Lindsay to the Black Hawks. "Jack Adams was a dictator," Wings executive Jimmy Devellano said in 2019. "That's how it was in those days. He found out Ted tried to organize the players for an association, and he was banished to the lowly Black Hawks."

But Adams didn't just trade Lindsay, he badmouthed him to reporters and spread rumors he was being paid double his actual salary of $13,000. Lindsay was very bitter over how Adams treated him. "As much as I admired Adams' achievements," Lindsay said in 1991, "he wouldn't last a season in today's world because of the way he treated the players."

Adams' recklessness proved costly. The Wings were swept in the first round of the 1958 playoffs and failed to quality in 1959. The 1960s began with another first-round exit. In 1960–61, despite a losing record, the Wings reached the Cup Finals. When the team failed to qualify in 1962, Bruce Norris finally fired Adams, ending his nearly four-decade association with the franchise. He had never had a contract.

Adams then helped found the Central Hockey League and was its president when he died in 1968 at 73. When the NHL introduced an annual trophy recognizing the top coach in 1974, the league named it the Jack Adams Award.

Adams was surpassed as the winningest coach in franchise history by Mike Babcock on April 8, 2014, when Babcock recorded his 414th victory.

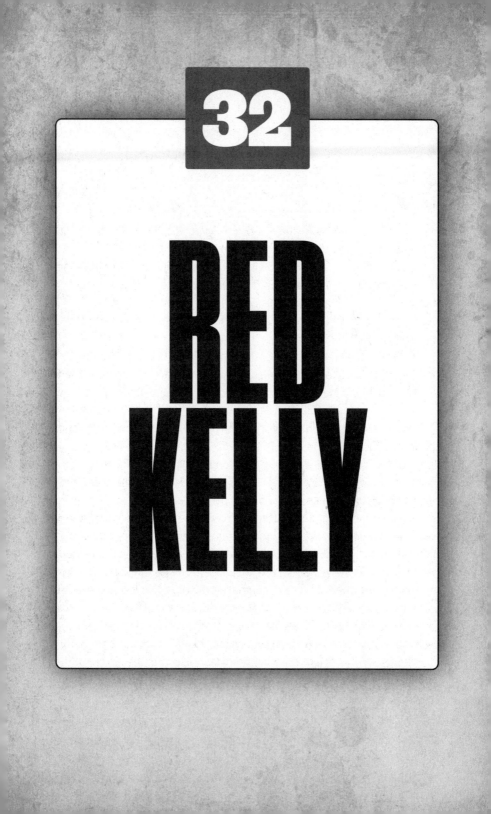

32

RED KELLY

On the night the Red Wings retired Red Kelly's No. 4, nearly six decades after he'd played his last game for them, Scotty Bowman made note that even in the golden age of hockey, headlined by stars such as Gordie Howe and Maurice "Rocket" Richard, Kelly stood out. "We are honoring a legend, a hero," Bowman said.

Kelly won four Stanley Cups with the Wings while revolutionizing the position of defenseman, his smooth skating and skilled hands at times making him seem more like a fourth forward. Then he won four Stanley Cups as a star forward with the Toronto Maple Leafs—two while a member of Canadian Parliament, no less.

Kelly was the first recipient of the James Norris Memorial Trophy, honoring the NHL's top defenseman. He's one of only three defensemen to win the Lady Byng Memorial Trophy, honoring gentlemanly conduct hand in hand with a high standard of playing ability.

Leonard Patrick "Red" Kelly was born July 9, 1927, in Simcoe, Ontario, roughly 200 miles northeast of Detroit and 100 miles southwest of Toronto, the two cities Kelly would call home during his legendary NHL career. He joined the Wings in 1947 after being rejected by the Leafs, and had an immediate impact. Kelly finished the 1947–48 season with 20 points in 60 games and was third in voting for the Calder Cup, recognizing the NHL's top rookie. Kelly was a strong skater who loved to carry the puck, mindful of coach Tommy Ivan's directive not to get caught up ice. He had played soccer at St. Michael's College School, a private, all-boys day school in Toronto, and was as nimble at controlling the puck with his skates as he was with his stick. When Benny Woit joined the Wings in 1951, he and Kelly formed a formidable pairing—Kelly the prototype offensive defenseman, Woit a physical force who made sure opponents felt it when he hit them.

"Red Kelly was one of the most dominant players in the history of the game," Steve Yzerman said after Kelly passed away at 91 on May 2, 2019. "He truly redefined how people viewed the defense position, and how it was played for decades to come."

Kelly was named an All-Star eight straight times from 1950 to 1957, six of those to the first team. From 1950 to 1957, Kelly led all NHL defensemen with 109 goals in 479 games. The next-closest guy, Bill Gadsby, had 48 goals. Kelly's 217 assists ranked second behind Doug Harvey's 232. Gadsby ranked third, with 163. Of the nine defensemen who played at least 400 games during that span, Kelly had the lowest penalty minutes, with 151. Harvey had the third-most, at 568, and Gus Mortson led the group with 835.

"Throughout the '50s, the two premier defensemen in the world, one was Doug Harvey of Montreal Canadiens and Red Kelly was the other," Wings senior vice president Jimmy Devellano told the *Detroit Free Press* in 2019. "Red Kelly was pretty remarkable—eight Stanley Cups. He was probably the first defenseman in the original six-team league that really carried the puck and would be considered an offensive defenseman."

Kelly was runner-up for the 1954 Hart Memorial Trophy, awarded to the player deemed most valuable to his team (he was edged out by goalie Al Rollins, who posted a 12–47–7 record for the last-place Black Hawks). His sportsmanlike conduct on ice led to his first Lady Byng in 1951 (he'd finished second in voting in 1950). He won it again in 1953 and 1954, and a fourth time, as a forward, in 1961. Kelly is one of four players who've won the Lady Byng at least four times, the others are Frank Boucher (seven), Wayne Gretzky (five), and Pavel Datsyuk (four).

Kelly lasted just shy of 13 seasons with the Wings, accumulating 162 goals and 310 assists (472 points). He served as captain from 1956–58.

Then came an honest answer to a fair question that upended his life. Midway through the 1959–60 season, Toronto sports writer Trent Frayne, asked Kelly why he was performing better than the previous season. Kelly answered that he'd played on a broken ankle in the previous season, at the behest of general manager Jack Adams. Kelly recalled what happened in January 2019. "In practice, one of the players shot the puck along the boards and it broke my ankle," Kelly told the *Free Press* in 2019. "They put it in a cast for three days. The team went on the road and lost three games. They asked me if I thought if I could take the cast off and tape it up and play because we were desperate. I said, 'Sure, I'll give it a try.' They taped it up to my knee and I played for the rest of the year. The ankle was stiff, wouldn't bend."

When the story broke, Adams was furious. "There was a big headline: 'Was Red Kelly forced to play on broken foot?'" Kelly recalled. "Ted Lindsay's wife called my wife, 'Got your bags packed?'"

Kelly played that night. He was traded midway through the game. Incensed Kelly would reveal he'd been asked to play while injured, Adams negotiated a trade with the New York Rangers that would send Kelly and forward Billy McNeill to the Rangers for Bill Gadsby, a fellow star defenseman, and forward Eddie Shack. But Kelly pushed back, telling Adams he'd retire rather than join a team that wasn't going to make the playoffs. "I know it means starting all over. But I have lots of friends in Detroit and I can go to work tomorrow if I want to on my job with Sam Graham," Kelly told the *Free Press* at the time. He called his employer at his summertime job, Sam Graham at Re-Nu Tool Company, and asked for a full-time job. He got it.

The trade was nullified. Instead, Adams worked out a deal with the Maple Leafs, sending Kelly to Toronto for Marc Reaume. It was a horrible deal for the Wings. Reaume was forgettable; he had two assists in 47 games before getting the boot. Kelly, meanwhile, would go on to play 470 games for the Leafs, adding to his legend thanks to an insightful request by Leafs coach Punch Imlach.

Knowing what a good skater Kelly was and how well he handled the puck, Imlach asked Kelly to switch from defense to forward. Imlach put Kelly with Frank Mahovlich and Bob Nevin. They'd finish the 1960–61 season 1-2-3 in scoring (Mahovlich was first with 84 points in 70 games, Kelly second with 70 points in 64 games). Kelly led the Leafs with 50 assists; Mahovlich with 48 goals. The only player in the six-team NHL to record more assists was legendary Montreal Canadiens center Jean Beliveau, who had 58 (Gordie Howe was third, with 49).

Kelly went from one dynasty to another. The Leafs won the Stanley Cup in 1962, repeating in 1963 and 1964. Kelly won his eighth and last Cup in 1967 (he had a former teammate in net, as Sawchuk had joined the Leafs in 1964–65). Kelly retired that spring having played 1,316 games with 281 goals, 542 assists, and only 327 penalty minutes. Kelly logged 164 playoff games, with 33 goals, 59 assists, and 92 points. He missed the playoffs only once in a 20-season career (with the Wings, in 1959). At the time of his retirement, Kelly ranked seventh all-time in points with 823, behind

Howe (1,501), Richard (966), Beliveau (944), Andy Bathgate (870), Alex Delvecchio (864), and Lindsay (851).

He transitioned immediately to coaching, spending two years with the expansion Los Angeles Kings, then four seasons with the Pittsburgh Penguins. He returned to Toronto in 1973, and coached the Leafs until 1977. Kelly went 278–330–134 in 742 games as a coach, making the playoffs eight times. (The Penguins failed to qualify in 1971, and Kelly was fired before the 1973 playoffs.)

As if his immense hockey career isn't a great story on its own, Kelly entered politics in 1962, elected to the House of Commons of Canada with the Liberal Party led by Lester B. Pearson. (Pearson has quite a story of his own: he'd been awarded the Nobel Peace Prize in 1957 for his role in

Red Kelly waves at his jersey retirement ceremony at Little Caesars Arena, February 1, 2019. (Junfu Han)

helping to solve the Suez Canal conflict. He was elected prime minister in 1963. The award for the NHL's most outstanding player, as judged by members of the NHL Players' Association, was named in Pearson's honor before being renamed the Ted Lindsay Award in 2010.) Kelly served in office until 1965.

He was inducted into the Hockey Hall of Fame in 1969. The Leafs retired his number on October 15, 2016. The Wings raised No. 4 to the rafters at Little Caesars Arena on February 1, 2019. Kelly attended with his wife, Andra (a former speedskater and figure skater), and their family (four children and eight grandchildren). It was an overdue honor, and a chance for Kelly to reflect on his time with the organization.

"We had 12½ great years in Detroit," Kelly said. "We had a great bunch of players. We stayed together off the ice and on the ice and had Red Wings stamped on our behinds."

33

A CAREER COMPETITOR

Chris Chelios was talking to reporters at the 2006 Winter Olympics when one asked whether having Peter Forsberg on their bench would help the Swedes.

Chelios paused and side-eyed the reporter. "I would say so," he answered. "Is this a trick question?"

That was Chelios at his core: outspoken and straightforward. He played with a fierceness that belied his 5'11", 190-pound frame, with an energy that never sagged even as he played into his mid-forties. He thrived on pushing back, against opponents and against their fans. Early in his career with the Red Wings, Chelios made a point of naming NHL players he considered divers (the list included Ron Francis, Paul Kariya, and Forsberg). Months later, at the 2002 Olympics in Salt Lake City, Chelios spotted Wings captain Steve Yzerman in a dining hall and sauntered over to chat. Yzerman was dining with Kariya, and later described how Chelios was baffled by Kariya's icy reception.

That was another trademark: as quickly as Chelios struck, he forgot.

He didn't soften after he finally conceded his professional playing days were over. Six years after he retired in 2010, Chelios threw on a Wings jersey and played in the Wings–Avalanche alumni game at Coors Field, part of the NHL Stadium Series of outdoor games in 2016. One by one the Wings players were introduced, soundly booed by partisan fans who still cherished the great rivalry from 10 years ago. When it was Chelios' turn, he booed right back. "I couldn't help myself," he said.

While he was with Chicago in 1995, Chelios scored an overtime goal in the playoffs at Vancouver. "They picked me for one of the stars of the game," he said in 2018. "I skated around the whole ice pumping my fist, and that didn't go over great."

When the Wings traded for Chelios, he already was 37 years old. Things had soured for him with his hometown Chicago Blackhawks— Chelios didn't like a new team directive that no children were allowed in the dressing room—and a move made sense for both sides. For the Wings, Chelios was another in a series of attempts to ameliorate the loss of defenseman Vladimir Konstantinov, who sustained career-ending injuries in a June 13, 1997, limousine accident. The Uwe Krupp experiment yielded 30 games spanning four seasons from 1998 to 2002 and was chiefly notable for degenerating into a sideshow involving dogsledding and depositions.

General manager Ken Holland put aside history and triggered the first trade between the Original Six rivals since the 1970s on March 23, 1999. Back then—before mobile phone alerts disseminated news in nanoseconds—word of the trade spread the old-fashioned way. Larry Murphy heard about it from his wife, who had heard it from a friend. Chris Osgood heard about it from Kris Draper. Sergei Fedorov heard about it from an attendant at a video arcade. "I was at GameWorks playing IndyCar and I was like, 'Yeah, dream on. Chicago would never trade Chris Chelios to us,'" Fedorov said at the time. "When I got home, my mom told me."

Brendan Shanahan was driving home from practice and pulled over to listen to the details on the radio.

Holland knew Chelios was hated in Detroit but gambled that Wings fans would embrace Chelios' passion once he put on a winged wheel sweater. They quickly did.

When the Wings paired off with the Anaheim Ducks in Round 1 of the 1999 playoffs, coach Scotty Bowman paired Chelios up with Nicklas Lidstrom and used them to defend against Ducks superstars Teemu Selanne and Kariya. In Game 3 of what would be a sweep, Chelios played 33 minutes and 52 seconds (Lidstrom played 34:37). Selanne had one assist. Kariya had no points.

The Wings lost in the second round to Colorado in 1999 and 2000. In November 2000, Chelios underwent surgery to reconstruct the anterior cruciate ligament in his left knee. He had torn it five years earlier, but in typical Chelios fashion kept playing. And playing. The ligament atrophied. Then one day in October 2000, Chelios twisted the knee while skating and the pain was too much even for Chelios. Surgeons took a tendon from his right knee and turned it into a ligament for his left knee.

On January 25, 2002—his 40th birthday—Chelios led the NHL with a plus-30 rating. In February, he captained the United States to a silver medal at the Olympics. He returned to the Wings and finished the season leading the league at plus-40. He was runner-up for the 2002 James Norris Memorial trophy, losing to Lidstrom.

The Wings stormed through the playoffs, and on June 13, 2002, Chelios set up Tomas Holmstrom to give the Wings a 1–0 lead in Game 5 of the Stanley Cup Finals against the Carolina Hurricanes. That night Chelios celebrated his second Stanley Cup championship. (He had won his first with the Montreal Canadiens in 1986.)

Even among fellow professional athletes, Chelios was famous for his devotion to fitness. He used to drag a stationary bike into the sauna at Joe Louis Arena to work up a sweat.

"We always knew when he was at the arena early because from where the ice tub was to where the sauna was, there was a trail of water," Kirk Maltby said in 2019. "He would go back and forth, back and forth. If you were walking around barefoot or in socks, your feet would get wet because he would leave a trail of water and the carpet would stay wet all day. He was a fitness freak.

"If you went to Chris Chelios when he's 80 and said, 'We have an NHL contract for you,' he would do anything in his power to play. I don't think I've ever met anyone who competed as hard. He was second to none."

Chelios couldn't stand the thought of spending a year without playing hockey, so when the 2004–05 season shaped up as an epic labor dispute between the NHL and its Players' Association, he risked playing for the low-level Motor City Mechanics. Chelios, who turned 43 in January 2005, didn't have an NHL contract and a serious injury could have ended his career.

It speaks to Chelios' competitiveness and durability that he was still with the Wings when they won the Cup again in 2008. He had turned 46 during the season. On April 12, Chelios became the NHL's all-time leader in playoff games, with 248. His teammates loved it. "The more we've gotten to know Cheli, it doesn't surprise us one bit," Kris Draper said at the time. "Not only does he love hockey, but he loves playing playoff hockey. He's an inspiration to everyone in this dressing room. He's just an unbelievable teammate to have."

Chelios played his final game in a Wings uniform May 27, 2009, in their second-round playoff series against the Blackhawks. The Wings cut ties with him in June. Chelios gave one more NHL season a shot and signed with the AHL's Chicago Wolves, and in March 2010, with the Atlanta Thrashers. He appeared in just seven games. Chelios relented and retired on August 31, 2010, in a ceremony at Joe Louis Arena. He was 48 years old.

The Wings hired him to mentor young defensemen in their system. It wasn't just that Chelios had invaluable experience to impart, it was how he emphasized unity. Players saw that all the time. "He was the ultimate team guy," Maltby said. "Even in training camp when we would mix veterans with new guys and young guys, he would make sure they were a team. He would take them out for dinner and the whole team had to go. It didn't matter if you were on a tryout or you had a contract. It didn't matter where you were from. It didn't matter if you wanted to."

Chelios held various positions with the organization until 2018, when he returned to Chicago to look after his mom. He played for three Original Six teams in his career, logging more than 400 games each for the Canadiens, Blackhawks, and Wings, but as he pondered his past, it wasn't a tricky question to answer which stop was his best: Detroit.

"Those 10 years of my career, nothing tops it," Chelios said. "I came to Detroit at the right time, with the ownership and the people accepting me. It could have been a disaster but it worked out great. If I was to look over my career with the Wings, there wasn't a thing I would change."

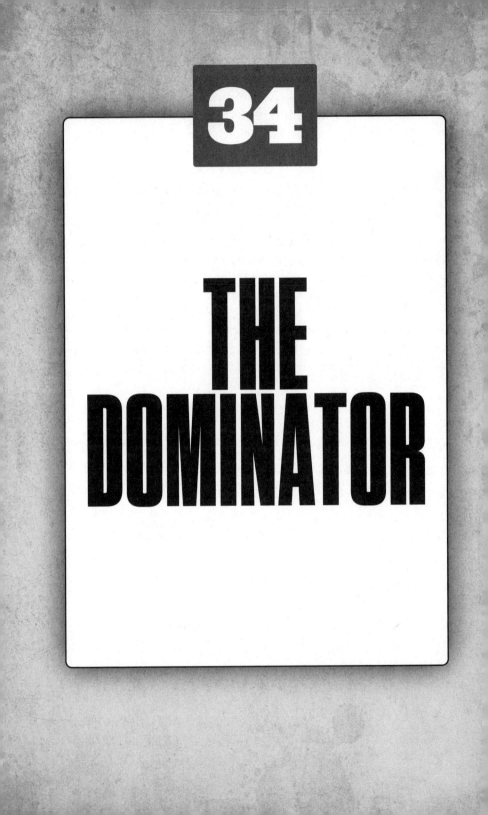

34

THE DOMINATOR

Dominik Hasek had just finished a game against the Columbus Blue Jackets, his Red Wings had won, and a reporter made a point of noting Hasek's performance. Hasek shrugged. It was no big deal, he said—there were not many good shots, so it was not much work for him.

Hasek made an impression on the ice because he was one of the best goaltenders to ever play the game, and off the ice he impressed with how guileless he was. He was unequivocally honest in assessing his play. Outsiders might think he was ripping the Blue Jackets, but those on the inside knew Hasek was one of the most accountable guys in the locker room. Goaltenders can be fickle—some hide behind quirks and refuse to talk to reporters on game days—but Hasek would talk on the morning of a Game 7. He was as self-assured as he was straightforward.

The Wings stunned the hockey world in the summer of 2001 when they added Hasek to their lineup. He was 36 and had spent nearly a decade in Buffalo, but the Sabres needed to shed salary and the Wings could not say no to adding a goaltender of Hasek's caliber. The previous season, the Wings had racked up 111 points, second best in the league, but they were upset by the Los Angeles Kings in Round 1. The Wings lost the last four games by one goal, capped by Adam Deadmarsh scoring on Chris Osgood in overtime in Game 6.

Bring the Dominator to Detroit? Yes, please. Hasek's résumé included six Vezina Trophies, two Hart Memorial Trophies, a trip to the 1999 Stanley Cup Finals, and a gold medal at the 1998 Olympics with the Czech Republic. General manager Ken Holland made one of the best trades of his career in giving the Sabres forward Vyacheslav Kozlov and a 2002 first-round pick. Osgood was lost on waivers when a trade did not materialize, but that was okay; Osgood would return to Detroit in later years and write his own storybook ending.

The trade reunited Hasek with Chris Chelios; a decade earlier they were with the Chicago Blackhawks. During one of his first practices with the Wings, Chelios reminded Hasek of a prediction he had made. "I said he was going to be one of the best goalies in the world back when he started with Chicago," Chelios said. Ed Belfour, the Blackhawks' starting goaltender at the time, overheard him and grew so incensed he didn't talk to Chelios for a month.

Hasek and Chelios were reunited in Detroit on a team boasting future Hall of Famers: themselves, Steve Yzerman, Nicklas Lidstrom, Sergei Fedorov, Brendan Shanahan, Luc Robitaille, Brett Hull, and Igor Larionov. And in Larionov, Hasek had a fellow devoted chess player.

Hasek was notorious for his on-ice intensity. When he had teammates battling opponents right in front of his net, Hasek would yell, "Must see, must see" in his thick accent.

Teammates came to dread scoring on him in practices. "If Dom thought that you got the better of him through the course of practice, when he knew practice was officially over, he would call your name and say, 'Let's go,'" Kirk Maltby said. "And it wasn't just you had to fire a shot at him and if he stopped it, it would be over. He would make you fire 10 shots and he had to stop all of them."

Hasek posted a career-best 41 victories, helping the 2001–02 Wings win the Presidents' Trophy. But the first two games of the playoffs were a disaster. Hasek allowed eight goals in back-to-back losses to the Vancouver Canucks at Joe Louis Arena. But then Lidstrom scored from center ice in Game 3 and the Wings, and Hasek, regained their superpowers. When the series returned to the Joe tied at two, Hasek came through with a shutout. Two more shutouts followed in the second-round, five-game series against the St. Louis Blues.

The Western Conference finals put the Wings face to face with Colorado again. In Game 3, Hasek became the first goalie to earn an assist on an overtime playoff goal when he passed the puck to Yzerman, who set up Fredrik Olausson's goal. Facing elimination in Game 6, Hasek made 24 saves to secure a 2–0 victory—on the road, no less. "The guy can win a playoff series on his own," Yzerman said afterward. His teammates took control of Game 7 in the first period, scoring four times on Patrick Roy en route to a 7–0 final. Hasek made 19 saves in his fifth shutout of the playoffs.

Hasek shut out the Carolina Hurricanes in Game 4 of the Stanley Cup Finals and hoisted the Cup one game later. Eleven months after the Wings saw him as a means to another Cup, Hasek finished the 2002 playoffs 16-7 with a 1.86 goals-against average and .920 save percentage.

Twelve days after winning the Cup, Hasek announced his retirement.

He spearheaded a weeklong Cup party that August in the Czech Republic, along with Czech teammates Jiri Fischer and Jiri Slegr. The celebrations included a public party in Hasek's hometown of Pardubice. He

Dominik Hasek makes a save during the Western Conference finals, May 11, 2007. (Julian H. Gonzalez)

held an auction for charity and then sent his own representatives into the crowd to make bids to help raise money.

Hasek's decision seemed grounded in a desire to pull back and enjoy private life in his homeland. He'd said no to an $8 million contract to keep playing for the Wings, and he'd turned down endorsements at home, save for stoking interest in his clothing line, Dominator. "Right now," Hasek said, "I don't feel like doing anything."

That feeling lasted a year. Hasek generated a heck of a headache for the Wings when, after watching them lose in the first round in 2003 to the Anaheim Ducks, Hasek aired his doubts about being done and set in motion a comeback. "I did not want to be 50 and thinking that I could have had another Stanley Cup," Hasek told *Free Press* columnist Mitch Albom. "There is nothing better than to win."

The Wings had signed Curtis Joseph for three years and $24 million in 2002 in an effort to fill the void left by Hasek. But if they didn't sign Hasek, there was a chance that hated rival Colorado would sign him because the Avalanche had lost Patrick Roy to retirement in 2003.

The Wings forged forward with three goaltenders; backup Manny Legace served as buffer as he sat between the two high-priced netminders. It was an awkward situation in the locker room. "It's an uncomfortable situation for myself and Dom and management," Joseph said, "but you make the best of it."

The Wings put Joseph on waivers December 3, 2003, but an ensuing stint in the minors lasted only one game. Fourteen games into his comeback, Hasek succumbed to a groin injury. The candor that was such a signature part of his persona showed in February when he announced he was done for the season, surprising management, and again when he revealed to reporters he had refused around $3 million of his $6 million salary because of his inability to play.

That was stint two with the Wings. Stint three commenced in 2006, when Hasek was 41. This time he signed for one year and $750,000. He won 38 games, the second most of his career.

The Wings brought him back for another year. By then, Osgood was back in the fold. Hasek and Osgood started 40 games apiece in 2007–08, pairing up to help the Wings allow an NHL-stingiest 184 goals. Hasek and Osgood shared the William M. Jennings Trophy, awarded to the goaltender(s) having played at least 25 games for the team with the fewest goals allowed.

Hasek was the starter when the playoffs began, but when he aallowed three goals on 14 shots in Game 4, he was pulled. It would be his last game in the NHL. Hasek's Dominator days in Detroit were over, though he played in Europe until age 46, but his place in Wings history was undoubtable.

35

SHANNYTOWN

Scotty Bowman picked up the phone and dialed the number for the equipment manager at Joe Louis Arena. Bowman wanted to know whether No. 14 was taken. It was, but never mind—the guy Bowman mentioned prompted an immediate reassignment.

Brendan Shanahan played for the Hartford Whalers on October 8, 1996, and the next night he was in a winged wheel jersey with No. 14 on the back and with an A on the front, the letter attached with double-sided tape by Paul Boyer, the Wings' longtime equipment manager. Shanahan was one of the game's most dominant left wingers, still only 27, and he was worth salvaging trade talks even though no one on the Wings wanted to go to Hartford.

In the fall of 1996, the Wings weren't far removed from the crushing finish to their 1996 playoffs, when they had been bullied out of the Western Conference finals by the Colorado Avalanche. There were also those—such as Bowman, the coach and director of player personnel—who remembered how the New Jersey Devils mowed over the Wings in the 1995 Stanley Cup Finals.

Shanahan was everything the Wings desired: a 6'3", 220-pound power forward with a dangerous shot who hit hard and hit back. He was a scorer and a scrapper, and he was worth a song. "We had had two tough years," Scotty Bowman said in 2019. "We were close but not good enough, and then Shanahan became available."

The Wings negotiated to send center Keith Primeau, defenseman Paul Coffey, and a first-round pick to the Whalers. The Wings had drafted Primeau at third overall in 1990, but he had soured on playing behind Steve Yzerman and Sergei Fedorov and had requested a trade. Primeau was holding out for a new contract, and when the Wings realized he wasn't going to relent, Primeau became expendable.

"He didn't want to sign," Bowman said. "When Brendan asked to be traded and his name came up, you had a package of a big guy who could score and be tough. He was one of those players that the other team has the utmost respect for because he had a mean streak in him. He was a big,

Brendan Shanahan during the 1998 playoffs. (Julian H. Gonzalez)

strong guy but the main thing was he had a special knack for putting the puck in the net. He had what we needed."

Still, the deal almost fell through. Coffey said he wouldn't report to Hartford. Then he relented, only for Primeau to have doubts. Finally, on October 9, the Wings and Whalers completed the deal.

Wings owner Mike Ilitch dispatched his private jet to pick up Shanahan in Hartford and fly him to Detroit for the home opener. Shanahan arrived at Joe Louis Arena at 6:44 PM and 11 minutes later he was on the ice with his new teammates. They had waited to take warm-ups until he was with them. Fans greeted Shanahan, a two-time 50-goal scorer, with a standing ovation. Everything about him signaled he was the shot in the arm needed to finally complete a Stanley Cup run.

"He was one of those types of players we were missing," Kirk Maltby said in 2019. "I heard it when I was in Edmonton—*the Wings were too soft, had too many Europeans, they can't win, playoff hockey is too tough for them*. You bring in a guy like Brendan, he is your typical power forward that any team would covet.

"He was tough. He's got that Irish in him and he'd snap and wouldn't remember it 30 seconds later. We referred to it as his wires touching. I remember there was one time he and Bob Boughner were jostling one another, they kept slashing one another. It was about five or six slashes—it stopped just short of being baseball swings at each other. Afterwards Shanny didn't even remember it happened."

Shanahan was used to pressure—he was drafted second overall in 1987 by New Jersey—and savored the new situation he had landed in. "Let's face it, I am joining a spectacular hockey team," he said. "Obviously their game plan is to win the Stanley Cup. That's my goal as well. There is pressure. I welcome it. It's what I want. I like being in the big game, big moments of a game. I'm looking forward to it."

In his Detroit debut, Shanahan started a fight with Edmonton's Greg de Vries at 3:31 of the first period. Shanahan scored his first goal in a Wings uniform on October 21. Two days later, he scored the team's first two power-play goals of the season. On November 27, he recorded his 300th career goal during his ninth career hat trick. He had quickly become a fan favorite and a franchise favorite, and the Wings picked up the two remaining option years on his contract in March 1997.

Shanahan finished the season with 46 goals and 87 points—and then the Wings really reaped the rewards of the trade. "The ultimate change wasn't really reflected until we got into the playoffs," Yzerman said in 2019.

"We had lost in '95, got swept by New Jersey, and they were a big, strong, physical team. By the time we got to that series, we had a lot of injuries. Guys were banged up and didn't play well and we got swept. But a year later we add Brendan Shanahan, who is 220 pounds. We have Joe Kocur, who is 220 pounds, and Darren McCarty, who is 215. Tomas Sandstrom was 215. Marty Lapointe was 215.

"We were a bigger, stronger, more physical team and on each line we had one of those guys. With each series, we were wearing the other team down. We just became a much harder team to play against, a physically stronger team. It was something we needed to become. Acquiring Shanny at the start of the season was part of it."

Shanahan collected six points in Round 1 against the Blues. He scored in double overtime of Game 4 to end the Round 2 series against Anaheim. As the Wings opened Round 3 against nemesis Colorado, Shanahan flashed the wit that was so integral to his persona. Speaking during an off-day in Denver, Shanahan said this was why he had requested a trade out of Hartford. To join the Wings, he was asked by a reporter, or simply to be in the playoffs? "No, to be right here in this hotel lobby," Shanahan replied. "I love these Marriotts."

During Game 2 of the Stanley Cup Finals against the Philadelphia Flyers, Shanahan tallied two goals. He scored his first 1:37 into the game when he fired a shot that deflected in off a Flyers defenseman. It was Paul Coffey—one of the pieces the Wings had given up to get Shanahan. One goal, one assist, and two games later, Shanahan hoisted the Stanley Cup. In 20 playoff games, he nine goals and 17 points.

"When I asked to be traded at the start of the season, I said I was looking for a home," Shanahan said at a ceremony at Joe Louis Arena honoring the Wings. "I found one."

When Shanahan stood up and mimicked lifting the Cup during the parade, thousands of fans lining Woodward Avenue joined in the fun. Shanahan's week also included an appearance on *The Tonight Show with Jay Leno*. "I love the Cup," Shanahan said on the show. "It's not about rings or money. I get to take it home and parade around with it."

Shanahan paraded with the Cup again in 1998 and 2002. The 2001–02 Wings were one of the greatest teams ever assembled. During the 2001 off-season, general manager Ken Holland traded for goaltender Dominik Hasek and signed Luc Robitaille and Brett Hull. That gave the Wings something no other team ever had: three 500-goal scorers, in Yzerman, Robitaille, and Hull. Shanahan joined the 500 club on March 23, 2002, breaking a scoreless tie in the third period against the Avalanche.

He led the 2001–02 Wings with 37 goals and 75 points. He struggled to score in the playoffs, with just four goals the first 16 games, but he scored three times in the last two games of the Stanley Cup Finals against the Hurricanes and on June 13 hoisted the Cup for the third time in six years. This time he took the Cup—and his wit—on *Live with Regis and Kelly*. Kelly Ripa asked Shanahan when he started skating. "Well, in Canada, I got a little bit of a late start," Shanahan quipped. "I was four. Most of the kids were three, so they laughed at me when I came out at four."

Shanahan made Detroit his home for nine seasons. He signaled in the summer of 2006 that it was time for him to move on, allowing himself to enter free agency. Yzerman had just retired, and centers Pavel Datsyuk and Henrik Zetterberg had begun their ascension as the team's next leaders. Yzerman tried to persuade Shanahan to stay. Ilitch called him personally.

"I gave it a lot of thought, and ultimately, my instincts were that I was more associated with Detroit's great past than necessarily the promising future they have," said Shanahan, now 37 but coming off a 40-goal, 81-point season. "As time has rolled on, I just felt that, with some of the departures of some of the players that were there when I started, I felt more and more identified with its past."

Shanahan left behind an indelible mark, a power forward worth the fanfare of his arrival.

36

THE DEAD WINGS

One day during the early 1970s, Bruce Martyn, the radio voice for the Red Wings, emerged from Olympia Stadium, walked to his car, and did a double take when he saw it. Somebody had stuck a DARKNESS WITH HARKNESS sticker on his bumper. Martyn immediately removed the bumper sticker; the damage Harkness inflicted on the franchise took years to repair.

Two games into the 1969–70 season, owner Bruce Norris fired coach Bill Gadsby, installing general manager Sid Abel on an interim basis. The decision was a curious one, considering the Wings had won both games. It was a telling start to the turbulence that would rattle the Wings during the coming decade. They were so awful fans took to calling them "Dead Wings."

But in 1969–70, the Wings still had Gordie Howe and Frank Mahovlich in the lineup and had a 40-goal scorer in Garry Unger. They had Roger Crozier and Roy Edwards in net. The Wings finished in third place in the East Division with 95 points, only four points behind first-place Chicago. The Black Hawks swept the Wings in the first round of the playoffs, each game by a 4–2 score. In what would be their last playoff appearances with the Wings, Howe had two goals and Alex Delvecchio two assists.

In May 1970, Norris replaced Abel behind the bench with Ned Harkness, a highly successful college hockey coach but far from Abel's choice. It was a disastrous move. The power Harkness had wielded over student players—dictating length of hair, rules about drinking—did not sit well in the Wings' locker room. By January 1971, Abel wanted to fire Harkness, but instead resigned when he realized he lacked the power to do so. The Wings were 12–21–4 and days earlier had suffered a 13–0 loss at Toronto—the worst in team history. Asked to assess Harkness as a coach, Abel quickly shot back: "I can't. I don't think he is one.... I cannot accept the fellow." Two days later, Norris promoted Harkness to general manager. Harkness declined also staying behind the bench and promoted Doug Barkley, coach at the Fort Worth farm team and a talented Wings defenseman whose career was cut short in 1966 by an eye injury. With his new power, Harkness resorted to trading players with a recklessness that recalled Jack Adams' ruinous moves of the mid-1950s. Harkness traded Mahovlich to the Montreal Canadiens in a package deal that brought Mickey Redmond to Detroit. Mahovlich won his fifth Stanley Cup with the Canadiens in 1971, and a sixth in 1973.

There was nothing but failure under Harkness. The Wings missed the playoffs every year with him as general manager. His ineptitude ranks among the worst in the history of the franchise, and "Darkness with Harkness" still resonates among a generation of Wings fans.

The 1973–74 season was Harkness' last. Delvecchio, Harkness' fourth coach, was also appointed general manager. He had logged 1,550 games in a Wings uniform and helped the franchise win three Stanley Cups. Unfortunately, he was not able to replicate that success as an executive. The Wings continued to miss the playoffs. In 1976–77, they finished at the bottom of the 18-team league with a record of 16–55–9 (41 points).

Norris released Delvecchio with 10 games left in the 1976–77 season, and looked to another former player for help, naming Ted Lindsay general manager. Lindsay had four Stanley Cups from his playing days and had earned the nickname "Terrible Ted" for his rugged play. Under new coach Bobby Kromm, the Wings sought to emulate Lindsay's demanding style and adopted the slogan "Aggressive Hockey Is Back in Town."

It was as if somebody stuck a defibrillator on Olympia Stadium and shocked the team back to life. The Wings finished second in the Norris Division at 32–34–14 and advanced to the playoffs for the first time in eight years. They faced a best-of-three preliminary round against the Atlanta Flames and won in two games—5–3 in Atlanta and 3–2 at Olympia. Bill Lochead, the Wings' selection at ninth overall in the 1974 draft (which was held in secret in an effort to prevent the World Hockey Association from poaching players) scored two of his three career NHL playoff goals in the game at Olympia. In the last two minutes, he skated up the left side and lured Flames goaltender Dan Bouchard from his crease, then flipped the puck in one-handed to win the series.

That earned the Wings a trip to the quarterfinals, where they faced the defending Stanley Cup champion Montreal. The Wings scored an upset in Game 2, shocking the Habs with a 4-2 victory at the Forum. Nick Libbett scored twice in Game 3, but Montreal rallied to a 4-2 victory. Game 4 would be the last playoff game at Olympia. The Wings lost 8-0, and were eliminated two nights later.

The revival was over. The next season the Wings won only 23 games and finished 15th out of 17 teams. They closed out the final full season at Olympia Stadium with a 1-0 victory over the Canadiens. They opened the next season at Olympia, but on December 27, 1979, they played their first game at Joe Louis Arena.

The excitement over a new home wasn't enough to invigorate the Wings. Jimmy Skinner, a Jack Adams protégé, had assumed general manager duties when Lindsay was demoted to coach only in July 1980. Just as Harkness had been detrimental to the Wings at the start of the 1970s, Skinner left a devastating imprint on the new decade. He swapped first-round choices with the Minnesota North Stars, also receiving Don Murdoch, a forward who finished the season in the minors, and Greg Smith, a journeyman defenseman. The North Stars ended up picking second overall and drafted Brian Bellows, who played nearly 1,200 NHL games, was picked for three All-Star Games, and won a Stanley Cup with Montreal. The Wings picked 17th, selecting Murray Craven, who they only kept for parts of two seasons. In December 1981, Skinner traded three former first-round picks (Mike Foligno, Dale McCourt, and Brent Peterson) to Buffalo for veterans Jim Schoenfeld, Derek Smith, and Danny Gare. The Wings won a paltry 19 games in 1980-81, and 21 the following season.

It was after the 1981-82 season that something finally happened that would lead the Wings back to glory. In 1982, the Wings had been owned by the Norris family for 50 years. Bruce Norris wanted to celebrate. But he misjudged that Wings fans wanted to celebrate a golden anniversary when they had not seen the silver of the Stanley Cup since 1955, when they had endured the Dead Wings. He was booed at a ceremony heralding the 50-year milestone. He had lost millions of dollars on the team, and decided to sell the franchise.

Norris had been mostly an absentee owner, with homes in Chicago, New York and Florida, but the man who purchased the franchise, Mike Ilitch, was hands-on and a Detroiter. The Wings would miss the playoffs the first year under Ilitch, but the era of the "Dead Wings" was in its last gasp.

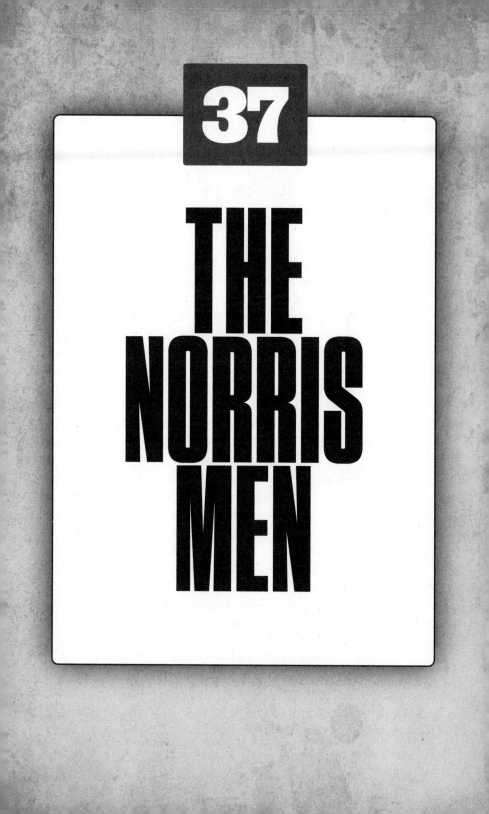

37

THE NORRIS MEN

James E. Norris parlayed his industrial wealth into ownership of a budding hockey franchise in Detroit in 1932, launching the birth of the Red Wings. A Montreal-born, Chicago-based businessman who played hockey in his youth, Norris had unsuccessfully bid for established teams in Chicago and St. Louis before investing his money in what was then the Detroit Falcons and their arena, Olympia Stadium, rescuing the franchise from receivership. It was the start of a prosperous adventure.

Norris rechristened the team, changing the name to the Red Wings and instituting the winged wheel logo after the Montreal team he once played for that bore the nickname the "Winged Wheelers."

Through grain and cattle companies, Norris had the financial means to ensure the Wings could succeed. By 1934 they were good enough to appear in the Stanley Cup Finals, which they lost to the Chicago Black Hawks. Two years later, Norris had his first Stanley Cup, as the Wings won the series against the Toronto Maple Leafs three games to one. April 18, 1936, was designated "Champions Day" in Michigan by governor Frank Fitzgerald to herald a growing list of accomplishments by Detroit sports teams and athletes, including the Wings' first Stanley Cup, Joe Louis being named the Most Outstanding Athlete of 1935 by the Associated Press, the Detroit Tigers' 1935 World Series title, and the Detroit Lions' 1935 NFL championship. Their successes comforted a city decimated by the Great Depression.

Norris, often referred to as Norris Sr., held extensive power in the NHL. In 1936, he bought Chicago Stadium, home of the Black Hawks. He also owned stock in Madison Square Garden, home of the New York Rangers. Norris lived in Chicago, where his father had relocated the family in 1897. A heart condition limited Norris' travel, but while he did not see the Wings in action very often, coach and general manager Jack Adams famously called Norris from the locker room after games to keep him updated. The Wings won five Cups under Norris' ownership.

Upon Norris' death on December 4, 1952, two of his children, Bruce and Marguerite, inherited the Wings. (A second son, James D. Norris, was

Marguerite Norris, Jack Adams, Ted Lindsay, and Bruce Norris with the Stanley Cup in 1954.

part of a group that purchased the Black Hawks in 1946.) Marguerite, 25, was named president as dictated by Norris' will. She earned the admiration of players—including Gordie Howe, Ted Lindsay, Alex Delvecchio, and Red Kelly—for standing up to Adams, who liked to operate with an arbitrary hand.

Shortly after the Wings won their second straight Stanley Cup title in 1955, Marguerite was ousted by Bruce. It was the beginning of the end of the glory years. Bruce let Adams dismantle the team, sending them into a decline during which they'd be known as the "Dead Wings."

MARVELOUS MARGUERITE

During the 1950s the Red Wings won seven straight regular season titles and four Stanley Cups. Had a certain woman retained control of the team, there might have more. Instead, the team entered a decline that would last four decades.

No less an authority than Gordie Howe made the case in his 2014 book, *Mr. Hockey: My Story*, that had Marguerite Norris continued in her position as the president of the Wings, the group of players who dominated the early-to-middle 1950s might have celebrated a decade-long dynasty.

In 1952, the Wings finished first overall for a fourth straight season. On April 15, they won the Stanley Cup for the second time in three years. On December 4, James E. Norris, who had owned the Wings since 1932, died at 72 after a heart attack. His will revealed that he wanted his youngest child, Marguerite, to become president of the Wings and Olympia Stadium. A graduate of Smith College, Marguerite attained business training with Dun & Bradstreet in New York and West Farm Management in Chicago. She had seen the Wings play on the road, but never at Olympia. She decided to reside in Detroit, unlike her father.

"Marguerite Ann was selected to follow the prescribed wishes of her father," general manager Jack Adams said in a brief statement, which he read to Detroit hockey writers by phone. On December 16, 1952, the *Detroit Free Press* heralded her arrival with a story titled "Madam President Looks Right for Her Part" that was the main piece on a page beneath the banner FOR AND ABOUT WOMEN.

"Marguerite Norris, new president of the Red Wings hockey team, might do only fairly well in stumping the *What's My Line* experts," the story began. "Marguerite is an athletic looking young woman, five feet, 11 inches tall. On the other hand Marguerite's scholastic background, if it were the only clew to her current occupation, would fool them completely. The girl first went to Smith and Oxford."

The article wemt on to describe that she arrived at Willow Run Airport "clad in gray wool and a mink jacket.... She was gracious and friendly, talking in a low-pitched tone and posing graciously." A photo of Marguerite descending the portable stair ran next to the story, along with two profile photos.

Marguerite's role in running an NHL team was unprecedented in hockey and a great success. The Wings finished first in all three seasons under Marguerite's leadership, and won the Cup in 1954 and 1955. Howe lauded her for her acumen and her ability to stand up for herself—something Howe was a master at himself on the ice.

Marguerite Ann Norris was born Feb. 16, 1927, in Chicago. She was only 25 years old when she took charge, yet she deftly handled Adams, the cantankerous, trade-happy veteran 33 years her senior who'd been appointed to the board of governors upon Norris' death. Writing in his memoir, Howe said of Marguerite:

> Her role with the team has been relegated to a footnote in sports history, but I think she was the first woman to ever run a professional team. I don't know how Mr. Adams felt about his new team president, but I'm sure he wasn't thrilled about a woman in her 20s handing down his marching orders.
>
> I found her to be both smart and capable. Others I talked to felt the same way. She was good for the club, but unfortunately she didn't stick around for as long as anyone would have liked. A few years into the job, she was ousted by her older brother, Bruce.

In *The Red Kelly Story*, Kelly echoed Howe's estimation, telling biographers, "Marguerite was more than capable in our eyes. She was a great lady."

None the less, Marguerite's tenure ended after the Wings won the Cup in 1955, when her shares were bought out by her brother Bruce. He remained sole owner until selling the team to Mike Ilitch in 1982. The Wings did not win the Cup again until 1997.

"In retrospect, it's easy to see how bad the family infighting was for the team," Howe wrote. "Marguerite was a much more thoughtful owner than her brother, who could be something of a bully. I don't think it's a coincidence that Marguerite's time in charge coincided with some of the greatest years in franchise history. As president, she had enough juice to check Trader Jack's instincts to upset the apple cart. It's hard to say how many Stanley Cups we might have won if she had stuck around longer."

Marguerite Norris passed away in 1994 at 67 from heart failure. She was the first woman to have her name engraved on the Stanley Cup, in 1954 and 1955. Her father was elected to the Hockey Hall of Fame in 1958. Her brother James D. Norris was inducted in 1962, and Bruce in 1969. Marguerite, despite her pioneering work as the first female executive in the NHL and her tenure as president of a two-time Stanley Cup champion, as of 2019 had yet to take her rightful place in the Hockey Hall of Fame.

Adams traded away Terry Sawchuk and Lindsay, among others. In his book *Mr. Hockey: My Story*, Howe revealed his bitterness over how the Wings finished the 1950s. "Sadly, we weren't left alone for long enough to find out what might have been," Howe wrote. "Bruce's hockey acumen was no match for his sister's, which was good for Mr. Adams but bad for the rest of us. Despite winning seven consecutive league championships and two straight Stanley Cups, Trader Jack decided to spend the 1955 off-season dismantling the team."

They returned to the Cup Finals in 1956, but lost 4–1, to Montreal. They went on to lose in the first round of the playoffs in 1957 and 1958. While the Wings began to grow used to leaving the playoffs disappointed, rival Montreal claimed the Cup every year from 1956 to 1960. When the Wings missed the playoffs in 1959, it was the first time in 21 years.

"The dismantling of the Red Wings juggernaut cleared the way for Montreal, who went on to win five Cups in a row," Howe continued. "We were still competitive, but it's easy now to see how those trades sapped us of the firepower we needed to win another championship."

Norris fired Adams in 1962. As the 1960s drew to a close, the Wings missed the playoffs three straight years before qualifying in 1970. They were tumultuous times. The Wings had four coaches— Adams, Tommy Ivan, Jimmy Skinner, and Sid Abel—from 1927 to 1968. Bill Gadsby was coach in 1968–69. Though he only lasted a season and two games in 1969–70, his stint is part of local folklore. Norris was a heavy drinker. When he was at games, he liked to meddle in coaching decisions, using the phone in his suite at Olympia. Finally one day, Gadsby had enough, and he broke the phone in the locker room.

In May 1970, Ned Harkness was hired as coach, replacing Abel, who had been an interim replacement for Gadsby, along with general manager. It was a detrimental decision. Harkness was a successful college coach, but was not a good fit in the NHL. In January 1971, Abel was resigned, and Harkness, despite a 12–22–4 coaching record, became the general manager. All that spurred the sobriquet "Darkness with Harkness."

The last decade under Norris ownership read like a manifesto of how to ruin a glorious franchise. Under Harkness, Howe quit in anger in 1971, ending his 25-year career with the Wings. The team failed to qualify for the playoffs from 1971 to 1977. They were known throughout the league as the worst team money could buy.

Ten men coached the Wings in the 1970s (Doug Barkley, Alex Delvecchio, and Billy Dea served at least two stints). Lindsay succeeded Delvecchio as GM in 1977, but it was Delvecchio who had hired Bobby Kromm in the summer of 1976 to coach when his contract with the WHA's Winnipeg Jets ended in 1977. Kromm guided the Wings into the playoffs in 1978, but then the team missed the playoffs the next four years.

Norris' breaking point came in 1982, when fans at Joe Louis Arena booed him at a 50th anniversary celebration of family ownership. He was 58 years old, and had had enough of being the fall guy for a failing franchise. "We have been pressured by the media for two or three years," Norris said in May. "We have decided to sell. We're tired of listening to this all the time."

Norris had rejected an $11 million bid from Detroit businessman Mike Ilitch in 1981. The Wings were in terrible shape—they finished 20th out of 21 teams in 1981–82. They hadn't made the playoffs since 1978. They were on their 12th coach since 1969. The team was old and slow. Average ticket sales were below the 13,000 break-even point. Norris was losing millions of dollars.

"You're not buying a No. 1 product right now, but few markets are better for hockey than Detroit," team counsel Robert Cavalieri said. "I think local people with money would realize the cable TV potential. A business like this should be headed by a dominant individual."

The sale went through in June in 1982. The Wings had finished last that spring in the Norris Division, which was formed in 1974 and named after James E. Norris. More famously, the named its annual award for best defenseman after Norris.

Norris Sr. was elected posthumously to the Hockey Hall of Fame in 1958. Bruce was elected in 1969. Bruce died of liver failure in 1986, at 61, a year after filing a bankruptcy claim.

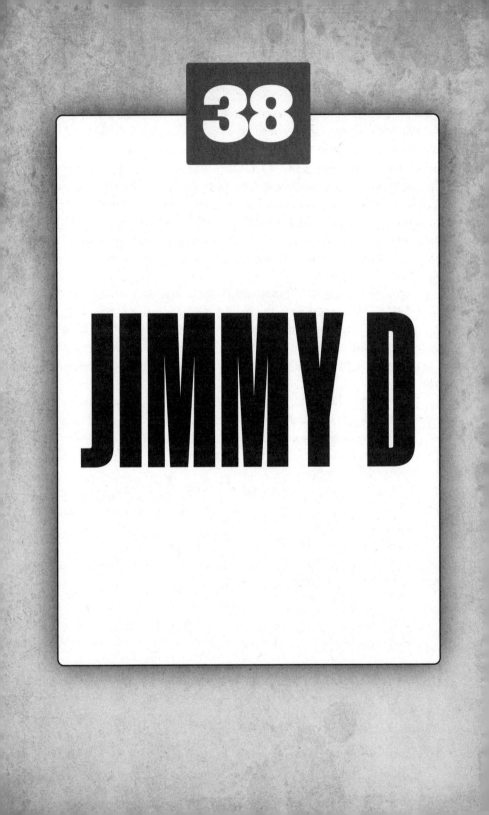

38

JIMMY D

When Jimmy Devellano was hired as general manager of the Detroit Red Wings in July 1982, he told his bosses he'd win them a championship in eight years.

Introduced a few weeks after the draft, Devellano was blunt about the work ahead: "What the Red Wings obviously lack," he said, "is a game-breaker type of player. When Detroit had its great teams, it had people like Gordie Howe, Sid Abel, Ted Lindsay, and Red Kelly. Those were winners. Nobody trades you a super player like that today. Our only answer is the draft."

Devellano was hired by Mike Ilitch, who finalized his purchase of the team in June 1982. It was a well-received hire in hockey circles—NHL president John Ziegler, born in Grosse Pointe, Michigan, called Devellano "first cabin all the way. Mike Ilitch made a very shrewdest decision. Being an old Red Wings fan, I think the fires of hope are properly rekindled."

Devellano first set eyes on the Red Wings in the 1950s when they played at Maple Leaf Gardens. As a Toronto native fan, Devellano was a huge Maple Leafs fan. (In 1976 he started using some of his earnings to buy stock in Maple Leaf Gardens, Ltd., the firm that owns the Gardens and the Leafs. It became known as Maple Leaf Sports & Entertainment in 1998.)

Three decades later, Devellano found himself rooting for the Wings. He was taking charge of a team that had missed the playoffs in 14 of the previous 16 seasons. Devellano was 39 years old and a veteran of the scouting life. He got his start in the NHL in 1967 after writing a letter to Lynn Patrick, the general manager of the expansion St. Louis Blues, offering free scouting services. Devellano worked for the Blues until he was let go in 1972. He immediately joined the New York Islanders, an expansion franchise readying itself for its first season. Devellano would turn in quarterly player progress reports, writing "Hockey is Happiness" at the bottom of each one. He was promoted to chief scout in 1974 and assistant general manager in 1981. His success with that franchise made him an attractive candidate: he had scouted such notable draft picks as Denis

JACQUES DEMERS

Jacques Demers coached the Red Wings out of decrepitude, guiding them to their first true playoff series victory in two decades. He was named the 21st coach of the team in June 1986, signing a five-year contract that signaled the team was done with a carousel which saw three coaches from 1985 to 1986. Demers brought respectability and likability, his work ethic befitting a city with a blue-collar image.

The Wings finished the 1985–86 season last among the NHL's 21 teams with 40 points. They improved by 38 points Demers' first year, winning 34 games. When they won their first game of the season, in the home opener on October 11, 1986, with a 4–3 final over the Blackhawks, Demers gave the puck to owner Mike Ilitch.

In 1987, the Wings won their first playoff series since 1966 (in 1978, the Wings had won what was a three-game preliminary round against the Atlanta Flames). The Wings advanced all the way to the third round, losing in the conference finals to eventual Cup champion Edmonton. Demers was recognized with the Jack Adams Trophy.

The next year, Demers became the only coach to win it back-to-back. The Wings won 41 games, banked 93 points and finished first in the Norris Division. They made another run to the conference finals, but again were unable to best the Oilers. The Edmonton series was tarnished when Bob Probert and Petr Klima were among half a dozen Wings players found drinking the night before Game 5. Demers was criticized for playing Probert in the game. (Klima was hurt.)

The incident was the beginning of the end for Demers. The Wings lasted one round in the 1989 playoffs. In 1990, they won 28 games and missed the playoffs altogether. Demers' popularity faded.

Hired on Friday, June 13, 1986, Demers was fired on Friday, July 13, 1990, summoned to Ilitch's house to have his heart broken. Demers was told key players said he could no longer motivate the team. "It's the coach's job to get them to respond," Ilitch said. "If you lose that ability you have a big problem. And that's the problem we faced."

Demers called it "one of the most disappointing moments" of his life. He held a news conference at his Jacques Demers restaurant in Southfield. "My pride is hurt," he declared. He'd gone his entire hockey career without ever being fired.

Demers received a standing ovation from fans when he returned to Joe Louis Arena as a radio analyst for the Quebec Nordiques in December 1990. In his four years with the Wings, Demers went 137–136–47, winning two division titles. He resurfaced in 1992 with the Montreal Canadiens, coaching them to the 1993 Stanley Cup championship; the Wings had been booted in the first round.

"He should feel good about himself, not only for winning the Stanley Cup but for what he did here," Devellano said. "He had a great impact on this franchise and this city. We won with him behind our bench and we filled the building. He had a profound marketing effect while he was here."

Potvin, Bryan Trottier, and Mike Bossy. Devellano had also suggested hiring Al Arbour as head coach.

Devellano flew to Detroit on July 1, 1982. Ilitch took him to one of the Little Caesars Pizza plants. Devellano met Marian Ilitch, met their seven children. One day turned into two days. Finally, over coffee at the airport—Ilitch had driven Devellano there himself—Ilitch offered Devellano the job.

Devellano's first summer with the Wings was very busy. He embraced Ilitch's push to re-engage fans, going to booster club meetings, calling in to sports talk radio shows, even calling back fans who'd leave messages with the switchboard at Joe Louis Arena. He tried out various slogans—"We're not easy anymore" and "We'll earn our Wings."

He worked 16 hours a day, his fingers weighed down by the three Stanley Cup rings he'd won with the Islanders. "I'm trying to improve that damn product on the ice," Devellano said in an August 1982 interview with *Detroit Free Press* reporter Joe Lapointe. "We'll be quite respectable in four years, and our long-term goal is the Stanley Cup. I'll save the other hand for Detroit rings. I'll be like Sammy Davis, Jr."

For more visual inspiration, Devellano hung a picture on his office wall of the 1980 U.S. Olympic hockey team celebrating its success over the Soviet Union. On his desk was a book titled *Winning Is Everything! Losing Is Nothing!: For the Nice Folks Who Want to Finish First.*

Ilitch endorsed Devellano's plan to build through the draft but naturally pined for a better product even sooner. "I'm hoping we can do it somewhere in the area of three years," Ilitch said.

First, the team needed a new coach. Devellano hired Nick Polano, describing him as a "proven winner and a hard-nosed guy." (Polano became the team's 13th coach in 14 years, replacing Billy Dea, an interim coach who served 11 games after Wayne Maxner was fired late in the 1981–

82 season.) Polano was a Wings fan as a boy, going so far as to wear a ring with a picture of Lindsay that he had gotten from an offer on the back of a cereal box. (He also served as an assistant with the Buffalo Sabres under future coach Scotty Bowman.)

"I think there's something new and fresh about the whole thing," Devellano said. It certainly fit a trend: Polano had never been a head coach in the NHL, Devellano had never been a GM of an NHL team, and Ilitch had never owned an NHL team.

The freshness grew stale as the Wings began the 1982–83 season 0–6–1. Devellano tried everything: he called out players in the press, he called them to his office. "I want to hear what they have to say about what the problems seem to be," he said. "It's a disappointing start. I'm mystified. I don't have an answer for it."

Back in those days, Devellano watched games from the stands, seated next to fans. He worried they might boo him, but they booed the product on the ice. Devellano was tempted to join in. "Frankly, I can only approach the Red Wings like a new expansion franchise," he said. "I told that to Mr. Ilitch. I know that's hard to accept for people who have bought season tickets for 15 years or more, but look at us. We have no superstars, only seven or eight bona fide NHL players and our farm system is almost barren." Devellano could blame his predecessor for that: Jimmy Skinner's trades included dealing away four first-round picks.

The Wings finally won in their eighth game, defeating Bowman's Sabres by a score of 6–2. "My heart couldn't have taken too many more losses," Devellano said afterward.

There were 44 losses in all in 1982–83, and just 21 victories. The Wings finished last in the Norris Division, 18th in the 21-team league.

Eleven months into the job, Devellano acquired that game-breaker he'd lamented the team lacked. After missing out on hometown star Pat LaFontaine at third overall, Devellano drafted Steve Yzerman at fourth. The 1983 draft also yielded Bob Probert, Joe Kocur, and Petr Klima, all of whom would play significant roles in changing the team's fortunes.

Devellano's Wings started to take flight. They made the playoffs in 1984 and 1985, and showed signs of rebirth as strong drafts infiltrated the roster (although 1985–86 was ugly: 17–57–6, dead last in the NHL). In 1987 the Wings advanced to the conference finals, and Devellano was rewarded with a three-year contract extension. The salary line was left blank. Team vice president Jim Lites told Devellano to fill it in himself. "I gave myself a raise," Devellano said.

As the decade came to a close, though, Devellano's job appeared to be in jeopardy. Two of the picks he made at the 1989 draft—Nicklas Lidstrom and Sergei Fedorov—would turn out to be first-ballot Hockey Hall of Famers, but no one knew that at the time. The Wings lost in the first round of the playoffs in 1989 and failed to quality in 1990. Devellano had been on the job for eight years, and the Wings were still thirsting for a Cup. "I'm sorry to disappoint so many people," he said in May 1990.

By July he had a new title: senior vice president. Bryan Murray took over as general manager, leaving Devellano responsible for the NHL entry draft and player development. "Jimmy D's a good scout," Ilitch said. "His health hasn't been great, he's in poor health. He had a lot of pressure on him in his job and he wanted to continue to do a little bit of scouting, so I allowed him to do so."

Devellano resumed GM duties in 1994, sharing managerial duties with Bowman, who was named director of player personnel a year after being named coach. Devellano's title was director of hockey operations. That was his role when, 15 years after being hired by Ilitch, the Wings won the Stanley Cup on June 7, 1997. Minutes after the buzzer sounded on Game 4 at Joe Louis Arena, Devellano was on the Wings' bench, hugging the Ilitches, hugging Yzerman.

Devellano had come to Detroit with three Stanley Cup rings. He won four more with the Wings, in 1997, 1998, 2002, and 2008.

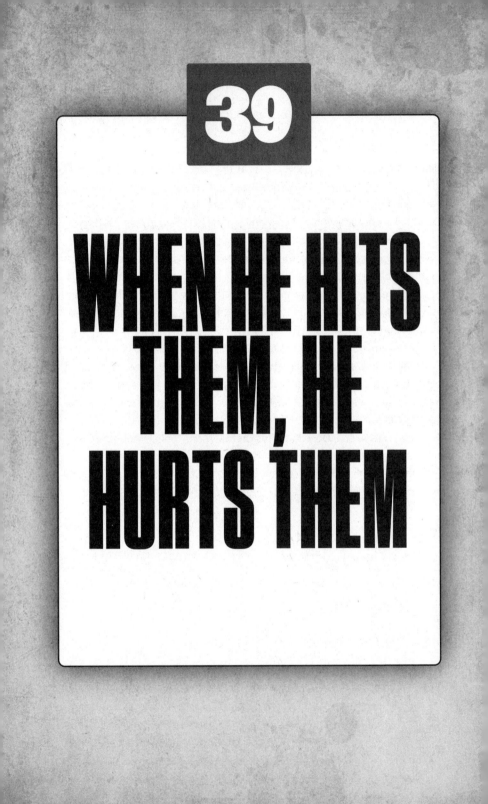

39

WHEN HE HITS THEM, HE HURTS THEM

Kirk Maltby couldn't figure out why the Red Wings wanted him. When the Wings traded for Maltby on March 20, 1996, they already had won 53 games and had a 20-point lead on first place in the NHL. What did they need with him? He hadn't even played in a month because of a scary injury.

"In my own head, I was like, *Why would I be traded here*?" Maltby said in a 2019 interview reflecting on his career. "I knew what kind of player I was. I was like, *Why aren't they adding more goal scoring or a defenseman? Why are they adding me?* I didn't know where I would fit in."

Maltby came to the Wings from the Edmonton Oilers, who were battling to make the playoffs. The Wings were trying to win the Stanley Cup, and they dealt collegiate defenseman Dan McGillis to the Oilers to acquire Maltby.

"We weren't going to sign McGillis," Scotty Bowman said in 2019. "Edmonton wanted him. Kirk became a really good player for us. He really developed. He really improved."

When Maltby, a left wing, arrived in Detroit, he hadn't played since January 30. He had suffered an eye injury when clipped by Oilers teammate Louie DeBrusk's stick during a practice, an incident that would require him to wear a visor for the rest of his career.

Only 23, Maltby had two goals, six assists, and a minus-16 rating in 49 games with the Oilers. He would look at those numbers and wonder where he fit, or how he fit, in Detroit, but it was his physicality that intrigued the Wings. Higher-ups in the organization still remembered Maltby's bone-rattling hit the previous season on Paul Coffey, which caused Coffey to sit out a few games with a back injury.

Maltby played eight games in the 1996 playoff run that ended when the Wings lost to the Colorado Avalanche in the Western Conference finals. It was a huge disappointment for a team that had set a record with 62 regular season victories, and once again Maltby had doubts about whether he would fit with the team.

"I remember coming to training camp in '96," Maltby said. "I was staying at the hotel at the Renaissance Center for the whole camp and exhibition season. I didn't know if I would make the team. I was in and out of the lineup the first half of the season."

But Maltby did make the team. He gave Bowman an option to reduce the wear and tear on Steve Yzerman and Brendan Shanahan. The two stars were taken off penalty-killing duties and Maltby and Kris Draper became regulars when the Wings were shorthanded. It was an ideal development, because it allowed Bowman to roll his line of Yzerman, Shanahan, and Darren McCarty without having to account for Yzerman and Shanahan killing penalties while McCarty was idle. Yzerman and Shanahan had started every penalty kill, seeing time against opposing star players. Now it was Maltby and Draper doing hard time.

The Wings had hired in Bowman in 1993 for the sole purpose of winning the Stanley Cup. He had added a cerebral center in Igor Larionov in 1995 and a premier power forward in Shanahan at the start of the 1996–97 season. Maltby was brought in for his physical play. During Christmastime in 1996, Bowman, on the suggestion of Yzerman, reached out to Joe Kocur. A former half of the Bruise Brothers had washed out of the NHL and was playing in a beer league. Kocur jumped at the chance to rejoin the Wings—and within a few months, Maltby knew where he fit.

"We signed Joey and shortly thereafter Scotty put me and Joey and Drapes on a line and things were going good," Maltby said. "Fast-forward to the playoffs—it was a lot of fun."

The trio stirred and scored. The line—at that time, it had not yet been dubbed "The Grind Line"—played with speed and strength, tenacity and toughness. Maltby especially had a knack for annoying opponents. "Guys spend their whole shift chasing Maltby around the rink," associate coach Barry Smith noted.

In Game 3 of the first-round series against the Blues, the score was 2–2 when Geoff Courtnall head-butted Maltby, drawing a match penalty and an automatic game misconduct. "Any time you put your team on a power play, it's a plus for us," Maltby said. "For our line, that's our job."

They contributed the first goal in the 3–2 victory when Draper backhanded the rebound from Maltby's slap shot past Grant Fuhr less than three minutes into the game.

After the Wings lost Game 4, Bowman retooled the Grind Line to feature Maltby, Draper, and McCarty. After the Wings won Game 5, Bowman called the line the key to the 5–2 victory. "It's fun that we're able to complement each other and read each other," Maltby said. "With our style, we get under teams' skin. It's good anytime you can get a guy to retaliate."

Maltby, who had tallied three goals in 66 games during the regular season, scored three times the first 14 games in the playoffs. That was a bonus. It was the way he mowed down opponents that stood out. "When he hits them, he hurts them," Ted Lindsay said. "They remember."

The Grind Line became such a success it spawned T-shirts, with images of the players depicted on the front. And when *Sports Illustrated* devoted its June 2, 1997, issue to the Red Wings, it was Maltby who was on the cover.

Maltby finally put any doubts he had about where he would fit to rest. He finished the playoffs with five goals, two assists, and a plus-6 rating in 20 games. "I went from not knowing if I would be on the Wings to being on a T-shirt as the Grind Line," he said. "Especially for a player like me, I was able to find a niche. When I look back, my moment of feeling like I belonged was Game 1 of the Stanley Cup Finals in Philadelphia. Me, Drapes, and Mac start against the Legion of Doom. I remember thinking, *I am starting against Eric Lindros, John LeClair, and Mikael Renberg. Holy Christ.* It gave me confidence. I felt like I belonged."

Maltby ended up spending 14 seasons with the Wings, winning the Stanley Cup in 1997, '98, '02, and '08. He played 908 games in a Wings uniform (1,072 in his career) and tallied 107 goals and 222 points. In 169 playoff games, all with the Wings, Maltby tallied 16 goals and 31 points. Two of 15 playoff assists came in the 2002 Western Conference finals, when he set up McCarty's second and third goals in the only hat trick of his career.

Maltby's role gradually diminished under coach Mike Babcock, and on October 12, 2010, Maltby made his retirement official at a news conference staged in the media lounge at Joe Louis Arena.

"I was a pain in the ass," he said, reflecting on his playing career as he segued into a job as a pro scout for the Wings. "I just like to think I was a guy who came and worked hard. All I wanted to do was win, and I did what I had to do to help my team win."

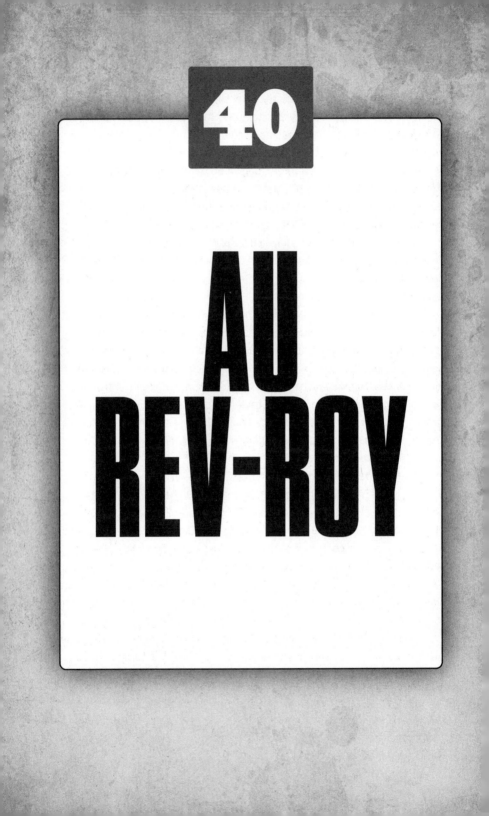

Players kept glancing up at the scoreboard as they left the ice and left the bench. There was no way that score was real, was there?

The 2001–02 Red Wings were one of the greatest teams ever assembled, a supernova of superstars assembled for one purpose: to win the Stanley Cup. There were future Hall of Famers at every position: Dominik Hasek in goal; Nicklas Lidstrom and Chris Chelios on defense; and Steve Yzerman, Sergei Fedorov, Brendan Shanahan, Brett Hull, Igor Larionov, and Luc Robitaille up front.

The team stumbled the first two games of the first round of the postseason, losing twice at home to Vancouver, but once the Wings regained their footing, they cruised past the Canucks and took care of the Blues in Round 2, in five games.

That set up another meeting with the Wings' nemesis. The 2001–02 Colorado Avalanche had a superstar goaltender in Patrick Roy and a highly respected captain in Joe Sakic; Rob Blake and Adam Foote on defense; and Peter Forsberg, Alex Tanguay, and Milan Hejduk up front. If there was one team that threatened the Wings for the silver chalice, it was the Avalanche.

And so the Avs did. Forsberg scored in overtime in Game 5, sending the series back to Denver with the Wings facing elimination at three games to two. Hasek responded by stopping all 24 shots and Shanahan and Darren McCarty provided the goals in a 2–0 victory that set up a final showdown at Joe Louis Arena.

The Wings prepared for what they believed would be the toughest game of the series. The Avalanche, after all, had won their last four Game 7s and had beaten the Wings in three out of their four playoff series.

"We knew they were going to give it their best, just like us," Kirk Maltby said in a 2019 interview. "This was winner takes all. It was probably going to be a 2–1 game or something like that. That's what we figured."

What no one figured was that it would be so one-sided that fans at the Joe started partying in the first period and serenading in the third. The Wings scored on their first shot, on their second shot, on their fifth shot.

Roy, winner of the Stanley Cup in 1986, '93, '96, and '01, let in the first goal less than two minutes after the puck dropped. Tomas Holmstrom managed to deflect a shot from the point even as he was tangled up with a defender, at 1:57. Eighty seconds later Fedorov fired a puck that bounced through traffic and slipped beneath Roy's right arm. Fans taunted Roy, dismissively chanting, "Pa-*trick*, Pa-*trick*."

Then Robitaille turned a pass from Larionov into a 3–0 lead, scoring five-hole on Roy at 10:25. Roy banged his stick. Avalanche coach Bob Hartley called a time-out and called Roy over to the bench. Did Roy want to come out? No? Okay, game on. It was 3–0, sure, but there was still almost 50 minutes of hockey left.

The time-out didn't help. Holmstrom scored again at 12:51, scooping up Robitaille's rebound and turning it into a 4–0 lead. If it was the first time in 240 playoff games that Roy had let in four goals in one period.

If Avalanche players couldn't believe it, well, neither could the guys who were ahead. "I remember going off the bench after the first period and as a group—it was almost like we were on the other side, that we were down 4–0," Maltby said. "We were in disbelief."

It was like holding a winning lottery ticket—you checked the numbers one more time, just to make sure it wasn't a dream. Then you checked again.

"You imagine and pray for something like this, but you don't realistically think it's going to happen," Hull said.

Hull scored 4:41 into the second period. The Wings were too savvy, too wary, to assume their victory was sealed. They knew the Avalanche had the talent to mount a rally, so better to make it even more insurmountable.

"The good thing about it was we didn't have just such a good leadership core, but we had so much experience from winning and being in so many different situations," Maltby said. "We knew we had to keep our foot on the gas because the team on the other side had such a high-quality team and the ability to score. We kept our foot down and put a few more in the net and made sure there was no chance of them coming back."

When Fredrik Olausson scored to make it 6–0 at 6:28 of the second period, the Avalanche pulled Roy. The future Hall of Fame goaltender had allowed 6 goals on 16 shots. His save percentage that night was .625. A headline in the *Detroit Free Press* the next day summed up his night: Au Rev-Roy!

While the Wings humbled Roy, Hasek basked in the blowout. He made six saves in the first period, three in the second. Chris Drury appeared to score at 12:50 of the third period but video replay showed he kicked in the puck, and Hasek's shutout remained intact. It was his NHL record fifth of the playoffs. Roy may have had the Cups, but Hasek had the last victory.

"To be honest, I felt good," Hasek said. "It was a relief for me. I wasn't going to have to see him anymore."

Soon after Pavel Datsyuk scored at 16:09 of the third period, fans sang along to Neil Diamond's "Sweet Caroline," eagerly anticipating the Stanley Cup Finals against the Carolina Hurricanes. All that was left was for the horn to sound on a 7–0 final. It was the most lopsided Game 7 in NHL playoff history, surpassing two six-goal-margin games.

"To be honest, we thought this would be an overtime game," Yzerman said. "After the first period, we were up 4–0, and we were still thinking, *This isn't how it's supposed to be*."

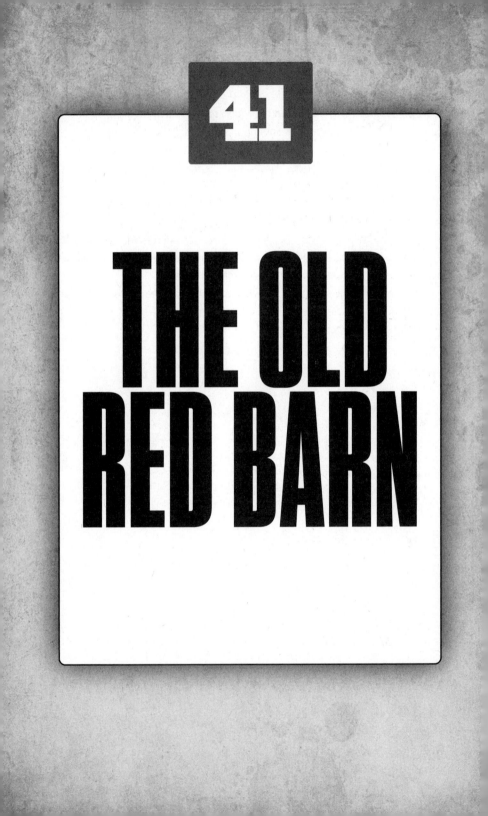

41

THE OLD RED BARN

Olympia Stadium was a red brick hockey barn, a place of character and charm and championships. It wasn't easily accessible and there wasn't much parking, but the Red Wings franchise called it home from 1927 to 1979 and won seven Stanley Cups beneath its roof.

"It was the greatest place in the world to work," longtime radio announcer Bruce Martyn said. "You were sitting on top of everything. It was a scary place when they had the riots, but it didn't have a bad sight line anywhere."

The fans loved it too. "Everybody was into the game from the moment it started," Martyn continued. "It was a friendly place."

It was where fans chanted "We want Howe" on April 23, 1950, when the Wings played the New York Rangers in Game 7 of the Stanley Cup Finals. Eight minutes into the second overtime, Pete Babando scored on a 15-foot backhand shot. NHL president Clarence Campbell presented the Stanley Cup to Wings captain Sid Abel at center ice. Fans whooped and cheered and wanted more, wanted Howe. He had suffered a near-fatal head injury in the first game of the playoffs, and when he walked onto the ice, his head bearing the stitches from the injury, fans erupted into a frenzy.

It was where Mike Ilitch watched the Wings as a kid, dreaming of one day owning them. It was where he took Marian Bayoff when he courted her. It was where, in 1947, Miller High defeated St. Joseph 47–34 before a crowd of 16,041 people, the largest in Michigan high school basketball history.

Olympia Stadium opened on October 15, 1927, seven months after Detroit mayor John W. Smith laid the cornerstone in a ceremony at the site on the corner of Grand River Avenue and McGraw Street. It was built to house the new hockey team a group of Detroit businessmen had purchased when the Western Hockey League dissolved and the Victoria Cougars became available. Initial capacity was 11,563, but renovations over the years expanded its seating to 15,000.

The renamed Detroit Cougars played their first game in their new home on November 22, 1927. Johnny Shephard gave fans a reason to cheer when he scored the first goal, but the Cougars fell to Ottawa Senators 2–1. The Cougars advanced to the playoffs in 1929, but a losing record the next season prompted a name change to the Detroit Falcons. When James E. Norris purchased the team in 1932, he renamed the team the Red Wings after an old club he played for in Montreal. He retained Jack Adams as coach and general manager. Four years later, in 1936, Olympia Stadium hosted its first Stanley Cup championship.

The arena hosted many notable events over the years, from boxing to the Beatles. It was where Jake LaMotta defeated Sugar Ray Robinson on February 5, 1943, pummeling his rival and knocking him through the ropes of the boxing ring. On September 6, 1964, 15,000 fans danced along to "Twist and Shout" in the first of two performances by the Beatles. Tickets were $3; they rose to $5.50 when the Beatles played at Olympia less than two years later.

That was the same year Martyn called the overtime conclusion to the Wings–Canadiens finale in the '66 playoffs, his sonorous voice sounding out a crushing finish: "It's Richard, Balon, and Talbot. Richard across the line, Balon moving in, a pass right in front and the Canadiens have scored! And Montreal has won the Stanley Cup! And the Canadiens move out onto the ice! And it was almost too sudden."

The Detroit Pistons were joint tenants from 1957 to 1961. When Bruce Norris took control of the team from his sister, Marguerite, in 1955, he refurbished the arena, adding padded seats.

The neighborhood went into decline after the deadly riots that shook the city in the summer of 1967, and the Wings went into decline under Bruce Norris. Fans started calling them the "Dead Wings" and "the worst team money can buy." Wings practices were open at Olympia Stadium, but the team wasn't worth watching. In 1977—50 years after they began playing at Olympia—there was talk of the Wings moving to Pontiac, but an agreement was reached on a new building along the Detroit riverfront. The city would own the building—the future Joe Louis Arena—but Norris would have operational control. The city threw in Cobo Hall and parking structures to avoid Norris moving the team from Detroit.

That set the clock ticking on Olympia. The Wings played their last game there on December 15, 1979. A capacity 15,609 fans jammed the old arena and watched the Wings tie the Quebec Nordiques 4–4. In February 1980, more than 14,000 fans came to see what was billed as the Old Red

Barn's final hockey game, an exhibition showcase between the Wings and alumni. The stadium closed for good that month.

In 1985 the city council voted to demolish the stadium. It was 58 years old and had fallen into disrepair since the Wings left, a sad and sorry-looking reminder of better days for the city and for the hockey team. In the 1950s, taxis would line up two deep and stretch half a mile waiting for games to be over. Now the stadium stood among boarded-up buildings painted with graffiti.

Olympia Stadium was torn down in September 1987, its sign put in storage. The state and federal government erected an armory, garage, and vehicle repair shop for Michigan National Guard's 1st battalion, 182nd artillery regiment on the site. An indoor rifle range was installed where Howe, Lindsay, and Abel once shot pucks.

Joe Louis Arena was home to the Wings until April 9, 2017. When the team moved into its brand-new home, Little Caesars Arena, the original Olympia Stadium marquee letters graced the concourse next to a mural of Gordie Howe.

42

KEN HOLLAND

Soon after he started a new job in 2019, Ken Holland walked into the media dining lounge at Rogers Place and picked out a table. It had to have a good view of a TV, but that was easy given how many screens were mounted on the walls. He also wanted a table big enough where people could join him for pregame meals. An employee crafted a RESERVED sign, and, when the Edmonton Oilers began the 2019-20 season, Holland had his new dining spot.

It was a stark contrast for reporters who covered the Oilers, who grew used to rarely seeing previous general managers outside of news conferences. Here was Holland—dining in their midst, milling about the press box during intermissions. But accessibility and gregariousness marked the start of Holland's tenure with the Oilers, just as they had marked his 22 years managing the Red Wings.

Holland loved to talk hockey. With anyone. With everyone. Hockey was his life.

He was elected to the Hockey Hall of Fame as a builder in 2020, one year after leaving the Wings—but there was a brief time after his playing days ended that Holland considered leaving the sport.

He tried to make it as a goaltender. He was 19 years old when he decided to attend the junior hockey camp of the Medicine Hat Tigers. He wanted one of their jerseys—Holland would later joke he was prepared to steal one—and got one when he earned a job. He spent two seasons with the Tigers, then embarked on a career as a minor-league goaltender that lasted until 1984-85. He spent his last two seasons in the Wings organization, making three of his four career NHL appearances in a winged wheel jersey.

Holland was 29 and out of work as a hockey player. Back in his hometown of Vernon, British Columbia, he had taken a summer job stocking shelves for a liquor store, but that wasn't much of a paycheck for a man with a wife and three children under five years old. He considered going to college and earning a degree in accounting, but that wasn't realistic given his need for an immediate income. He talked it over with his family.

"My mom told me I needed to get a job right away," Holland said in 2019. "She and my grandmother both needed a new vacuum cleaner, and she suggested I get into selling vacuum cleaners door-to-door. That sounded good, but then I wondered, where is the *third* sale coming from? I pictured myself the next day with doors slamming in my face. I was going to have to make a decision. You don't know what's out there for you."

He soon found out. Bill Dineen, who had coached Holland with the AHL's Adirondack Red Wings, recommended him as a scout to Wings general manager Jimmy Devellano. Devellano balked at first, wary that Holland had no scouting experience. After talking with Holland on the phone, Devellano changed his mind and offered him the job.

Holland drove through ice storms and snowstorms, drove hundreds of miles in a day. He filed impressively detailed reports that reminded Devellano of his own days starting out as a scout with the St. Louis Blues. "Kenny was very, very detailed," Devellano said in 2019. "That is what scouting is all about. He did a wonderful job."

In 1989, Devellano promoted Holland to director of scouting. In 1993, Bob Clarke tried to hire Holland as assistant general manager of the Florida Panthers, but the Wings refused to let Holland out of his contract. Devellano had plans of his own for Holland; he was named assistant general manager in 1994, with assurances he would one day rise another rung.

Holland was named the 10th general manager of the Wings on July 18, 1997, a month after the Wings won the Stanley Cup. "I think he'll have a tremendous run in Detroit," Devellano said at the time.

Scotty Bowman had carried dual titles of coach and director of player personnel, and Holland did not accept the GM job until he was certain that he would have control of the team and that Bowman would be coach and coach alone.

One of Holland's first moves was a bold one. He traded Mike Vernon, the 1997 playoff MVP, to San Jose. Holland was confident that Chris Osgood—whom Holland had scouted in western Canada and pushed for in the 1991 draft—was ready to be the team's bona fide starter.

"I wasn't nervous about it, but it meant a lot to me," Osgood said in 2019. "I was confident I could handle the pressure."

Holland had a monumental task in the summer of 1997: find a physical, top-pairing defenseman in the prime of his career. Vladimir Konstantinov was fighting for his life after sustaining career-ending injuries in a limousine accident. Then there was Sergei Fedorov's holdout with which to contend.

Holland remained for 22 years as manager of the Wings, during which time he engineered dozens of trades. In March 1999, with the Wings pushing for a third straight Stanley Cup, Holland acquired Chris Chelios, Ulf Samuelsson, Wendel Clark, and Bill Ranford. Chelios spent a decade with the Wings, helping them to win the Stanley Cup in 2002 and '08. In December 2000, Holland reacquired Igor Larionov, whose decision to sign with Florida was a disaster. Larionov played a significant role in the 2002 Cup run, centering a fourth line that featured fellow future Hockey Hall of Fame member Luc Robitaille on one wing and Tomas Holmstrom on the other.

Another crucial member of the 2002 team was acquired in June 2001, when Holland negotiated deep into the night with his colleague in Buffalo, Sabres general manager Darcy Regier. For Vyacheslav Kozlov and a first-round pick, Holland landed one of the greatest goaltenders ever in Dominik Hasek. Then with Hasek on board, Holland went out and signed Robitaille and Brett Hull.

"Kenny was pretty sharp on that regard," Bowman said in 2019. "He would sign guys to one or two years. Then if you're wrong, you're wrong—but he wasn't wrong."

That same summer, Holland traded defenseman Aaron Ward to Carolina for a 2002 second-round pick. That selection yielded forward Jiri Hudler, who would go on to play a key role in the 2008 Stanley Cup championship.

Another trade that aided that Cup effort came at the 2008 deadline, when Holland acquired defenseman Brad Stuart. Stuart formed a fierce pairing with Niklas Kronwall, the gritty follow-up to the finesse pairing of Nicklas Lidstrom and Brian Rafalski. Rafalski was one of Holland's free-agent signings, from the summer of 2007.

Of course, there were duds along the way. Uwe Krupp, signed to ameliorate the loss of Konstantinov, played just 30 games after being signed to a four-year contract. He claimed back pain prevented him from playing, but when the Wings found out he was dogsledding, it led to a series of suspensions and arbitration hearings. Stephen Weiss, signed at the request of coach Mike Babcock to a five-year deal in the summer of 2013, was such a disaster the Wings bought out his contract in 2015. There were also trades—Kyle Quincey in 2012, David Legwand in 2014, Erik Cole in 2015—which did not pan out.

One of Holland's last actions as GM of the Red Wings came in autumn 2018. When Steve Yzerman announced he would be stepping back as general manager of the Tampa Bay Lightning in September 2018, just as he was entering the last year of his contract, Holland knew what needed to come next. Should Yzerman be available in spring 2019, Holland wanted him to be the next general manager of the Red Wings.

That came to pass April 19, 2019. Holland accepted a role as advisor, but he grew restless after a few weeks. When the Oilers came calling, he found an ideal landing place. Had it been a team in the Atlantic Division—or even the Eastern Conference—Holland said in fall 2019 that he would not have accepted. "I root for the Wings, I root for Steve Yzerman—except when we're playing them," Holland said.

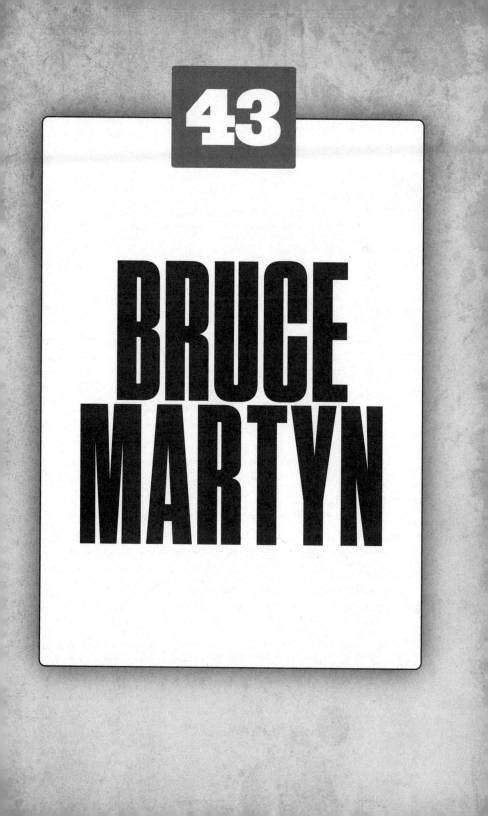

43

BRUCE MARTYN

Bruce Martyn had been retired for two years when he finally called a game on the radio on a night the Red Wings won a Stanley Cup.

Martyn had been the radio voice of the Wings from 1964 to 1995. He called games at Olympia Stadium, Joe Louis Arena, and countless arenas on the road—called them back when radio announcers didn't need a lineup sheet because players didn't wear helmets and there were only six teams.

Martyn has his favorite stories from those days. One of them, of course, involved Gordie Howe. "I've been asked a hundred times: Who is a better player, Wayne Gretzky or Gordie Howe?" Martyn, still sharp as a tack at age 90, said in a 2019 interview. "And I've always said, 'Well, you take five Wayne Gretzkys and put them on the ice and I'll take five Gordie Howes, and I'll beat you 40–0. Because you will be down on the ice and Gordie will be putting the puck in the net.' Gordie was such a natural athlete. He just covered everything."

Martyn first met Howe in the early 1950s, back when the Production Line—Howe, Sid Abel, and Ted Lindsay—reigned in the NHL. Martyn got his start in radio in his hometown of Sault Ste. Marie, Michigan. "My wife and I had a little radio station there, doing a little bit of the Northern Ontario Hockey Association games," Martyn said. "The Red Wings were training there. Eventually, it came to be we met everybody. As a fledging announcer, I interviewed the Production Line. I said about three words, I was so nervous. They carried the interview. It was such a thrill for me."

The Martyns moved to the Detroit area in 1953, and Martyn began calling games for the Detroit Lions, the Detroit Pistons, and Michigan State football for WCAR-AM (1130). He later worked for WKBD-TV (Channel 50). In 1964, the Wings called. Martyn teamed with Budd Lynch, and later Abel, calling games for 31 seasons. He exclaimed, "He shoots, he scores!" thousands of times, his melodious voice cracking an octave higher. He saw generations of the greatest players in the game along the way.

His career with the Wings, though, was bookended by bittersweet events.

"My second year and last year were two of my greatest disappointments," Martyn said. "We went into Montreal in 1966 and won the first two games at the Forum, which is hardly ever done. Andy Bathgate, who had been picked up by the Red Wings, I sat with him on the bus going out to the airport. Andy was saying, 'Boy, they're going to throw you in the shower as soon as we get that Cup.' Then they proceeded to lose the next four games, including a real heartbreaker in Detroit.

"Then in 1995, they looked like they were going to go right down the line for a Stanley Cup, which I never got in 31 years. That's when they went in and New Jersey beat them four straight games."

Those playoffs ended in disappointment, but at least the Wings were in the playoffs. The toughest stretch of Martyn's career with the Wings was the 1970s—the "Darkness with Harkness" years under Ned Harkness, whose coaching career with the Wings ended after a 12–22–4 mark in 1971 but who lasted three-and-a-half more seasons as general manager.

When Ted Lindsay was named GM in 1977, the Wings still couldn't win, plus Martyn's travel arrangements worsened. "Originally everything was commercial flights," he said. "The announcers and coaching staff would ride in first class and the players had their spot in the rear, which they liked because it separated them from being observed all the time. When Ted Lindsay became general manager of the team, he made the announcement that 'I will not sit anywhere my players can't sit, and that goes for the rest of you.' So that was the end of first class."

Mostly Martyn remembered how much he loved his job and the people he worked with. Lynch became a lifelong friend. So did Abel.

Martyn, born June 24, 1929, was like many of the players back in the day: he had a second job. He worked as a manufacturers' representative for Fred Harris & Associates. "I worked days and nights," Martyn remembered.

Martyn was at a party in the summer of 1982 when he found out that pizza baron Mike Ilitch had bought the Wings from Bruce Norris, ending 50 years of Norris ownership of the franchise. Norris was a part-timer, a guy who relied on one of his executives, Lincoln Cavalieri, to keep him up to date on what was going on with the Wings. Ilitch was at Joe Louis Arena every day.

LAST MINUTE OF PLAY IN THIS PERIOD

Budd Lynch was living history for the Red Wings, a link between their first dynasty and their second 40 years later. He was a link between Gordie Howe and Steve Yzerman, Tommy Ivan and Scotty Bowman, James Norris and Mike Ilitch.

Lynch began working for the Wings in 1949, just when they were starting their string of seven straight first-place finishes and four Stanley Cups. He broadcast games on the radio and sometimes on television. The latter, at that time, was a nascent phenomenon. Lynch once estimated there were 500 TV sets in Detroit when he started.

He called Wings games for 26 seasons and broke in Bruce Martyn in the mid-1960s. The two became the best of friends, often traveling with the team.

"Budd was always close to the players," Martyn remembered. "We were coming out of Toronto one time and the Red Wings had lost the game pretty badly and it was a pretty dark trip between the hockey rink and the airport. Budd and I were seated in the front seats like we always did. Alex Delvecchio was the captain of the team; he sat way in the back. It was so quiet you couldn't believe it.

"All of a sudden there's a voice in the back and sure enough, it was Delvecchio. He said, 'Budd! Budd! We've got a question for you.' Budd started getting his briefcase out and said, 'Yes, yes, what is it?' They said, 'Budd, how do you wind your watch?' Budd just had a left arm."

Frank Joseph James "Budd" Lynch lost his right arm and shoulder serving in the Canadian Army in World War II. He was part of the third wave at Juno Beach on D-Day in 1944. Three weeks later Lynch and his outfit were near Caen, France, when a German shell exploded and lacerated Lynch's body as he dragged a fellow solider to safety.

Lynch did play-by-play until 1975, when he was named director of public relations. In 1985, he was named arena announcer.

Lynch died at 95 on October 9, 2012. The Wings continued to use a recording of Lynch announcing "last minute of play in this period" until their last game at Joe Louis Arena on April 9, 2017.

"Mike Ilitch took a very close interest in the team, whereas Bruce Norris just traveled back and forth from Chicago and got his information from Lincoln Cavalieri mostly," Martyn said. "He was the absent owner, where Mike Ilitch was the hands-on. It made a big difference."

While at that party, Lefty Wilson, the team's longtime trainer, occasional spare goaltender, and general jack-of-all-trades, found out he had been released by the team. "They wanted a more professional-type trainer," Martyn said. "He was the only trainer there, and one of his methods was to say, 'Get up, you're not hurt.' It worked in those days. Guys would go in, get a shot of cortisone, and be right back on the ice."

Medical treatment was one of the things Martyn saw change dramatically over his years. So was the makeup of the roster. It was North American when he started; decidedly more worldly when he left. One of his favorite players from the later generation he saw was Sergei Fedorov, a prize pick from the 1989 draft. They gambled and picked him in the fourth round, even though there was no guarantee they could get him out of Russia. Fedorov was with the Wings a year later.

"When Sergei came in, this was his first year, it was a game on the West Coast," Martyn said. "He went out of his way to speak English. He really worked on it. We sat down at breakfast and he said, 'I don't feel very good.' Well, the team had taken him out and made him buy dinner the night before. I guess they had some beers Sergei wasn't used to. I said to go up to his room and order a milkshake and just sit down and relax, which he did. The next day he came and said, 'Oh, thank you.' That was Dr. Martyn's first cure."

Martyn was inducted into the Hockey Hall of Fame in 1991, the unanimous winner of the Foster Hewitt Memorial Award for excellence in hockey broadcasting.

"When I heard it was the award named for Foster Hewitt, well, that was what really makes it an honor," Martyn said at the time. "When I was a kid, that was it. He was my dream."

Martyn retired in 1995 but realized a dream two years later. When the Wings were ahead three-games-to-none in the 1997 Stanley Cup Finals against the Philadelphia Flyers, Martyn's voice once again sounded on the Wings' radio broadcast. "Ken Kal, a beautiful young guy, invited me to do the second period of the game," Martyn said. Kal had become the team's play-by-play announcer after Martyn's retirement. "Lo and behold, that is when Darren McCarty scored his goal that won the series," Martyn said at the time. "That's the first time I had ever been to a Stanley Cup party. It was a tremendous experience for me because I dreamed of something like this most of my life."

44

THE JOE

One of the first actions Mike Ilitch took after purchasing the Red Wings in 1982 was to redecorate.

Joe Louis Arena was only a couple years old, completed in 1979 to house the Wings after 52 years at Olympia Stadium. It opened to less than favorable reviews for lacking Olympia's character, for looking like a warehouse on the riverfront, for its steep steps at the entrances, for its higher prices and for not being totally finished. Ilitch wanted to send a message, one that exorcised the stagnant atmosphere that had descended during previous owner Bruce Norris. Ilitch wanted the Joe to impress, "so people will want to be a part of the team and the family," Ilitch said in October 1982. "It's my job as leader of the franchise to produce the proper environment. This is my way of doing things. I want to do things that are going to stimulate the fans along with the team members and the staff."

Ilitch signed off on renovating the locker room, lining the weight room with mirrors, buying fancy new exercise machines. He revamped the press room and the pro shop, added a Little Caesars outlet (of course), and put up murals in the concourse. He ordered new buttons for the coats worn by arena ushers. He greenighted a team mascot, a bird dressed in red feathers and nicknamed "The Red Winger." (The guy wearing the costume on opening night, Jim Wilczak, slipped and fell on the ice, but delighted fans as he signed autographs and threw pucks to children.) The mascot lasted only a short time.

To further attract fans as he sought to move forward from the "Dead Wings" era, Ilitch authorized a season-long promotion: a new car would be given away at each home game.

Ilitch invited fans to watch Wings practices at the Joe, but the first attempt went awry because it had not been cleared with the arena's landlord. Norris' Olympia Stadium Corporation still managed the Joe and Cobo Hall, city-owned buildings under the control of executive Lincoln Cavalieri. It was a confusing time for arena employees: there was a new tenant (the Wings), the landlord (Olympia Corp.) was the previous owner,

Steve Yzerman and Lane Lambert in front of Joe Louis Arena in 1984.
(Mary Schroeder)

and the city owned the property. Things became easier in December 1982, when Ilitch paid an estimated $15 million for the operating contracts to Joe Louis Arena and Cobo Hall and renamed the corporation Olympia Arenas. In 1996, the name was changed to Olympia Entertainment.

Joe Louis Arena hosted its first Wings game on December 27, 1979. The cost was $57 million and was the city's capitulation to Norris' threat to move the team to Pontiac in 1977. It had great sight lines, spacious corridors, and concession stands with closed-circuit TVs showing the night's event. The press box famously was forgotten, and workers

THE RED WINGS' OWN

She has been suspended in a harness and hung below the rafters at Joe Louis Arena, her aerial arrival part of the playoff pregame show. Mostly, though, Karen Newman is known for standing on a red carpet at the Joe and at Little Caesars Arena, her melodious voice doing justice to the U.S. and sometimes Canadian anthems. In 2015, she celebrated a quarter century as "the Red Wings' own Karen Newman," as she is introduced by the public address announcer.

Newman grew up in metro Detroit and received a full scholarship to Oakland University. She went to Los Angeles in hopes of making it big in the music business, but she was back home when she got her big break. She was dating her former husband, Freddy Cohen, a hairdresser who had been hired to work a Little Caesars pro tennis tournament at Cobo Arena in 1988. When Cohen heard tournament organizers were going to use a recording of "The Star-Spangled Banner," he pitched Newman.

The event featured John McEnroe and among the fans was John Oates, a big tennis follower and one-half of Hall & Oates, the top-selling musical duo in history. When he saw how nervous Newman was, Oates tried to ease her fears. "I literally was having a breakdown backstage before I had to go out and sing for the first time ever," Newman recalled in 2014. "I was a nervous wreck, and I remember him saying, 'Calm down. You're going to be fine.' I'll never forget that. Now I'm really nervous because John Oates just talked to me, right? But that's what started it. So I went out and sang."

Ironically enough, she caught the Wings' attention when she performed the anthem at Pistons games. By 1991, she was the Wings' own.

scrambled to knock out the top rows of seats to build a makeshift one that was so narrow that two people could not walk side by side.

The arena was erected before it became common practice to sell naming rights and was named in honor of Joe Louis, the legendary "Brown Bomber" from Detroit who reigned as heavyweight boxing champion from 1937 to 1949. The arena was dedicated to Louis in October 1983, two years after Louis' death and four years after the arena opened for business. It was heralded as a friendlier and safer experience than Olympia Stadium, with nearby parking structures, and shuttles to area restaurants and bars, surrounded by well-lit streets and accessible from major freeways.

The new arena was awarded the 1980 NHL All-Star Game. It could not have been better timing, as it was Gordie Howe's farewell season. A then–NHL record 21,002 fans watched Howe in the last of his 23 All-Star appearances. When his name was announced, fans gave Howe a thunderous standing ovation.

After taking over the building, Ilitch poured $2.5 million into renovations and improvements. Suites boasted plush red velvet-upholstered furnishings, a jukebox, and a private bar. There were two rows of six seats, each overlooking the ice, so that suite holders felt like a part of the crowd. Even the hot dogs were heralded as "the best in the NHL and perhaps the world" by the *Toronto Globe and Mail* in 1982.

The arena hosted its first playoff games in April 1984—for both the NHL and the NBA. The Wings lost a best-of-five first-round series to the Jacques Demers' Blues, eliminated at the Joe by dropping Game 3 in double overtime and Game 4 in overtime. The Detroit Pistons played Game 5 of their best-of-five first-round series against the New York Knicks at the Joe because of a scheduling conflict at their usual home, the Pontiac Silverdome. A then-record crowd of 21,208 watched as Isiah Thomas scored 16 points in the final 1:34 to tie the game at 114–114. Fans erupted in a frenzy when Thomas sank a three-pointer with 23 seconds to go in regulation. The Pistons, though, lost in overtime 127–123.

As the Wings rolled, the Joe rocked. "It was such a fun arena to play in because you could feed off the crowd so easily when they were engaged," Kirk Maltby said. "Before they raised the glass, they could reach over the glass and yell at you. It was just so much fun to play in that you couldn't help but get caught up in the atmosphere. It was definitely a home-ice

LITTLE CAESARS ARENA

Players spent the first week trying not to get lost. Their new facilities spanned 20,000 square feet of locker stalls, training facilities, a kitchen and dining area, equipment room, coaches' offices, and a video room set up a like a luxury theater.

After 38 years at Joe Louis Arena, the Red Wings moved to a palatial new home at the start of the 2017–18 season. Located on Woodward Avenue not far from the Fox Theatre, Comerica Park and Ford Field, Little Caesars Arena was the best of everything modern and innovative, but it is also a nod to the city's past.

One of the primary directives in constructing the arena was to model it after Bell Centre in Montreal. Build steep, rather than slanted. Players raved about how it felt as if fans were right on top of them at the Joe, about how much of an advantage that was in the playoffs.

When Joe Louis Arena opened in 1979, at a cost of $57 million, it was billed as an improvement over Olympia Stadium. Four decades later, Little Caesars Arena cost $863 million and was heralded as a high-water mark for new arenas. The main concourse is wide enough to stage ballroom dancing classes, there were five restaurants and numerous food stalls, and plenty for the fan to enjoy beyond the activity on the main floor. LCA features a cool transparent roof on the southwest side, plus a sort of "skin" wall on the outside of the arena where images from events inside could be projected.

LCA seats 19,515 for Wings games, 20,332 for Pistons games, and 12,000–22,000 for concerts. The Jumbotron, which is square, retracts into the ceiling if performers prefer. Seats were originally red, but were changed to black during the second year of operation.

LCA stands as an homage to Detroit's legendary athletes and entertainers. Murals of Joe Louis, Isiah Thomas, and Aretha Franklin grace the building's edifice along Sproat Street. One of the most nostalgic features is the old Olympia Stadium marquee letters on the concourse, next to a mural of Gordie Howe. The main concourse also features manhole covers immortalizing past Wings and Pistons players.

If ice wasn't available at the Joe because of concert or other event, players used to go through what they called "dress and drive"—change into their gear at the Joe, drive to another rink, then repeat in reverse, wearing now smelly gear. If the ice isn't available at LCA, players only have to walk a few feet from their locker room to a below-ground practice facility.

advantage for us to have a rink like that, where it felt like the crowd was right on top of you. It was awesome."

In 1999, the *Detroit Free Press* reported Ilitch was buying land behind the Fox Theatre, presumably for a new arena. Twenty years after it had opened, the Joe already was outdated, lacking lucrative mid-level suites and the general luxuries that marked new arenas. At the same time, there was talk of expanding neighboring Cobo Hall to create more space for the annual North American International Auto Show, and combining Cobo and the Joe into one big center had its logic. When an option arose to automatically renew the lease for Joe Louis Arena in 2009, the club negotiated a shorter-term lease. Plans for a new arena were announced in 2012.

The Wings' final game at the Joe was April 9, 2017. It was a beautifully sunny Sunday, the weather perfect for the pomp that began outside. Players current and former walked a red carpet. Dani Probert, the wife of former Wings forward Bob Probert, brought some of his ashes and scattered them in the home penalty box. Bruce Martyn, the team's former longtime broadcaster, attended. Actor Dave Coulier, a well-known Wings fan, made an appearance.

The opposing team was the New Jersey Devils—not much in the way of a rival, but it didn't matter. The Wings were celebrating their history at the Joe, and there was one last big milestone to add to the books. The game was the 1,000th of Henrik Zetterberg's career, and the Wings held a ceremony to honor his accomplishment before the puck dropped.

Steve Yzerman, the beloved icon who left the organization in 2010 to manage the Tampa Bay Lightning, dropped the last ceremonial puck. After Detroit's 4–1 victory, workers rushed onto the ice to place a red carpet that spelled out Joe.

Demolition on the arena began in 2019, 40 years after it opened. It was just a shell by then, gutted after the Wings moved to their ritzier home. But on that April day in 2017, Yzerman delivered the arena's best epithet, describing Joe Louis Arena as "beautiful in its simplicity."

45

OUTDOOR FUN

The alumni hydrated with beer. They had put in their dues and reached retirement. Most kept fit afterward, and these games felt like an awesome reunion under the best of circumstances.

The Red Wings first ventured outside in 1954, in an exhibition game against inmates at Michigan's Marquette Branch Prison. Scorekeepers gave up after the Wings went ahead 18–0 in the first period. That was the last time the franchise went outdoors for 55 years.

Around the late 2000s, the NHL realized it had a gold mine in returning hockey to where it began: outdoors. Staging a game beneath an open sky beckoned nostalgia. Players harkened back to their childhoods, and fans could sit in the stands, their hands wrapped around a cup of hot chocolate.

The tradition gained traction in 2008, when the Winter Classic was added to the NHL schedule. The Pittsburgh Penguins and Buffalo Sabres played in the inaugural game, at Ralph Wilson Stadium in upstate New York. The next year, the league staged a marquee matchup between Original Six rivals Chicago and Detroit at Wrigley Field. On New Year's Day 2009, 40,818 fans packed into the baseball stadium and watched the Wings rally to a 6–4 victory. Before the game, fireworks shot into the air from the outfield during the national anthem, and two jets flew over as the last notes sounded on "The Star-Spangled Banner."

"You can't say enough about this whole atmosphere, this whole environment," Kris Draper said afterward. "It was so much fun. We didn't really know what to expect, we didn't know how the ice conditions were going to be, we didn't know how the weather was going to be, and everything just turned out great."

Tomas Holmstrom skated off at the end, reluctantly. "I've never had the planes coming over you like that," he said. "The crowd got going too. It was fun. You just want to do it again."

The Wings let the NHL know the next day that they wanted to host a Winter Classic. Three years later they were still pushing for a game on home soil. Comerica Park was one option. Michigan Stadium in Ann Arbor looked even better.

"Everyone here would just love it, and people in Michigan would really enjoy it too," defenseman Niklas Kronwall said on New Year's Eve 2011. "Everybody would relish it and have a good time." At the time, the list of teams that had hosted outdoor games numbered Buffalo, Chicago, Boston (2010, Fenway Park), and Pittsburgh (2011, Heinz Field). That New Year's Day, Philadelphia hosted the Rangers at Citizens Bank Park.

Coach Mike Babcock was hopeful. "We're a good franchise," he said. "I think we've got a good market, we've got a good brand."

The Wings' efforts were successful. They were awarded the 2013 Winter Classic, but the game was wiped out by the labor dispute that left the 2012–13 season a 48-game sprint that began in January 2013. Instead, the Wings would get the 2014 edition, at Michigan Stadium, against Original Six rival Toronto.

Brendan Shanahan, Nicklas Lidstrom, Steve Yzerman, Mickey Redmond, and Kris Draper at the Alumni Showdown Game at Comerica Park, December 31, 2013. (Julian H. Gonzalez)

The area became a hotbed of outdoor hockey that week. The Great Lakes Invitational, an annual four-team college hockey event held at Joe Louis Arena, took place December 28 at Comerica Park in Detroit. On December 29, there were two junior hockey games at the baseball park, and Detroit's and Toronto's American Hockey League teams met December 30.

Alumni games became part of the tradition of NHL outdoor games in 2010. So many Wings and Maple Leafs alumni wanted to play that the teams ended up organizing not one but two games at Comerica Park, on December 31. A crowd of 33,425 was treated to two Wings victories. When Steve Yzerman was introduced, fans cheered on their feet.

"I remember it being really fun," Yzerman recalled in 2019. "I wanted to retire raising the Stanley Cup, but that didn't happen. Going out on the ice one more time like that was really cool. It was a great atmosphere."

Joe Kocur honored his late Bruise Brother, Bob Probert, by wearing his No. 24 in the second game. Probert had passed away four years earlier. Kocur said he had thought about doing so for a long time, and made sure to get the approval of Probert's widow, Dani. Kocur gave the sweater to Probert's son, Jack.

It was an emotional day. Before the second game started, Slava Fetisov, Igor Larionov, Vyacheslav Kozlov, and Sergei Fedorov gathered around Vladimir Konstantinov as he clasped a hockey stick. Konstantinov nearly died in a limousine accident six days after the Wings won the Stanley Cup in 1997. For a brief moment, the Russian Five were reunited.

Gordie Howe and Ted Lindsay, two of the greatest legends in Wings history, appeared together to perform a ceremonial puck drop with Yzerman. When Howe made as if he wanted to play, fans happily chanted, "*Gor-die! Gor-die!*"

"That's the pride that hockey players have," Kris Draper said. "Gordie wanted to step on the ice and Vladdie didn't want to get off the ice. It was great, it was great to see them all back. It was a heck of an effort by Sergei, Kozzie, and Slava to come back over and be a part of this. It meant a lot for everybody to be here, and I think the fans really appreciated it."

There had been four days of outdoor hockey already, and the big game at the Big House was still on the slate. Current players had to miss the Alumni Showdown because December 31 was their only opportunity to get in a practice on the rink inside Michigan Stadium on the University of Michigan campus. Snow flurries fell as they skated. Justin Abdelkader fetched a shovel and cleared in front of the nets, then dropped the shovel in a corner. Within minutes, Todd Bertuzzi tripped over it. Delighted teammates banged their sticks as he got back up.

The forecast for Ann Arbor on January 1 was 18 degrees. Previous Winter Classics had never been colder than 31. It was cold, it was windy, ilt snowed all game and snowed most of the day. Players loved it. The brutal weather didn't deter fans either. They tailgated, staged impromptu hockey games of their own, and drank beer that didn't need to be in a cooler.

The snow slowed the game. Players tried to appreciate the atmosphere during stoppages in play—it took 10 skaters with shovels to clear the snow at regular intervals—and peered at the crowd through wet, heavy snowflakes. "It was almost like a blizzard out there," Abdelkader said.

The crowd was announced as 105,491, but there was some controversy about how many people actually attended and it was not certified by *Guinness World Records* as a record crowd at an outdoor hockey game. However, the game did set an NHL attendance record.

"This might be one of the best experiences in life," Tomas Tatar said, despite the fact the Wings lost 3–2 in a shootout.

"An unbelievable experience," Kronwall said. "Something I don't think any of us will ever forget. One of the best experiences I've ever had."

When the Wings next ventured outdoors to play in 2016, it was a sunny day in February. They played at Coors Field in Denver, and the alumni game was the highlight of the Stadium Series event. By 2016, the rivalry that had captured the hockey world from 1996 to 2002 was a distant memory—but the men who made those memories flocked to play once more. Draper took charge of assembling the Wings' roster. He got Yzerman on board during a visit to his cottage in the summer of 2015, a feat considering the Monday preceding the game was the NHL trade deadline and Yzerman at that time was general manager of the Tampa Bay Lightning. Soon Nicklas Lidstrom, Tomas Holmstrom, Chris Chelios, Darren McCarty, Kirk Maltby, Martin Lapointe, and Larionov signed on. So did Brendan Shanahan, the president of the Toronto Maple Leafs. Chris Osgood deferred because he underwent hernia surgery in January 2016. Joe Sakic, Patrick Roy, Peter Forsberg, and Claude Lemieux—the premier villain of the rivalry—were among the Avalanche alumni.

DETROIT RED WINGS

A crowd of 43,319 packed into the baseball stadium. It was 58.8 degrees when the game began around 5:30 PM local time. The crowd booed when Draper was introduced. Fans booed Chelios; Chelios booed back. During the third period, a video paying tribute to the rivalry played on the scoreboard. Fans stood and cheered. Players paused, raised their sticks in salute.

Afterward the veteran Wings sat shoulder to shoulder in a small locker room. Lapointe hoisted a beer and grinned. He wasn't the only one. It was a fabulous evening, even though the Avalanche prevailed 5–2.

"It was really fun to be out there. It reminded me of how much fun playing the game as a kid was, going to outdoor rinks and playing with your friends," Yzerman said in 2019. "I enjoyed both games I played in, at Comerica and Coors, enjoyed seeing all the guys I used to play with. That was great. They're fun to be a part of."

The younger Wings fared better, winning 5–3 in the Winter Classic before a sellout crowd of 50,095. It was 65 degrees and still sunny when the game began at 6:21 PM. As evening fell and the wind picked up, the sheets of cotton staged to mimic a snowy scene shredded and blew around the stadium. "You are looking up and the foam is everywhere," Tatar said. "It was a little weird."

The Wings and Maple Leafs met again outdoors in the 2017 Centennial Classic at BMO Field in Toronto. This time Draper persuaded Osgood to play by going through his son. Max, five years old at the time, never saw his father play in the NHL. "I played a little dirty pool," Draper admitted. "Within 48 hours, he was convinced."

The Wings alumni beat Toronto 4–3 as Draper scored the game-winner with 65 seconds left. "I love these things," Draper said. The NHL Wings lost 5–4 in overtime on January 1. Before 40,148 fans, bright sunshine delayed the start and the game finished in darkness. Seven goals were scored in the third period, and Anthony Mantha tied it at 4–4 with 1.1 seconds left. Toronto rookie Auston Matthews scored at 3:40 of overtime. "It's fun to play outdoors, play in front of a big crowd," Mantha said. "It's something you need to do at least once in your career."

Tomas Holmstrom and Nicklas Lidstrom smiled as they posed with Red Wings legend Alex Delvecchio. It was a special night for the Swedish teammates and close friends, and it couldn't have come at a sweeter time.

From November 5, 2011, to February 19, 2012, the Wings won a record 23 consecutive games at Joe Louis Arena. On February 10, they beat the Anaheim Ducks 2-1 in a shootout. It was Holmstrom's 1,000th career game, and Delvecchio was on hand to honor Lidstrom for tying Delvecchio's 1,549 games played in a Wings uniform, second behind Gordie Howe's 1,687. (However, it was much later determined that Delvecchio actually played in 1,550 games—a stat mistake dating to the 1954–55 season.)

Holmstrom's nose was bloodied in a collision with Ducks forward George Parros, but a disregard for physical contact played a big part in why Holmstrom reached 1,000 games. Delvecchio—one of the cleanest players of his day—paid Holmstrom an enormous compliment that night. "He said that if I played during their era, they win more Stanley Cup," a beaming Holmstrom said.

It was a fun time to be at home. On December 8, the Wings hosted the Phoenix Coyotes. Fans who arrived early to the Joe were gifted a Johan Franzen bobblehead. Henrik Zetterberg wondered out loud after the morning skate whether Franzen's big head could fit on a bobblehead. The Wings went out and scored five goals in the first period.

Two nights later, the Winnipeg Jets were in town. It was 2-1 after the first period, 6-1 after the second period, 7-1 at the buzzer. The Wings won their next home game, December 17 against Los Angeles, 8-2.

The Wings rolled into a new year after besting the Blues 3-0 on a Jimmy Howard shutout—their 12th straight home victory. They opened 2012 with four games on the road, then preserved their home streak with a shootout victory over the Coyotes and an overtime victory against the Blackhawks. When the Blues reappeared at the Joe on January 23, teammates delighted in the hit defenseman Brad Stuart put on defenseman Alex Pietrangelo, sending the St. Louis defender into the boards in the last minute of the first period. Blues forward Chris Stewart grew so irate he jumped Stuart.

"That hit changed our game," Pavel Datsyuk said after scoring while Stewart cooled off in the penalty box. The Wings won 3–1, nabbing their 17th straight victory at the Joe.

When the Wings beat Philadelphia on February 12, they tied the all-time NHL single-season record for most consecutive home victories at 20, set by the Boston Bruins in 1929–30 and the Flyers in 1975–76. (The Bruins also won their first two home games of the 1930–31 season to win a record 22 straight home games.) The month of February is usually ripe for trade speculation in the NHL, but the Wings' roll at the Joe was the talk of the town. When they beat the Dallas Stars 3–1 on February 14 to set a single-season record, fans chanted, "*21! 21! 21!*"

"We're thrilled that this has happened for our team," coach Mike Babcock said. "I think it's really good for our logo, it's really good for our ownership and our team. I'm proud of the guys."

Fans gave the Wings a standing ovation. The Wings gathered at center ice and saluted with their sticks.

"It is pretty cool now that we first of all were able to tie it in the last game, and more now that we really pulled it off and got the record," Zetterberg said. "It was awesome."

The Wings beat Nashville and San Jose in the next two home games— their 23rd straight at the Joe, setting the NHL record for longest home streak including multiple seasons. On February 21, they lost Pavel Datsyuk to arthroscopic knee surgery. The streak ended February 23 in a 4–3 shootout loss to the Vancouver Canucks, who forced overtime on Daniel Sedin's goal with 16 seconds left. Had the Wings won, they would have tied the 1978 Pittsburgh Pirates and 1988 Boston Red Sox, who hold the third-longest home winning streak in the history among North America's four major pro sports with 24 consecutive victories.

47

SCARY MOMENTS AT THE JOE

Joe Louis Arena bore witness to championship moments—and to multiple frightening ones.

One of the scariest moments occurred November 21, 2005, during a game against the Nashville Predators. Defenseman Jiri Fischer collapsed on the Wings bench during the first period while play was ongoing. He suffered a seizure, requiring CPR and the use of a defibrillator.

Steve Yzerman described what it was like on the bench. "Fear," he said. "You see the guy lying there and the doctors doing what they're doing. You fear for the guy's life at that moment."

Fischer's heart had stopped. He had no pulse. "They hooked up the auto defibrillator, and they shocked him," coach Mike Babcock said. "The heartbeat that leads to death, they got that stopped and going, and they continued with the CPR."

Fischer, only 25 but a six-year veteran, was seated on the far end of the bench when he fell over around 8:07 PM. Babcock waved his arm toward the Zamboni entrance, where an ambulance was stationed. Officials halted play. "I think a couple of us jumped on the ice and started screaming for the referees to blow the whistle, and they were confused," Brendan Shanahan said.

Team doctor Anthony Colucci, who sits directly behind the bench in the stands, jumped down and administered CPR. Team doctor Douglas Plagens and trainer Piet Van Zant also tended to Fischer.

"Everybody was caught by surprise," Yzerman said. "I'm not sure the players were aware of the circumstances. We turn and see Jiri lying between the boards and the bench and we're really not sure why he's lying there. For us, we were basically helpless to stand there and watch. You're just sitting back hoping that this is going to work out all right."

About 45 minutes after his collapse, the Wings announced Fischer was stable. Fans clapped, filling the arena with noise again. Officials postponed the game.

Fischer was taken to Detroit Receiving Hospital. He was released November 25 but readmitted to hospital after suffering a brief cardiac episode on November 28. Fischer had an abnormal electrocardiogram (EKG) during a physical September 12, 2002, at training camp, but he passed follow-up tests.

The November 2005 episodes forced Fischer to retire. He took a job with the Wings as director of player development and evaluation, but he suited up in a Wings uniform once more on December 31, 2013, in one of the Alumni Showdown games at Comerica Park.

There had also been a heart scare involving St. Louis Blues defenseman Chris Pronger at the Joe in 1998. During a playoff game on May 10, Pronger was struck by a puck from Dmitri Mironov on the left chest wall and fell unconscious for 30 seconds. Trainers and doctors from both teams rushed to Pronger. "To see him lying there like that was really scary," teammate Geoff Courtnall said.

Doctors kept Pronger at Henry Ford Hospital overnight, but there were almost immediate reports from the Blues that Pronger was okay. He played 41 minutes and 35 seconds the next game, on May 12, a 3–2 double overtime Wings vicory.

During the 2004 playoffs, fans at the Joe experienced another grim moment. They grew silent in the second period of Game 5 of the Calgary series when a puck hit Yzerman in the face. Wings defenseman Mathieu Schneider's shot from the right point had deflected off Flames defenseman Rhett Warrener's shin pad and the puck slammed into Yzerman. He immediately threw his stick and dropped to the ice. He skated off clutching a towel to his left eye.

"It was pretty scary for a few minutes," Schneider said afterward.

Yzerman underwent 4½ hours of surgery that same day at Henry Ford Hospital. He suffered a scratched cornea and multiple fractures to the orbital bone around his left eye. The Wings, the Presidents' Trophy winner, lost Game 5 1–0, and were eliminated from the second-round series two days later 1–0 in overtime.

By September, only bright sunshine bothered his left eye. The NHL declared a lockout September 15 as the league and the Players' Association feuded over a salary cap. Yzerman spent that fall ferrying his three daughters to and from school and various other activities. On December 2, he played in a charity game at Yost Arena in Ann Arbor wearing a visor that was slightly tinted to protect his left eye from bright light. Yzerman had worn a visor at times before in his career, but when the NHL resumed in 2005–06, Yzerman wore a visor full-time.

Teammate Nicklas Lidstrom followed Yzerman's example after a similar scare in 2008. During an exhibition game against the Montreal Canadiens on September 24, Lidstrom suffered a cut above his right eye when he was hit by a puck. "I saw the point shot from the blue line, and I saw Nick," teammate Tomas Kopecky said. "He was covered with lots of blood." Lidstrom needed 25 stitches under his right eyebrow and had a broken nose.

When the Wings found out Lidstrom's eye wasn't damaged, Kris Draper suggested the team fill Lidstrom's locker with visors. He had recently donned one himself after a scare. "I remember getting stitched up and not being able to see and with all the blood in my eye," Draper said. "The one thing I said was, if everything is all right, I'll throw a visor on, and it's never coming off again."

One of the bloodiest moments at the Joe occurred November 26, 1986, during a game against the Toronto Maple Leafs. Midway through the third period, Leafs defenseman Borje Salming was part of a goalmouth scramble. Wings forward Gerard Gallant was knocked over Salming while he was on the ice, and accidentally caught Salming with his skate. Salming suffered a 5½-inch gash that began over his right eye, missed the corner of his eye, and continued down his cheek to the right corner of his mouth. He was rushed to Detroit Osteopathic Hospital, where he underwent a three-hour operation. Surgeons stopped counting after 200 stitches. (In a cruel bit of irony, the accident happened the same week Salming stopped wearing a visor; he had played with one to protect a broken orbital bone.)

Remarkably, Salming left the hospital and went back to the team hotel. He was back playing December 10. Salming, a future Hall of Famer, finished his NHL career with the Wings, playing his final season in 1989–90.

48

THE REBUILD

On April 19, 2019, Detroit's Superman returned. Nine years after he'd left the organization to gain experience as a general manager in the Sunshine State, Steve Yzerman was back where he belonged: as a Red Wing.

The man who played through the "Dead Wings" era and led the franchise in its resurgence to glory as captain was named general manager in a news conference that fell on Good Friday. If anyone could resurrect the Wings, it had to be Yzerman.

Two years had passed since the Wings' historic 25-season playoff streak ended.

On March 28, 2017, the Wings played their third game in three days. They had spent an evening the previous December in Raleigh, North Carolina, waiting for the ice at PNC Arena to sufficiently freeze, only to have the game postponed when it became apparent that would not happen by 9:00 PM, thus violating the 22-hour window mandated between start times. The Wings and Hurricanes settled on meeting March 27, since the Wings already were scheduled to be in town for a March 28 game. They left for Carolina following a March 26 home matinee against Minnesota.

The three games in three days scenario was notable on its own, but what really garnered attention was the result: when the March 28 game ended with the Wings losing 4–1, while the Boston Bruins and Toronto Maple Leafs won, it marked the first time since 1991 the Wings failed to make the playoffs.

The attention shifted full tilt to rebuilding the Wings. They had it coming.

Were it not for hitting the draft jackpot in 1998 and 1999, the end would have come as the players responsible for the Cups between 1997 and 2002 aged into retirement. But in 1998 the Wings selected Pavel Datsyuk at 171st overall and in 1999 they found Henrik Zetterberg at 210th. Datsyuk joined the team in the fall of 2001 and Zetterberg came on board in the fall of 2002. While the retirement of Nicklas Lidstrom in

2012—one year after Brian Rafalski had quit with a year left on his contract —weakened the defense, the Wings had two superstars among their forwards and Niklas Kronwall anchoring the defense.

That prompted general manager Ken Holland to deal assets at trade deadlines, even as the playoff runs shortened. The 2012 trade for defenseman Kyle Quincey looked especially bad in hindsight because the Wings were done five games into the first round, while the deal (which was swung with Colorado via Tampa Bay) landed the Lightning a first-round pick they turned into franchise goaltender Andrei Vasilevskiy. At the time, though, the Wings needed depth on defense, and Quincey was a familiar option, having come up through the farm system and having helped them reach the Western Conference finals in 2007.

It was the last time Holland sought to improve the Wings at the cost of a first-round pick. Lower-round picks and prospects were used to bring in players at the 2014 and 2015 trade deadlines, but from 2013 on Holland balanced trades with stocking the farm system.

The Wings picked 6'5" winger Anthony Mantha at 20th overall in 2013. He was an outstanding juniors player coming off a 50-goal, 89-point season with Val-d'Or in the Quebec league. The pick looked even better when Mantha produced 120 points in 57 games in 2013–14. He turned pro in 2014 but struggled to translate his prowess as he adjusted to playing against men instead of teenagers. After two years in the minors, Mantha joined the Wings as a regular during 2016–17, scoring 17 goals in 60 games. The following season he led the team with 24 goals and nine power-play goals.

Mantha had been the subject of frustration at times—after a Thanksgiving eve loss to the Oilers in 2017, coach Jeff Blashill ripped Mantha in postgame comments, saying "It's not okay to just be a passenger when you are given the opportunity to be an impact player."

Mantha acknowledged his reputation in an October 2018 interview, saying he needed to "get it in my mind that I need to be the best player I can be every night."

One veteran teammate who saw Mantha as a rookie and again in 2018–19 had especially high regard for his potential. "I think he can become the next power forward in this league," Thomas Vanek said. "His size, his skill set, his skating—you don't see that combination that much. I don't think he realizes how strong he is. I think once he figures that part out, then the game will come easier for him."

The pick that appears to be a central block in the rebuild happened in 2014, when the Wings drafted Dylan Larkin at 15th overall. Five years after the draft, at the conclusion of the 2018–19 season, Larkin ranked third in his class with 213 points.

He made the Wings at 19, and on October 9, 2015, he became the team's first teenager to score in his NHL debut since Steve Yzerman in 1983. Larkin led the team with 23 goals as a rookie in 2015–16, finding success as a wing on a line with Zetterberg at center. His sophomore season was less successful, as Larkin struggled to hold his own at center until late in the season. But something clicked at the 2017 World Championships, where Larkin thrived playing for Blashill on the U.S. team. A trust was established, and Larkin brought the confidence and leadership earned at that tournament with him to the 2017–18 season. He more than doubled his personal best with 47 assists, and went from producing 32 points in 2016–17 to 63 points. Reward came in the shape of a five-year, $30.5 million contract in the summer of 2018 that made him the highest-paid player on the team.

Larkin revealed in March 2019 that his contract negotiations played a role in how well he played in 2018–19. He's a high-character guy who works extremely hard to be the best player he can be. (During the 2018 NHL All-Star break, Larkin texted Kris Draper to ask whether he could skate with Draper's 15-year-old son's team. Larkin practiced for an hour and 20 minutes with the Little Caesars team the next day.) He found extra motivation in hearing, as he put it, that "people said I wasn't a goal-scorer." He spent the summer working on his shot, and saw it pay off with 32 goals.

To those who knew him, Larkin's accomplishment wasn't a surprise. "Everybody works hard, everybody trains in the gym, everybody skates," Blashill said. "But are you willing to go and just shoot pucks over and over and over again and get better at a skill? A lot of guys aren't; he is. That's why he's continued to get better and exceeded a lot of people's expectations. I can't put a ceiling on him. When you have that kind of inner drive, you can never put a ceiling on a player."

Larkin became the Wings' first 30-goal scorer since 2008–09. "Any player wants to score goals," he said. "It's one of the greatest joys of this game. You want to score goals, you want to have the puck on your stick and make plays."

It was the first time in a decade the Wings had a player reach 30 goals.

More first-round picks followed: forwards Evgeny Svechnikov (2015), Michael Rasmussen (2017), Filip Zadina and Joe Veleno (2018), and defensemen Dennis Cholowski (2016) and Moritz Seider (2019). But it wasn't just about banking first-round picks. As it became apparent during the 2017–18 season, when the Wings missed the playoffs for a second straight season, Holland used the trade deadline to flip Tomas Tatar for three picks.

In all, the Wings made four picks between sixth and 36 in the 2018 draft. On March 12, 2019, the Wings were eliminated from playoff contention for a third straight year. A little more than a month later, on April 19, Yzerman was named general manager and tasked with taking charge of the rebuild. His first message was one gleaned by a young man who played through the Dead Wings era before a series of good drafts— and one superb one, in 1989—led the Red Wings to rise once again to Stanley Cup glory.

"We want to be a team that can compete for the Stanley Cup championship," Yzerman said. "That takes time. We have a lot of draft picks, we have some good kids coming. How well we draft and how quickly these players develop into impact players in the NHL will determine our success."

49

RETIRED NUMBERS

When Gordie Howe passed away in 2016, Wayne Gretzky shared his opinion that the NHL should retire Howe's No. 9 leaguewide. Select players have such an impact on their sport, are such ambassadors of their game, that their number is synonymous with their name. Major League Baseball did it with Jackie Robinson's No. 42. The NHL did it with Gretzky's No. 99 (which Gretzky had picked in honor of Howe, a childhood hero who became like a second father to him).

Howe's number was the first one retired by the Wings—and they did it almost a decade before he stopped playing professional hockey. He made the Wings in 1946 at age 18 and played a quarter of a century for the franchise. He won four Stanley Cups, six MVP trophies, and six scoring titles.

He announced his retirement after the 1970–71 season and accepted a job as a club vice president. The Wings staged a ceremony to retire his number on March 12, 1972, at Olympia Stadium that featured vice president Spiro Agnew. "There wasn't a dry eye in the place when the Number 9 banner went up," son Mark Howe wrote in his 2014 book, *Gordie Howe's Son: A Hall of Fame Life in the Shadow of Mr. Hockey.*

Howe ended his retirement a year later when he joined the World Hockey Association, but his No. 9 stayed where it was at Olympia Stadium. Howe's was the only number retired and hung in the rafters while the Norris family owned the Wings.

On November 10, 1991—nine years after Mike Ilitch purchased the Wings from Bruce Norris—the Wings retired Ted Lindsay's No. 7 and Alex Delvecchio's No. 10. "When they raise the sweater, well, what more can they do for you?" Lindsay quipped that night. "That means you've been hung."

Lindsay was part of the famed Production Line that reigned in the NHL from 1947–48 to 1951–52. Delvecchio—who starred between Lindsay and Howe on the Production Line II—spent his entire 24-season career with the Wings. The ceremony lasted 20 minutes. Jimmy Carson, who had been wearing No. 10, switched to No. 12 and presented Delvecchio a No.

NO. 6

Larry Aurie holds a special place in the history of the Red Wings. He helped the team win its first Stanley Cup championship, in 1936, and was a favorite of owner James E. Norris and coach Jack Adams.

Aurie joined the franchise in 1927, when it was known as the Detroit Cougars. He scored 13 goals in his rookie season, in the days when teams played fewer than 50 games. In 1933–34, he led the Red Wings (Norris renamed the team in 1932) with 19 assists and 35 points. He and left wing Herbie Lewis represented the Wings in 1934 at an All-Star benefit game for Ace Bailey, a precursor to the NHL All-Star Game that started in the 1940s.

A right wing, Aurie stood only 5'6" and weighed less than 150 pounds, but he paired skill with intense fierceness. He gained the nickname "The Little Rag Man" for the way he would rag the puck, or control it and keep it from opponents, while killing penalties. He captained the Wings in 1932–33 and led them in playoff scoring in 1934 with 10 points in nine games, when they lost in the Stanley Cup Finals to the Chicago Black Hawks, three games to one.

Aurie tallied 16 goals and 34 points in 1935–36 in a 48-game season. That spring, he had a hand in Lewis' goal during Game 2 of the Stanley Cup Finals, helping the Wings defeat the Toronto Maple Leafs in a best-of-five series. In the first round, the Wings swept the Montreal Maroons, starting with a 1–0, six-overtime triumph in Game 1.

Aurie reached a career-high 23 goals, tied for the league lead, the following season, and was selected the first-team All-Star right wing. But he suffered a fractured leg on March 11, 1937, that ended his season. The injury marred the rest of his career, and Aurie retired after the 1937–38 season. He was 33 years old. Aurie returned from Pittsburgh, where he was a player-coach, to play one last game for the injury-riddled Wings on January 10, 1939, and scored in the 3–0 victory over the Canadiens.

Aurie originally wore No. 12, but switched to No. 6 in his second season. Norris retired Aurie's number, but back in the 1930s, that did not include hanging it from the rafters.

"All I knew was that Jack Adams really admired him and didn't want anyone else to wear the jersey," Alex Delvecchio told the *Detroit Free Press* in 1997. "Jack Adams said he was great, and he knew great talent.... My thoughts are that Adams probably was too wrapped up in winning hockey games to hang jerseys from the rafters."

Cummy Burton, Aurie's cousin, wore No. 6 from 1957 to 1959, but neither Norris nor the Ilitch family, who purchased the Wings in 1982, has issued it since then. When asked why No. 6 was not hanging from the rafters, the Wings, under Ilitch owership, pointed to the fact Aurie, who died in 1952 a few days after Norris, was not in the Hockey Hall of Fame.

10 sweater. Steve Yzerman presented a No. 7 to Lindsay. Then banners bearing their names and numbers were raised to the rafters, joining Howe's. "What really counts," Lindsay said, "is who we're hung with: the greatest athlete in any sport that I've ever seen."

The franchise's greatest goaltender was honored on March 6, 1994, when the Wings retired Terry Sawchuk's No. 1. Sawchuk helped the Wings win three Stanley Cups. At the time of his death in 1970, he held NHL records with 445 victories and 103 shutouts. The Hockey Hall of Fame waived its three-year waiting period and inducted him in 1971. Howe, Lindsay, and Delvecchio attended the ceremony at Joe Louis Arena, along with six of Sawchuk's seven children.

Abel's No. 12 rose to the rafters on April 29, 1995. He centered the famed Production Line and also served the Wings as coach, general manager, and broadcaster during a career that spanned the 1930s to the 1980s. When he found out his number would join his old linemates', Abel said, "I'll look forward to being up there in the rafters with them."

That marked the last Original Six player number the Wings retired until Red Kelly's No. 4 on February 1, 2019. Kelly was the first Wing to have his number retired at Little Caesars Arena.

When the time came to retire Yzerman's No. 19 on January 2, 2007—almost six months to the day after he had announced his retirement—the pomp and circumstance befitted the man who had led the franchise to its second dynasty. The previous banners—those honoring Howe, Lindsay, Delvecchio, Abel, and Sawchuk—were lowered, then re-raised to the rafters while "Also Sprach Zarathustra" (the theme from *2001: A Space Odyssey*) played over loudspeakers.

Yzerman walked out onto a C-shaped red carpet to "Simply the Best," by Tina Turner. Fans cheered as Howe came out, cheered Bob Probert, cheered Igor Larionov and Brett Hull and Scotty Bowman. One of the most touching moments of the night was when Vladimir Konstantinov came onto the carpet using a walker. The ceremony lasted nearly 90 minutes.

The NHL squad also wore No. 19 jerseys during warm-ups—but not just winged wheel ones. Yzerman's history dating to his junior days and to international play was honored as some players wore Team Canada sweaters, some wore Campbell Conference All-Star sweaters, and some wore Peterborough Petes sweaters. Players gifted Yzerman a family trip to the 2008 European soccer championship in Austria. The Ilitch family gifted Yzerman a Chevy Tahoe.

"What you don't see in the record books is how Stevie won the respect of his teammates by doing the right thing day after day," owner Mike Ilitch said. "He led without arrogance or self-indulgence. Steve Yzerman, you helped build Hockeytown."

As Yzerman began talking, fans roared and clapped, they chanted "Ste-*vie*, Ste-*vie*." A minute went by, then another. Yzerman turned, waved, and clutched his hands. "You never disappoint me," he said."The Red Wings organization, I'm not sure I can fully express my pride, my gratitude. They allowed me to grow up. They supported me when I was down. They encouraged me when I needed encouragement."

Just before his banner went up, Yzerman turned his remarks to fans again. "You look up there, give yourselves a pat on the back because I really feel you're a huge reason, a big reason why it's up there," he said. "From the bottom of my heart, I am sincerely grateful to you all."

Joe Louis Arena bore witness to one last number retirement ceremony on March 6, 2014. Nicklas Lidstrom, the greatest defenseman in franchise history, hung up his skates after the 2011–12 season, but the lockout-shortened 2013 season prompted the Wings to postpone his ceremony a year. Lidstrom retired with four Stanley Cup championships, seven Norris Trophies, and a Conn Smythe Trophy among his hardware.

Brendan Shanahan summed up Lidstrom perfectly. "You always say it's a game of mistakes," Shanahan said, "but Nick proved us all wrong."

Lidstrom smiled and cast a sweet look at his wife and children as his No. 5 banner joined the lofty legends.

Mickey Redmond has broadcast some awful hockey in his career. He has always tried to find the greatness within it.

Redmond is a two-time Stanley Cup champion and two-time 50-goal scorer who turned early retirement into a roaring good time. His affable personality and affinity for turning a phrase have made him a favorite with Red Wings fans.

Redmond joined the organization in his second career as a broadcaster in 1985. Mike Ilitch had purchased the franchise from Bruce Norris in 1982, and the Wings wanted to expand coverage. Redmond, who was born December 27, 1947, in Kirkland Lake, Ontario, was announcing Canadiens games for CBC's *Hockey Night in Canada*. Redmond was teamed with Dave Strader to broadcast Wings games on Channel 20 (WXON-TV), while Bruce Martyn and Sid Abel would broadcast over the radio on WJR-AM (760). Previously, radio and TV had been simulcast.

That first season was rough. The Wings finished 17–57–6 with 40 points, their franchise-worst record, which placed them at the bottom of the standings.

It was around this time Redmond remembered the words of his father, Eddie Redmond. "My dad a long time ago told me, you can't allow the outcome with every team you're with to dictate the way you broadcast the game," Redmond said in a 2019 interview. "It was when I was doing the Leafs, doing some midweek games for Toronto in the mid-'80s. They were floundering, and my dad said, you can't allow the way they're playing to affect the way you broadcast the game.

"You look at the other team, you turn over more stones and you'll find the greatness in the game. You just have to look harder for it sometimes. I've always carried that with me."

Redmond played in the NHL from 1967 to 1976. He spent 3½ seasons with the Montreal Canadiens, winning Stanley Cups in 1968 and '69. Halfway through the 1970–71 season, the Wings acquired Redmond in a trade that sent Frank Mahovlich to Montreal. In 1972–73, Redmond's 52 goals broke Gordie Howe's single-season franchise record of 49 goals and stood as a record until John Ogrodnick scored 55 goals in 1984–85. Redmond began his Wings career playing with Alex Delvecchio and when Delvecchio retired to coach during the 1973–74 season, Redmond played with Marcel Dionne. Another 50-goal season followed in 1973–74.

A back injury forced Redmond to retire at age 28. A friend suggested he explore broadcasting, figuring it was a good fit for an ex-player with a keen mind and a colorful personality. Redmond spent five years broadcasting NHL games on CBC's *Hockey Night in Canada* alongside legends Bob Cole and Dick Irvin Jr. "It was five great years learning from great men," Redmond said.

Redmond was a natural on TV and did national broadcasts for ABC, ESPN, and the USA Network. In 2011, he was recognized with the prestigious Foster Hewitt Memorial Award during the Hockey Hall of Fame induction weekend.

Redmond's success stemmed from his ability to blend insight with entertainment. "All I know is that when the puck is dropped, even though it's the same game, it's a different script every night," he said. "That's what I do. I'm not really big on stats because what happens out there is really going to dictate what I do."

What Redmond is big on are signature phrases like "bingo-bango" and "B.C. two-hander," "oh, baby" and "holy mackerel" and "holy jumpin'."

Redmond has broadcasted to viewers through enormous disappointments—the sweep in the 1995 Stanley Cup Finals, that dismal 1985–86 season, the 62-victory season in 1995–96 that ultimately saw the Wings eliminated in the Western Conference finals—and through great times too, including the Stanley Cups in 1997, '98, '02, and '08.

"The championships are highlights, but I also appreciate the disappointments you face getting to the Cup and try to share that," Redmond said. "You see the frustration in players, and you hear it from fans, when a team gets 131 points and then loses in the playoffs. I try to tell people: enjoy the journey."

The 2019–20 season was Redmond's 41st in broadcasting. He found himself once again covering a team that struggled, and once again remembered the words of his father: "Always look for the greatness in the game, because it is the greatest game in the world."